New British poetries

New British poetries

The scope of the possible

Robert Hampson
Peter Barry *editors*

> Hang a painting by Carlo Dolci beside a Cosimo Tura. You cannot prevent Mr Buggins from preferring the former, but you can very seriously impede his setting up a false tradition of teaching on the assumption that Tura has never existed, or that the qualities of the Tura are non-existent or outside the scope of the possible.
>
> Ezra Pound, *ABC of Reading*

Manchester University Press

Manchester and New York

distributed exclusively in the USA and Canada by St. Martin's Press

Copyright © Manchester University Press 1993

While copyright in the volume as a whole is vested in Manchester
University Press, copyright in individual chapters belongs to their res-
pective authors, and chapter may be reproduced wholly or in part
without the express permission in writing of both author and publisher.

Published by Manchester University Press
Oxford Road, Manchester M13 9NR, UK
and Room 400, 175 Fifth Avenue, New York, NY 10010, USA

Distributed exclusively in the USA and Canada
by St. Martin's Press, Inc.,
175 Fifth Avenue, New York, NY 10010, USA

British Library Cataloguing-in-Publication Data

A catalogue record for this book is available from the British Library.

Library of Congress Cataloging-in-Publication Data applied for

ISBN 0 7190 4692 0 paperback

Paperback edition published 1995

Photoset in Linotron Joanna
by Northern Phototypesetting Co, Ltd, Bolton
Printed in Great Britain
by Biddles Ltd, Guildford and King's Lynn

1003538812

Contents

CASE STUDIES

Notes on contributors

Fred D'Aguiar is of Guyanese descent. His two books of poetry, *Mama Dot* and *British Citizen*, are published by Chatto. A play, *A Jamaican Airman Foresees his Death*, was performed at the Royal Court in 1990.

Peter Barry is Senior Lecturer in English at LSU College of Higher Education, Southampton and joint editor of *English*, the journal of the English Association.

R. J. Ellis is a lecturer and critic who has written extensively on contemporary poetry.

Robert Hampson is a Lecturer in English at Royal Holloway and Bedford New College, University of London. He is the author of *Joseph Conrad: Betrayal and Identity* (Macmillan, 1992). He has also published several pamphlets of poetry, including *A Feast of Friends* (Pig Press, 1982), *A Human Measure* (hardPressed Poetry, 1989), *Unicorns: 7 Studies in Velocity* (Pushtika Press, 1989).

Helen Kidd co-edited the *Virago Book of Women's Love Poetry* and contributed an essay to *Contemporary Poetry Meets Modern Theory* (Harvester, 1991). She teaches at Oxford Polytechnic.

Peter Middleton is a Lecturer in English at the University of Southampton. He has published widely on contemporary British and American poetry.

David Miller is a poet and critic whose books include *Malcolm Lowry: the Voyage that Never Ends* (Enitharmon, 1976) and *W. H. Hudson and the Elusive Paradise* (Macmillan, 1990).

Eric Mottram was, until his recent retirement, Professor of American Literature at King's College, London. He is Visiting Fellow in Poetics at SUNY, Buffalo for 1992–93, a former editor of *Poetry Review*, and co-editor of the anthology *The New British Poetry*.

Robert Sheppard co-edited (with Adrian Clarke) the anthology *Floating Capital: New Poets from London* (Potes and Poets Press, Connecticut, 1991).

Peter Barry
Robert Hampson

Introduction

The scope
of the possible

I
'Nothing difficult'

At the end of his recent book, *Under Briggflatts*, Donald Davie remarks:

> Foreign observers have been persuaded that the British have com-
> fortably opted out from twentieth century endeavour in poetry . . .
> British poetry has chosen to turn inwards, becoming parochial,
> self-comforting, serviceable, content to address no public outside
> the tight little islands.[1]

Hugh Kenner is one such 'foreign observer'. In *A Sinking Island*, he set out to chart what he saw as the decline of British writing from the high point of its involvement in international modernism in the early decades of the century to its present state of mediocrity, philistinism, and media-manipulation.[2] Kenner constructs a myth of decline with the great modernists – Conrad, Ford, Pound, Joyce, Wyndham Lewis – constituting an earthly paradise, and the creation of a mass reading-public figuring as the fall. Writing in the modernist tradition makes great demands on the reader, but, in the post-war period, readers seem to have become less willing to accept such demands. Kenner argues, in his final chapter, that a contributing factor has been the insistence by the 'Movement' poets on easy intelligibility, which was a way of selling poetry (and its readers) short:

> For Milton had assumed, and so had Dante, that what was *expected* of a poet was a work of learning, something to occupy readers all their lives ... The resistant book was a norm for many centuries. The strange newcomer was not twentieth century 'modernism' ... What was relatively new was the 'easy' book. (SI, pp. 240–1)

He presents the cult of Larkin as creating a readership which preferred, as Larkin himself did, to find 'nothing difficult' in its reading matter.[3] Kenner also addresses contemporary poetry: he notes that very few major English publishing houses now maintain 'active' poetry lists (i.e. very few are willing to publish collections by new poets of unestablished reputation).[4] The few that do (Chatto, Faber, Secker, and, to some extent, OUP), he sees as under the control of a 'Martian Mafia' (SI, p. 256):

> The machinery, for those both knowledgeable and lucky runs more reliably than at any time in the past ... few publishers maintain poetry lists at all, and what gets selected for review, or for publication in the weekly journals, is consequently of much significance. Tie together publishing and reviewing and you have a lot of the action sewn up. (SI, pp. 254–5)

Davie too offers an explanation for British poetry's low international standing, for its being seen as an off-shore irrelevance, a service industry, or a slightly shoddy branch of the entertainment business, but, unlike Kenner, he is also concerned to challenge this perception by promoting other poets than those in the official pantheon – poets, such as Charles Tomlinson and F. T. Prince, who have 'reached for the ambitious objectives that we associate with modernism' (UB, p. 256). Basil Bunting, of course, is one of Davie's prime examples, for 'Bunting did have, as every great poet must have, a politics, and a philosophy of history' (UB, p. 238). The technical components of this modernism gradually emerge in the course of the book: it involves, for instance, a poetics of juxtaposition rather than discursiveness, whereby, as in Bunting, 'words ... are set flush one by another, the syntactical connections between them elided or suppressed, enriched, if never quite supplanted, by connectives of melody, of rhythm' (UB, pp. 39–40). It is 'a poetry of statement', deploying a certain verbal sparseness, the 'spare and stripped down language of Robert Creeley, Lorine Niedecker and Louis Zukofsky, or in Britain of Bunting or Tom Pickard' (UB, p. 240). But there are always invisible barriers which Davie's kind of modernist doesn't attempt to cross: 'Bunting . . . though he strenuously condenses his sentences, never abandons the subject-verb-object structure of the English sentence, whereas in Oppen and Pound what we read is quite often a series of disjunct phrases pulled free of any syntactical anchorage' (UB, p. 42). In the same way, MacDiarmid's 'engagement with history is one of the things we expect of a great poet' (UB, p. 20), but his ignoring 'the more far-reaching structural innovations of Eliot's *Waste Land*' was, according to Davie, 'not necessarily a bad thing' (UB, p. 15). Davie is similarly wary of something he sees Norman McCaig just holding back from, namely the writing of 'another modern poem from which the perceiving subject, the magisterial ego, has been more scrupulously eliminated' (UB, p. 20). Elaine Feinstein is approved for having learned 'from American models certain devices and certain mannerisms, notably an extremely sparse and idiosyncratic punctuation' (UB, p. 50); she has learned ('from the Black Mountain poets, perhaps Ed Dorn') how to combine the 'throw-away colloquialism' with a more elevated kind of language which can accommodate, for instance, classical allusions and material from the sphere of science; but Davie responds 'with foreboding' when he senses the influence of Charles Olson's 'discontinuous and exclamatory English' (UB, p. 93). Davie, then, argues for the use of a certain kind of 'moderate modernism' as well as for the need to include a political, philosophical, or historical dimension which will move the poet out beyond the mere registering of personal experience and will make a gesture, at least, towards what might be called the transcendence of the transcendent subject.

Davie's account of modernism suggests very well the qualities of much of the British poetry which remains almost totally excluded from both popular and academic awareness. If even Davie's moderately modernist poets are undervalued, then pushing across the border between what Davie sees as the acceptable and the unacceptable versions of modernism is to invite complete exclusion, certainly from the major publishing houses, but also from the lists of presses like Carcanet and Bloodaxe. Davie is much concerned with the way a small group of poets achieve a public (Heaney, Hughes, Larkin), while most never achieve more than a following. The abiding problem, according to him, is that the poetry-buying public wants 'nothing difficult', and, 'conceiving poetry as a service industry such a reader expects service . . . expects the experience to be brought all the way over to him, not left halfway' (UB, p. 85). Put another way, it seems as if the general poetry reader will tolerate a degree of surface difficulty, but only so long as the subject matter remains essentially familiar, domestic, and re-assuring. What is not tolerated is the combination of this surface difficulty with Davie's other requirement, that informing sense of politics, philosophy, and history which, he says, every great poet must have. Join this to the kind of verbal difficulty characteristic of 'hard' modernism and not even a following could be hoped for, merely the kind of readers, as Roy Fisher once ruefully said, who are addicted to your method. Yet plenty of poetry is being written in Britain which has precisely this combination of qualities. (Prominent recent examples would include Allen Fisher's *Place* sequence, with its wide range of social, political and historical material, and Iain Sinclair's *Lud Heat* with its intricate interweave of myth and history.) It is, however, too easy to blame 'poetry readers': it is necessary to consider further the business of poetry publication and distribution.

II
Patterns of exclusion

The anthology *The Penguin Book of Contemporary British Poetry* (1982) provides a useful starting point. The narrowness of poetic taste evidenced in the anthology's selection of poets and poems clashes with the representative claim implicit in the title, and the

editors make this worse by further explicit claims in their Introduction: 'A shift of sensibility has taken place very recently in
British poetry. It follows a stretch, occupying much of the 1960s
and 1970s, when very little – in England at any rate – seemed to be
happening.[5] By contrast, two more recent anthologies – *A Various
Art* and *The New British Poetry* – not only show the different kinds of
poetry excluded from the Penguin anthology but also reveal the
attempt made in the Introduction to paint whole areas of poetic
activity out of the picture.[6] The different sections of *The New British
Poetry* indicate some of the areas of poetry that Morrison and
Motion ignore: black British poetry; feminist poetry; the poetry of
the British Poetry Revival of the '1960s and 70s'; and the younger
poets who developed in the context of that 'Poetry Revival'.
Unlike the Penguin anthology, both *A Various Art* and *The New British
Poetry* draw on the wealth of poetic production that was enabled,
in the sixties and seventies, by cheapish mimeo and offset litho.
As Geoffrey Soar and R. J. Ellis have noted 'the 1960s and 1970s
witnessed a great increase in little magazine and small press
activity' in Britain, and it was within this area of *samizdat* publishing
that the 'Poetry Revival' took place.[7] Andrew Crozier, in his Introduction to *A Various Art*, suggests that much of this small-press
poetic production was consciously in opposition to the official
British poetry of the fifties. Crozier pithily summarises the pre-
vailing orthodoxy of the time: 'Poetry was seen as an art in relation
to its own conventions – and a pusillanimous set of conventions
at that. It was not to be ambitious, or to seek to articulate ambition
through the complex deployment of its technical means.' To
establish this orthodoxy a 'shift in taste' had been engineered, and
this had involved 'the wholesale rewriting' of the history of
modern poetry and 'the virtual suppression of parts of it'.
Morrison's full-length study of 'the Movement' supplies ample
evidence in support of Crozier's brief synopsis. This describes
how the poets of 'the Movement' (Amis, Larkin, Wain, Davie etc.)
presented themselves as 'a radical departure' from the poetry of
the forties by constructing 'a distorted picture' of that decade in
order to define themselves against it.[8] Morrison's careful research
also shows exactly how a small group of Oxbridge writers,

through a network of Oxbridge contacts, came to shift the taste of the fifties. In particular, where the modernist movement (and the British Poetry Revival later) forged its identity through 'little magazines', 'the Movement' concentrated on the weekly periodicals – the *Spectator*, the *Listener*, the *New Statesman* – which immediately gave access to a larger audience. As Davie noted in 'The Varsity Match': 'Precisely because the positions that matter are so few, it is entirely feasible for a group to secure one or two sub-editorial chairs and a few reviewing "spots", so as to impose their shared proclivities and opinions as the reigning orthodoxy of a decade.'[9]

In this context, Crozier records, one escape route was provided by American poetry and its tradition: 'not that of Pound and Eliot but that of Pound and Williams'. Eric Mottram describes a similar response to this situation in the Introduction to his section of *The New British Poetry*: his generation were very conscious of the example of 'senior figures' like MacDiarmid, Bunting, and David Jones ('all poets deeply aware of and affected by the poetics of modernism'); in addition, poets of the 'British Poetry Revival' looked to Gael Turnbull's Migrant Press, Stuart Montgomery's Fulcrum Press and Tom Raworth/Barry Hall/Nathaniel Tarn's Goliard Press, which made available a range of contemporary North American poets. Similarly, twenty years later, according to Ken Edwards, the younger poets in his section of the anthology 'started by discovering the work of Prynne, Mottram, Raworth, Harwood, Cobbing or Roy Fisher, only then proceeding backwards through these to Pound, Williams, Olson, Ashbery or O'Hara, and then perhaps on to the current work being done in America or Europe'. What is noticeable here is an engagement with modernist poetics and a consciously internationalist stance quite at odds with the 'little Englandism' of the official poetry of the 50s. Pound, in particular, acts as a marker. Larkin, for example, offered the following praise of Betjeman's verses: 'For him there has been no symbolism, no objective correlative, no T. S. Eliot or Ezra Pound'. And Heaney, the poet whom Morrison and Motion describe as the 'most important new poet of the last fifteen years' has elsewhere been described by Morrison as 'inhabiting a world in which Ezra Pound and "making it new" might never have happened'.[10] Davie's conclusion, in his early, extended study of Pound, *Pound: The Poet as Sculptor*, provides a clue to both the reason and the excuse for this attitude to Pound: 'Whatever more long term effect Pound's disastrous career may have on American and British poetry, it seems inevitable that it will rule out (has ruled out already, for serious writers) any idea that poetry can or should operate in the dimension of history.'[11] Pound's fascism provides an excuse for ignoring his poetry, perhaps precisely because his 'disastrous career' raises unavoidably the question of the relations between poetry, history and politics, a question that Eliot's poetry or Larkin's occludes and mystifies. On the other hand, the tradition that Crozier mentions, which includes poets like Oppen, Zukofsky and Olson, repudiates Pound's fascism through an engagement with the issues of politics and poetics.[12]

III
The site and the struggle

If Kenner can see the limitations of the official British poetry ('it's not to their system that you look for anything vital' [SI, p. 263]), the pattern of resistance to the hegemonic culture seems harder for him to read. He criticises the official neglect of Bunting, unpublished in Britain until Fulcrum Press published *Briggflatts* in 1966, but he seems unaware of Bunting's relation to the 'British Poetry Revival' and of the way in which the Objectivists (Oppen and Zukofsky, in particular), with whom Bunting was associated in America, were also taken up by this group of British poets.[13] Indeed, he seems unaware of the great quantity of poetry published in little magazines and small presses in recent decades.

To do justice to the 'new British poetries' of the last twenty years in a single volume is an impossible task. Instead, we have concentrated on that area of poetic production that developed in the 1970s and 1980s in poetry readings, performances, and, in particular, in a wealth of small press and little magazine activity. The first stage of this poetry production was recorded, at the time, in the extensive listings in Peter Finch's *Second Aeon* (1966–74) and in successive volumes of Peter Hodgkiss's invaluable *Poetry Information* (1970–79). It was briefly visible at the Poetry Society (1969–74) and in the pages of *Poetry Review* (1971–77); it was the subject of a couple of conferences on Modern British Poetry at the Polytechnic of Central London (1974, 1977); it was sporadically evidenced at the Cambridge Poetry Festival (1973–85); but these were only the more publicised manifestations of an extensive network of poetry publishing and performance up and down the country. This range of activities was not autochthonous: it grew out of a tradition of little magazine publication that is particularly associated with modernism, and out of patterns of publication and performance established in the 1960s.[14] (The Association of Little Presses set up by Bob Cobbing and others at the end of the 1960s is one example of the informal systems of information and cooperation that had been established.) It was also consciously internationalist, both in its networking and in its awareness of American and other European traditions. Through poets such as Paul Brown, Vivienne Finch, Lee Harwood and Peter Robinson, there was an engagement with dada and surrealism: Harwood's translations of Tzara, Brown's work on Benjamin Peret, Robinson's and Finch's translations of Reverdy. Through other poets there was an engagement with more recent French writing, and here Paul Buck and Glenda George's *Curtains* (1971–78) was outstanding: from *French Curtains* (No.5) to the final issue *bal:le:d curtains*, Buck and George published a rich mixture of French, English and American writing. Throughout the 1970s there was also a constant dialogue and interaction with a range of American poetries and poetics which operated through a similarly extensive small press/ little magazine movement. This was evidenced in such magazines as Michael Horovitz's *New Departures*, Jim Burns's *Palantir*, Pierre Joris's *Sixpack* and Allen Fisher's *Spanner*. Tim Longville's *Grosseteste Review*, for example, published work by English poets such as Anthony Barnett, Andrew Crozier, Peter Riley and J. H. Prynne alongside the work of the Objectivists, George Oppen and Carl Rakosi, as well as younger North American poets such as Larry Eigner, Barbara Guest and Gilbert Sorrentino.

Through the 1980s there seems to have been an overall

shrinkage in this area of little magazine production, although there have been a number of magazines that have significantly developed the work done in the 1970s, including Rod Mengham and John Wilkinson's *Equofinality*, Tony Baker's *Figs*, Martin Stannard's *joe soap's canoe*, John Welch's *The Many Review*, Tony Frazer, Ian Robinson and Robert Vas Dias's *Ninth Decade*, Robert Sheppard's *Pages*, Ken Edwards' *Reality Studios*, Paul Green's *Spectacular Diseases*, and Ric Caddel's *Staple Diet*. In England, the main areas of activity seem to have been London, Cambridge and the North-East. In London, for example, there have been the regular Sub Voicive readings organised by Gilbert Adair; Bob Cobbing's continuing Writers Forum Workshop; events organised by North and South Press; and the poetry workshop run successively by Paul Brown, Allen Fisher and Robert Sheppard. In Cambridge, a fitting culmination to the decade's writing and publishing activity was the 1991 three-day 'Cambridge Conference of Contemporary Poetry'.[15] Another development in the 1980s is that groups that were politically marginalised in that decade – the Welsh, the Scots, blacks and women – seem to have forged stronger cultural identities. In 'Inheritance Landscape Location: Data for British Poetry 1977', commenting on the complexity of 'location' as an issue for poets, Eric Mottram noted the presence, at the 1977 PCL 'British Poetry Conference', of groups of poets with particular geographical associations: Tom Leonard, Hugh MacDiarmid and Edwin Morgan from Scotland; Peter Finch, John Freeman, and J. P. Ward from Wales; Allen Fisher, Bill Griffiths and Iain Sinclair from London; and Basil Bunting, Barry MacSweeney, Tom Pickard, Colin Simms and Ken Smith from the North East.[16] But there was no sense that geographical location was the overriding factor for these poets. By contrast, developments in Scottish poetry in the 1980s, in the context of Scotland's new political and cultural self-definition, would now require a separate book.

One striking feature of small press poetry in England in this period is the relatively minor role of women: very few of the poets or editors were female. Wendy Mulford has raised the question why 'the work produced by women writing in the British Isles should be less formally adventurous'.[17] Poets such as

Gillian Clarke, Medbh McGuckian, Liz Lochhead and Anne Stevenson, she observes, are 'largely tied to a familiar poetics', in which language itself is not seen to be 'problematic'. On the other hand, she instances poets such as Glenda George, Carlyle Reedy, Geraldine Monk and Maggie O'Sullivan as having abandoned narrative and the unified lyric voice for 'a poetics of play and gesture'. Instead of 'saying things' about themselves or about a world conceived as 'out there', these poets explore 'the border or edge between the inconsequential and the significant', producing a contradictory play of sign, cancellation and gap to elicit the reader's involvement. Helen Kidd's article explores some of the pressures that have prevented women from playing a significant part in this particular area of poetic production. Other essays in this volume attempt to map specific areas of poetic activity, engage with theoretical and technical issues relating to this poetry or examine the work of particular poets. The volume has, therefore, been divided into three sections: 'Mapping the field', 'Poetics, politics, procedures', and 'Case studies'. Given the large number of poets included in *A Various Art* and *The New British Poetry* (not to mention many more not included in either volume), the editors are only too conscious of how selective the second and third sections, in particular, have had to be.

Notes

1 Donald Davie, Under Briggflatts: A History of Poetry in Great Britain, 1960–1988, Carcanet Press, Manchester, 1989.

2 Hugh Kenner, A Sinking Island: The Modern English Writers, Barrie and Jenkins, London, 1988. Hereafter cited in the text as SI.

3 Philip Larkin, Required Writing, Faber & Faber, London, 1984, p. 70.

4 It is also worth noting that, for Secker at least, the average print-run for a poetry book is only 500 copies. (See Blake Morrison, 'Poetry and the poetry business', Granta, 4, 1981, p. 101.) This is about the same size as the print-run of many 'small press' poetry books.

5 Andrew Motion and Blake Morrison, The Penguin Book of Contemporary British Poetry, Penguin, Harmondsworth, 1982, p.11.

6 Andrew Crozier and Tim Longville (eds.), A Various Art, Carcanet, Manchester, 1987; Gillian Allnutt, Fred D'Aguiar, Eric Mottram and Ken Edwards, The New British Poetry, Paladin, London, 1988. See also Pierre Joris and Paul Buck (eds.), Matières d'Angleterre, Trois Cailloux, Paris, 1984, and

Adrian Clarke and Robert Sheppard (eds.), *Floating Capital: New Poets from London*, Potes and Poets Press, Elmwood, Connecticut, 1981.

7 Geoffrey Soar and R. J. Ellis, 'Little magazines in the British Isles today', *British Book News*, December 1983, pp. 728–33; and 'U.K. little magazines: an introductory survey', *Serials Review*, Spring 1982, pp.15–28.

8 Blake Morrison, *The Movement: English Poetry and Fiction of the 1950s*, Oxford University Press, 1980, p. 25.

9 Donald Davie, 'The Varsity Match', *Poetry Nation*, 2, 1974, p. 74.

10 Blake Morrison, *Seamus Heaney*, Methuen, New York, 1982, pp. 14–15.

11 Donald Davie, *Pound: The Poet as Sculptor*, Oxford University Press, New York, 1964, p. 244.

12 See, in particular, Catherine Seelye (ed.), *Charles Olson and Ezra Pound: An Encounter at St Elizabeths*, Grossman Publishers, New York, 1975.

13 The most recent evidences of this are Peter Dent (ed.), *Not Comforts / But Vision: Essays on the Poetry of George Oppen*, Interim Press, Budleigh Salterton, 1985, and Harry Gilonis (ed.), *Louis Zukofsky, or Whoever Someone Else Thought He Was*, North and South Press, Twickenham and Wakefield, 1988.

14 See the Geoffrey Soars/David Miller catalogue to the Poetry Library exhibition, 'Little magazines and how they got that way', September/October 1990, for the tradition of 'little magazines'. Martin Booth's *British Poetry 1964–84*, (Routledge and Kegan Paul, London, 1985), contains an anecdotal account of small press and little magazine activity in this period that catches something of the atmosphere and the excitement of the poetry scene. Magazines that helped create the context for this poetic expansion include Jon Silkin's *Stand* (1952–), which has consistently published foreign work in translation, and Michael Horovitz's *New Departures* (1959–), with its attention to the Beats and to live performance. Other influential magazines included Ian Hamilton Finlay's *Poor. Old. Tired. Horse.* (1962–67), Dave Cunliffe and Tina Morris's *Poetmeat* (1963–67), Lee Harwood's *Horde* (1964), *Soho* (1964) and *Tzarad* (1965–67), and Andrew Crozier and Peter Riley's *The English Intelligencer* (1966–67).

15 See Geoffrey Ward, 'Serious poets return to Cambridge', *PN Review*, vol. 17, no. 6, July/August 1991, pp. 14–5.

16 Eric Mottram, 'Inheritance landscape location: Data for British Poetry 1977', *PCL British Poetry Conference*, pp. 85–101.

17 Wendy Mulford, ' "Curved, Odd . . . Irregular": A vision of contemporary poetry by women', *Women: A Cultural Review*, vol. 1, no. 3, Winter 1990, pp. 261–74, p. 261.

Mapping the field

Eric Mottram

1

The British Poetry
Revival, 1960–75

In June 1974, and again in June 1977, the Centre for Extra Mural
Studies (by 1977 called the Cultural and Community Studies Unit)
of the Polytechnic of Central London held two British Poetry
Conferences. These events signalled the maturity of a contemporary British poetry, viable in an innovative and developed
poetics and substantial in range of materials, constituting a power
to be placed with contemporary poetry in America and Europe.
This state of British poetic art existed largely unrecognised by the
literary establishment, that is the big controlling presses, the universities and schools, and the reviewing fraternity. The new
poetry acknowledged no enclosure in self-styled 'schools',
although it already showed a variety of small group differences.
The work was published by a large number of small presses and
magazines, and therefore was easily available to anyone really
interested in poetry, although not, of course, at the controlling
High Street booksellers. The new poetry was also ignored or
attacked by charity-giving bodies like the Arts Council and the
radio and television comptrollers and censors. These and the rest
of the establishment were, and remain, mainly a flaccid hangover
from the dominant tastes of the thirties, forties and fifties. In
spring 1971, TriQuarterly 21, a major American journal, published a
collection of the new poetry that later became a book, Twenty-three

Modern British Poets, edited by John Matthias, an American poet with considerable experience of the British scene.[1] Owing to publisher's demands, it was not available in Britain, according to a note by the journal's regular editors. Although American reviews were enthusiastic, in this country the *Times Literary Supplement*, *Agenda* and *Stand* were hostile, according to a letter from Matthias to the present writer.

This collection contained work from the older generation – Basil Bunting, David Jones and Hugh MacDiarmid – major work by poets ignored by the apes of the thirties and the Movement's antecedents. (At Faber, Eliot had turned down Bunting but had at least published Jones). The middle generation was represented by Christopher Middleton, Charles Tomlinson, Gael Turnbull, Roy Fisher, Ted Hughes, Ian Hamilton Finlay, Christopher Logue, Matthew Mead and Nathaniel Tarn; and the younger poets by Anselm Hollo, Ken Smith, Lee Harwood, Harry Guest and Tom Raworth, some of whom were included in the first representative collection of the Revival, *The New British Poetry* (Paladin, London), in 1988. Their range of style remains wide, and, despite at least one attempt to foster a group called (of all things) 'Floating Capital', they are not restricted to London. Their education and class origins vary. Their political attitudes range from Communist to liberal-neutral. Their information and language resources are wide enough to justify Matthias's basis of choice: 'variety and change of pace'. The sheer range of other poets needed to make a later, completer list would have to include, at least, Jim Burns, David Chaloner, cris cheek, Bob Cobbing, Andrew Crozier, Ken Edwards, Elaine Feinstein, Allen Fisher, John Hall, Robert Hampson, Dom Silvester Houédard, Michael Horovitz, John James, Barry MacSweeney, Stuart Montgomery, Edwin Morgan, Wendy Mulford, Jeff Nuttall, Douglas Oliver, Tom Pickard, Denise Riley, Peter Riley, Elaine Randell, Gavin Selerie, Chris Torrance, Lawrence Upton . . .

The list is incomplete, invidious by its very brevity. These poets write within the current range of forms in world poetry – open field, projective verse, sound text, concrete poetry, surrealist and dada developments, pop lyrics, and various conceptual forms. Imitation and school are relegated; the skills develop free awareness and usage of a wide range of procedures. It is exactly that range that establishment restrictors wish to curtail by narrow critical dogma and restrictive publishing and reviewing. Under their own enterprise and financing, with a little help from the Arts Council where it fits its establishment judgement, and within as much hindrance for the future as possible, the small presses have ignored the 1950s biases and developed a wide range of contemporary poetics. The Catalogue of Little Press Books in Print, compiled by the Association of Little Presses (London, 1974) was a guide to the finest poetry, but it could not list the magazines and hundreds of significant books necessarily out of print. Small presses initiate, but the financial problems of reprinting rather than printing new work are formidable. As Stefan Themerson, for many years the centre of initiation at the Gabberbocchus Press, observed in his preface to the Catalogue, the big press 'starts with Market Research', while the small press 'exercises unprofitable freedom'. Establishment reviewers and committee members of grant-giving bodies are adjuncts of the market system and in fact form a club of advisers to the big presses. A list of poets published by these presses and of the reviewers in the posh weeklies and quarterlies, plus the publishers' advising editors, would reveal their close similarities and their relations with those who give and receive public grants.

The bookshop problem is closely related. By 1974 in London, for example, only Compendium Books stocked a range of poetry with any breadth of enterprise. Better Books, once a large store whose poetry selection came successively under the aegis of poetmanagers – Bill Butler and Bob Cobbing, and then Lee Harwood and Paul Selby – became increasingly smaller as market values moved in. They even managed to organise regular poetry readings in their cramped spaces. This enterprise was wiped out. The only other bookshop with anywhere near such enterprise was Bernard Stone's Turret bookshops in Kensington Church Walk, from which were published the Turret Books series.

The small press situation could be quickly estimated from a

feature, 'The Small Press' in *Time Out* for July 27–August 1, 1973, which concerned Gaberbocchus, Fulcrum and Trigram presses,provided facts on the Association of Little Presses (the ALP), the death-rate of small press publishing and the methods by which the Arts Council handles taxpayers' money intended for new publishing. It was and is, of course, notorious what a tiny percentage of the Council's funds reach living creative writing as distinct from the prestige spectaculars such as Covent Garden. *Time Out* demonstrated the amount of time, energy and humiliation entailed in appealing to the Council for funds. The Council's commissar for literature, Charles Osborne, replied in a celebratedly infamous letter, printed in the issue of August 17–23, signing himself, precisely, 'chief undertaker and literature director, The Arts Council'. But this institution was and is advised basically by establishment figures for decisions on poetry, and, what is more, poetry as a market consumption article like a double scotch or a cigarette. But small press poetry within the period 1960–75 did not cater to the middle-class rapid-reader, untrained in contemporary poetics and looking for instant significance and alibis with established, authenticated products. Poetry for contemporary writers and readers as parts of a significantly enterprising culture needed to be something other: the creation of artists whose notations of form, feeling and observation might take months or years of trained appreciation to understand, with a considerable outlay of time and energy. Nor will such poetry probably appear with the external trappings which signify leisure in consumer-product advertising terms: hard covers with big press signatures. Most librarians and practically the whole of the decreasing 'reading public' do not buy small press poetry, and little educational training encourages a young public to read at all once they have 'grown up'. Many 'little presses' use modern inexpensive techniques to produce decent, often elegant, books and pamphlets of poetry, in both hard and soft cover editions, but this productivity is largely ignored by the agents of information and distribution.

Large-scale poetry readings have never reached the extent and power of those in the American campus and city café scene from the later 1950s into the 1960s and 1970s. The neglect of the presence of living poets and poetry by British universities was and remains a scandal, compared to the American practice.

During the fifteen years of the Revival, it became obvious to anyone paying serious attention to European and American poetry that we had a major poetry in Britain. This developed strongly and confidently during the 1970s. Even the minimal help from official organisations had an extent unknown in previous decades.

The life of poetry had traditionally been left to chance and market exigencies of taste. Two signs of better conditions appeared in the 1960s – the Poets Conference and the London Poetry Secretariat. The first was convened by writers as different in literary concern as William Plomer, Asa Benveniste, George MacBeth, and Adrian Henri, with Bob Cobbing as secretary. All poets were invited to participate, but especially those professionals who earned at least part of their living from poetry or regarded it as their main occupation. The Conference leaflet stated: 'it is the nearest poets have got to having a trade union'. The ninth conference was held in 1974. The London Poetry Secretariat's brochure declared: 'Poetry is no longer the preserve of a cultural elite – it has become an art which is widely enjoyed . . . the poet has gained a new audience through reading his work in public.' Readings series need sound organisation; two organisations, *Poets in Public* and the Greater London Arts Association joined 'to promote readings and to help look after the interests of poets giving readings of their work' and to help arts administrators, educational authorities and the public. Later, under the aegis of a reformed Poetry Society, the National Poetry Secretariat functioned similarly, but, at least initially, with a wider range of poetic styles. The Poetry Society, which used to be considered the centre of reaction and tediously restricted conservativism, moved into the twentieth century in the early 1970s with a fresh and innovative organisation voted into control by people deeply concerned with making it a centre of the Revival. It was not long before the Arts Council moved in to quash this action, by threatening to withdraw funds unless its own unelected representatives were placed on the committee of management and certain members of the organisation sacked. (See Appendix.)

But for nearly a decade the Poetry Society gained a reputation for representing the finest in the Revival. The presidential chair was accepted by a major poet of the older generation, Basil Bunting, a remarkable man, with direct links to Pound, Zukofsky and Ford Madox Ford, with connections with young poets in his own region of the North East, and a wide-ranging sense of the history of poetic forms, manifest in his seminars and lectures – the latter only too few, owing to the radical conservativism of the academic and educational world. The ugly attack on his work and influence in British Poetry since 1960 (edited by Michael Schmidt and Grevel Lindop in 1972) is both spiteful and inaccurate.[2] Stuart Montgomery, distinguished poet and organiser, with his wife Deirdre, of the excellent Fulcrum Press, was at one time treasurer, a post later held by Bob Cobbing, the senior British soundtext poet with an international reputation, and editor of the Writers Forum series, today reaching its celebration of 500 texts. Members of the General Council included a range of excellent poets including Roy Fisher, Elaine Feinstein, Harry Guest, Peter Finch, Anthony Rudolph, Martin Booth, Jeremy Adler, Peter Hodgkiss, editor of Poetry Information, who later made it into the primary source the Revival needed, and Daniel Weissbort, one of the editors of Modern Poetry in Translation. The range of poets and speakers at the Poetry Society respected the Revival, and so did the new editorship of Poetry Review, journal of the Society, in the hand of the present writer, generously helped by Bob Cobbing.

But the official British poetry continued to be a peculiar axis, formed from a handful of dominant sources within a single frame, later in their history called, characteristically, The Movement. Listen (II, 3, 1957), edited by George Hartley from Hessle, Yorkshire, contained the types: Larkin, Lerner, Fraser, Auden, Amis, Conquest, Fuller, Enright, et. al. G. S. Fraser, writing in Post-War Trends in English Literature (Tokyo, 1959) claimed: if 'we have no common style, today', it is because 'we have no common vision', and that is because of 'the decay and division of the Christian faith since the Renaissance, to the humanist arrogance that will not accept mystery'. But since unity of custom is, in Britain, unity of culture, this tolerance will enable 'the growing vision . . . to take care of itself.' The English writer does not need 'artificial props' of 'ideologies, systems, schools' – except, presumably, Christianity – 'he finds his moral support and the nourishment of his sensibility in the large society in which he lives . . . It is not good for a nation, anymore than it is good for a man, to be for ever dragging up to the light, and scrutinising and questioning the principles by which he lives. It is habit which gives life strength and ease and unity, so long as it is a healthy habit, so long as it is informed by a living principle of growth'. This woolly, reactionary rhetoric impregnated the poets in Robert Conquest's New Lines (1956), and his official list remained in place for decades: Elizabeth Jennings, Larkin, Thom Gunn, Amis, D. J. Enright, Donald Davie, John Wain . . .[3] The thin coherence is Conquest's 'refusal to abandon a rational structure and comprehensible language, even when the verse is most highly charged with sensuous or emotional intent', and his need for 'an intellectual skeleton . . . given the flesh of humanity, irony, passion or sanity'. These were the partly hilarious bases of the Movement's dance of death, anthologised by Fraser in Poetry Now (1956).[4] His list was slightly broader than Conquest's and contained first-rate poets such as W. S. Graham, F. T. Prince, and the early Charles Tomlinson (his first book, The Necklace, at least influenced by Wallace Stevens, appeared in 1955 with an introduction by Davie).[5] The rest were much duller: Bergonzi, Alvarez, Brownjohn, Durrell, Heath-Stubbs, MacBeth and R. S. Thomas. Fraser's introduction acknowledges the group's allegiance to the thirties poets who invented no new forms but adapted existing ones, and worked for 'a new Augustanism'; he cites Conquest's criticism of Dylan Thomas, the influence of William Empson's metrical forms, and Larkin as 'a chastened Yeats – a Yeats "done over again" in water-colour'. The desired common tone is 'sobriety' and 'strictness' – 'the most assured level of accomplishment seems to me rather that of wit or fancy or sensitive description than that of profound or soaring imagination'.[6]

Part of the reason this lot swerved away from the twentieth

century is given in Robin Skelton's introduction to *Poetry of the Thirties* in 1964.[7] He disparages 'the paraphernalia of surrealism' and the 'iconoclastic effects' of Freud and Marx, who both 'upset the *bourgeoisie* and laid bare the springs of action'. He goes on ambivalently about 'the surrealistic, or near-surrealistic poetry of David Gascoyne, Hugh Sykes Davies, Phillip O'Connor, and others', Gascoyne's *A Short Survey of Surrealism* (1935) and the Surrealist Exhibition of 1936, but he then declares Auden 'the clear Master of the Period', cited for his 'often schoolboy knowingness, an eager relishing of the audience's probably shocked response', and he quotes Dylan Thomas from the Auden number of *New Verse* in 1937: 'I sometimes think of his poetry as a great war, admire intensely the mature, religious, and logical fighter, and deprecate the boy bushranger'. In fact, the scene in the forties inherited this interwar search for authority and foundation. But some of the better artists knew what they needed. Gascoyne's *Poems 1937–42* worked with plates by Graham Sutherland, and such connections with Picasso and expressionism were to be taken up by Jeff Nuttall in the sixties.[8] Auden's poems of moral and political landscape became a departure for John Ashbery and Lee Harwood in the sixties, and both Harwood and the New York poets respected F. T. Prince's *The Doors of Stone: Poems, 1938–1962* (1963).[9]

David Wright's *The Mid-Century: English Poetry, 1940–60* (1965) constituted a kind of who's who of official verse from Auden and Betjeman to Abse, Hughes and Thwaite, a trio with authority in the establishment.[10] The introduction also signals the anti-Americanism of the later sixties and seventies, which enabled the establishment to attack the Revival, with its clear grasp of American poetics: 'There are no American poets in this anthology. American and English poetry is no longer homogeneous, though written in approximately the same language'. If that clumsy account of the facts were not daft enough, Wright continues: 'Contemporary American poetry – which, thanks to the excessive interest taken in it by the American universities, is now an industry rather than art – seems to be wandering off in the direction of the decorative, where style and technique is all and thought, if anything, a peg on which to hang a Chinese box of semantic ingenuities.' So much for Olson, Stevens, Duncan, Ashbery, Ginsberg and Rexroth.

In his introduction to *Poetry of the Committed Individual* (1973), Jon Silkin states that the magazine *Stand* was started in 1962 partly to rectify the narrowness and laziness which typify the 1950s Axis of Conquest–Fraser–Larkin.[11] The issues formed up between *New Lines* and *Mavericks* (edited by Howard Sergeant and Dannie Abse), devoted to a more romantic and dionysian utterance but under 'discipline and form and style'. Silkin regarded this as a struggle for the ascendancy of a single set of received aesthetic criteria, as 'the continuing basis for a lasting autonomy', and therefore a 'senti-mental tyranny'. Although he believed it was no longer necessary, 'it may return', since no set of criteria then dominated – we have 'relative openness' within 'the comparative rigidity of English society and its culture'. We may look forward to criteria emerging from 'the practice of the writers, and not from the imposition upon them of well-worn absolutes'.

In fact the tyranny continued to operate with increased power as the small presses brought through a radical change in British poetry. At least Silkin was correct that the practice of writers would take charge, and he knew that American poetry's effect on British poetry was at least a ten-year fact: our poetry 'shares the language on different points of a lengthening spectrum, the extension of which is no longer within the sole dictation of England'. There are poets who have accommodated the 'cultural shock' and 're-examine what (they) have in relation to these others, and develop it in mutual interaction'. Silkin was aware of the benefits of refusing the Movement's narrow nationalism: 'The quicker and more thoroughly we learn, in however limited a way, something of what the sensuous powers and moral entrapments feel like in Iowa, Teesside, or Prague (quite apart from what Amman, Jaffa and Hanoi can tell us) the more insistently can our preparations be made for a continuingly vigorous and changing culture.'

Ezra Pound offered a clear example of how useful could be; a variety of formal procedures release from inherited forms and their radical transformation; a thorough choice of contemporary and historical life that might be used in poetry; a sense of the limitations of symbol and metaphor – that nothing can really stand for another thing; a continuous awareness of the poet's function within finance capitalism, political corruption and concepts of law, and of the nature of erotic love and desire for power and their traditions within the morphology of social and personal energies. But his concern for order was a response, like those of Eliot, Yeats, MacDiarmid, David Jones and Auden, that could only too swiftly move towards the authoritarian, paradoxically within an art that could be a full-blooded articulation of inventive imagination. At least it was not the thin Tory–Liberal rationalism and whining of the Angry Young Men of the 1950s, and their rapid metamorphosis into middle-brow rigidities and safeties in the 1960s and 1970s. Pablo Neruda's life as a Communist political eminence in Chile juxtaposed his intense inventiveness of form and his dedicated attention to an extraordinarily wide range of materials. Latin American poetry, in fact, could exemplify for young British poets the nature of commitment to new poetics – the work of Vallejo, Huidobro, Guillen, Castillo and Cardenal, available through issues of *El Cornu Emplumado* (that reached Britain through Better Books) and texts from an extraordinary publishing enterprise in the sixties: *Our Word: Guerrilla Poems from Latin America* and *Con Cuba: A Cuban Anthology*, were both published by Cape Goliard in 1968, edited respectively by Edward Dorn, the American poet, and Gordon Brotherstone, a major British university figure in the Latin American field, and by Nathaniel Tarn, the British poet and anthropologist, who also edited *Selected Poems of Pablo Neruda* for Cape in 1970.

The nearest to total commitment to invention and social consciousness in Britain was the poetry of Hugh MacDiarmid, the product of a lifetime of creative imagination and social consciousness, and a wide-ranging linguist and informed intellect, finely registered in his autobiography, *Lucky Poet: A Self-Study in Literature and Political Ideas . . .* (1942; reissued by Cape in 1972) and his *Collected Poems* (published in New York in 1962).[12]

David Jones's large-scale palimpsestic patterns of mythical

and religious history, Celtic, Arthurian and Roman Catholic, placed in his own invented forms, inherited and developed the ambits of C. S. Lewis, Charles Williams, Eric Gill and Stanley Spencer, that is, of major Christian allegory in the inter-war years. Jones's skilled movement between remote and recent history, between the present and the eternal, was related to the scale of invention and inspiration in the *Cantos*, but was entirely British: *In Parenthesis* (1937), under Eliot's patronage at Faber; *The Anathemata* (1952); *The Tribune's Visitation* (Fulcrum, 1969).[13] The support for Jones in William Cookson's *Agenda* magazine was outstanding, and for some time virtually unique. The nearest in prose to MacDiarmid and Jones was *Finnegans Wake* and in lyric poetry Dylan Thomas's 'The Ballad of the Long-Legged Bait' and 'Vision and Prayer' in *Deaths and Entrances* (1946).[14]

The liberatory action of these poets began to grow again in the 1960s, exemplifying and instigating the invention of forms and poetics rather than endless adaptations and repetitions within a classicist attitude towards poetry under some policing from a critical school or tyrannical ideology of restriction. As Rilke wrote in one of his *Sonnets to Orpheus* (Ruth Speirs' translation in Erich Neumann's *Art and the Creative Unconscious*, (1959):

> . . . what locks itself in endurance grows rigid; sheltered
> in assuming greyness, does it feel safe?
> Wait, from the distance hardness is menaced by something still
> harder.
> Alas – : a remote hammer is poised to strike.
> Knowledge knows him who pours forth a spring;
> delighted she guides him, showing him what was created in joy
> and often concludes with beginning and starts with end.
>
> Every happy space they traverse in wonder
> is child or grandchild of parting. And Daphne, transformed,
> feeling herself laurel, wants you to change into wind.[15]

Or as Norbert Wiener wrote in *The Human Use of Human Beings* (1950): 'to be alive is to participate in a continuous stream of influences from the outer world and acts on the outer world . . . to participate in a continual development of knowledge and its unhampered exchange'.[16] Academics and architectural offices could find no formal dogmas or recipes in Wittgenstein's Kundmanngasse house because it went beyond limits and 'demonstrates how enriching "unprofessional encroachment" can be, and questions the limits of a profession that are mainly set by the very members of that profession' (Bernard Leitner, 'Wittgenstein's Architecture', *Art Forum*, February 1970).

Since the 1930s, officially-sanctioned British poetry had favoured minimal invention and information, and maximum ironic finesse, with personal anecdote, covered with a social veneer or location of elements in the country. It favoured the urbanely witty or baroquely emotional rather than the thoroughly informed intelligence willing and eager to risk imaginative forms. Official preference could not tolerate an art that went beyond a leisure-hours consumer inclination to rapid reading; work which might necessitate concentration, trained ability to read, and a willingness to entertain the prospect of new forms and materials. Poetry of the official preference had become a mere adjunct to politics, business and academic scholarship, in distinct enmity to the inclusive and exhilarating forces in, for example, Lawrence, Pound, William Carlos Williams, MacDiarmid, Jones and Bunting. Those taking part – as poets, publishers and readers – in the British Poetry Revival that took place all over Britain, irrespective of schools', universities' and reviewers' orthodoxies, recognised that poetry was not a consumer product to be easily ingested. The performances of the Liverpool poets (those 'pop' poets partly recorded in Edward Lucie-Smith's *The Liverpool Scene* [1967]) at least showed that there could be an audience for poetry outside the study, the university library and the tradition-bound classroom.[17] In the summer of 1965, the Albert Hall reading by poets from a number of countries, including Britain (later registered in a text entitled *Wholly Communion*) demonstrated that it might not be too late for an exciting growth of live poetry readings such as had become common in the United States during the past decade. *Live New Departures*, organised by Michael Horovitz and Pete Brown, showed that poetry and music in combined performance could open new audiences. They produced over a thousand such shows in about eight years, and their total audiences were large. As Adrian Mitchell wrote in 'Poetry Explodes' (*The Listener*, May 14, 1970): 'Mike Horovitz has done one hundred times more than the Arts Council to encourage poetry in this country. The informality and excitement of these concerts has brought into the open a huge new audience for poetry, as well as many new poets. Other people have helped to discover this audience, but Horovitz is the man most responsible'.

But power in a hierarchy favours those whose ideal is the invariant, the self-maintaining system in the dreams of a totalitarian mind, and an aristocraticism of culture. The artist who creates rather than adapts to a predictive system and invents forms which resist custom is quickly identified as the enemy. The desire for a cut-off nationalist culture is part of this desire. Many young British poets learned a great deal about the variety of possible poetics from contemporary American examples, and often from poets visiting this country – for example, the exuberant, hearty and Whitmanesque Allen Ginsberg, the meticulous and erudite Charles Olson, the passionately bardic and highly informed Robert Duncan, the radically political and formally inventive Louis Zukofsky and George Oppen, and the astonishing cultural erudition and startling performance skills of Jerome Rothenberg. But the establishment were scared of what it considered to be an invasion of exclusive territory. From the lyrics of the Beatles and other rock groups, and from Bob Dylan and a few other soloists, poets could learn that lyrical forms, too, could be reinvented to give contemporary force. Poetic space need not be rigidly enclosed or shaped under hard linear dimensions, restricted to traditional sentence logic and grammatical usage. The completion of a poem could include a reader's consciousness. The poet's meeting a reader in a formative process need not be dependent on a straight-jacketing notation and the eyes following print on a silent page. A poem need not illustrate dogmas but can enact with gestures flexible enough to hold potentiality as well as ascertained experience and prior formed knowledge. A poem could be a proposition of energies that suggested their sources and need not terminate them in insistent limits. Instead of being marketed as a consumerist item, a poem could be part of the world of physics and philosophy in inter-action, requiring an attention beyond instant recognition and reaction. Instead of being an item in a school of rhetoric, a poem could have a variety of articulations, continuity and discontinuity, sentence and parataxis, and an awareness of the imaginative pos-sibilities of relationships between particle, measure, line and paragraph, between existent and new forms. The gentle but firm terseness of Carl Rakosi's and George Oppen's short measures suggested possibilities of the social personal lyric. When Neruda read at King's College, University of London, the audience con-fronted a poet as a national, political and personal presence conveyed through varied poetics unknown in this country.

The poets of the Revival understood the risks of ambitious form and multiple experience. It was not at all a matter of impositions of American and other poetries as claimed by some chauvinist critics of the 1960s new poetry – a panic reaction based on petty nationalism. The new poets realised that poetry could be a usable body of vision and example from which new experience and new forms had not been edited out in the name of custom and fear of imagination and the body's senses. The new poets came towards that definition in J. Z. Young's wonderful book *Doubt and Certainty in Science*: 'The creative artist is an observer whose brain works in new ways, making it possible for him to convey information to others about matters that were not a sub-ject for communication before. It is by search for means of communication that we sharpen our powers of observation. The discoveries of the artist and scientist are exactly alike in this respect.'[18] The parameters of poetry and poetics were recognised afresh as geology, geography, etymology, history and the erotic – materials manifest in Pound, Zukofsky, Neruda, Trakl, Olson, Pasolini, Vallejo, Rothenberg – all readily to hand. The axes of proprioceptive poetic action (readily accessible in Olson's *Human Universe*, for example) and a reader's attention to it included both individual response (Duncan's 'ability to respond' as a definition of responsibility) and group action within actual economics, politics and anti-Freudian psychology, the interactions of person and process (Whitehead's writings gained a fresh lease of life), an answer to Rimbaud's question 'What is on the other side of despair?', and a new recognition of mythology to be used hermeneutically and heuristically, bearing an active relationship with Carl Sauer's definition of morphology.[19] That is, a multiple and practical understanding of the discovery of coherences and locations for a renewal of civic poetry in the culture – 'civic' in the sense that William Carlos Williams consciously inherited from Dante, for example ('Against the weather', 1939).[20]

Poetic action under such possibilities rejects the precepts of the 1950s Movement poets and their 1955 spokesman Kingsley Amis, whose dictum was: 'nobody wants any more poems on the grander themes for a few years'. For 'nobody' read the reader as rapid consumer or lazy academic who resists attention to the complex contemporary. For 'a few years' read for ever, or at least Amis's lifetime. Under such a *diktat*, it was clear why MacDiarmid, for instance, had been neglected. The range of interests and sources for poetry offered in chapter three of *Lucky Poet*, 'The Kind of Poetry I Want', and chapter six, 'The Ideas Behind My Work', would constitute anathema for the Movement. It would be a matter of poetry requiring attention to form in the widest sense of that term, and informed intelligence – in the Scottish poet's case, to a degree unimaginable by any Movement versifier. It is the requirement of this kind of attention that relegated Bunting's work, with the honorable exception of its publication in Peter Russell's magazine *Nine*, its rediscovery by *Poetry* (Chicago) which published 'Briggflatts' in its January 1966 issue, Stuart Montgomery's Fulcrum Press, and Tom Pickard in Newcastle with his one-off magazine recording Bunting's life and work, *King Ida's Watch Chain* (1965) (which included appreciations from Gael Turnbull, Hugh Kenner and Louis Zukofsky, among others). But criteria for acceptable establishment poetry required that it be easily teachable; its form so nearly a transparent vehicle that it can be read rapidly without interference. A poem must be reviewable reassuringly in the posh papers and journals and contain some kind of utilitarian reference which is not too disturbing. It should have an easily paraphrasable meaning. Most of the Revival work did not wish to meet such criteria.

In the absence of large representative anthologies of Revival work between 1960 and 1975, any full account would have to be based on the long listing of magazines, presses, publications and events in Part 4 of the essay accompanying the programme of the 1974 Modern British Poetry Conference at the Polytechnic of Central London. This shows clearly that a large number of people understood that an abundance of good poetry needed publishing, and that they were prepared to place together British, American and continental European poetry, militating against the provincialism of the Movement and the containing officialdom. The list is not so much a totally complete map as an invitation to notice and explore. It could have been double its present size. The variety of poetry is as remarkable as the general level of ability is extraordinarily high. And most of the publications were financed out of personal funds. It can only be recommended here that an interested scholar of the Revival should study the document. It is a matter of sixteen and a half large pages of materials. Some of the items are housed in the library of University College, University of London, but there is, of course, no representatively full collection anywhere in this country, beyond perhaps two or three large private collections, which no library is prepared to purchase and maintain under proper curatorship.

The list includes, for example, some account of: New Departures, Agenda, Writers Forum, Tarasque, My Own Mag, Tzarad, Ambit, Kroklok, The Journal of Pierre Menard, Grosseteste Review, Second Aeon, the Big Venus series of titles, and the Ice series, The Wivenhoe Park Review and Ferry Press, Fulcrum Press, Goliard and Cape Goliard, Earthship, Curtains, Sesheta, Strange Faeces, Juillard, Collection, Schmuck, Aloes Press, Sixpack, Akros Publications, and, for soundtext work, Stereo Headphones, Mindplay, Typewriter Poems, Trigram Press, Turret, Albion Village, Joe Dimaggio, Penguin Modern Poets, (an almost unique big press enterprise), Poetry Review (particularly from 1970 to 1976). This is part of the needed demonstration without the necessary full analysis. The listings in Second Aeon, Poetry Review, Poetry Information,

and *Little Press Books in Print*, (Association of Little Presses) supply
further facts. Facts which expose the ignorant stupidity of Stephen
Berg and Robert Mezey's foreword to *Naked Poetry* (New York,
1969): 'with a few exceptions (mainly Ted Hughes) nothing much
new has happened in English poetry since Lawrence laid down
his pen and died'.[21] For such American and other foreign
opinions and their British counterparts, we have partly to thank
the British Council and official distribution and propaganda in the
weeklies and academic quarterlies, and teachers trained in academic traditions of caution, waiting for a poet to be safely dead
before you even begin to contemplate studying, even teaching,
him or her – provided the poet fits established definitions of the
catch-all term for conservative panics, 'tradition'.

In 'Syllogism and Censorshit' (*Poetry Information*, 8, 1973),
Horovitz quoted Anthony Thwaite from *The Listener* (Thwaite
being a typical poetry powerman in the trade) writing that there
are two poetries: one believes in 'shape, form and control' and is
led by Fuller, Larkin and Hamilton; the other believes in 'spontaneity, immediacy, an energy released by both poet and audience in a flash communion' and is exemplified by Ginsberg,
Horovitz, Nuttall and Brian Patten. Ginsberg's *Reality Sandwiches*,
according to Thwaite, ('reveals all its facets and depths and resonances at a single reading or hearing'. Apart from the careless
arrogance of his own self-appraisal, such a belief is easily dis-
proved. But Thwaite needs a division stemming from an
inaccurate notion of the processes of reading and hearing poetry,
of kinds of poetry and kinds of training to receive it. The poets he
mentions have different prosodies and complexities and ranges
of materials. These he ignores, but his opinion carries
officialdom's weight. The Revival poets managed very well without his deliberations, except that grants, publication that might
bring in some funds, the possibility of reviews and of purchasing
in libraries and educational places, the chance of reaching
potential readers with tastes for the unconventional, all depended
on the Thwaite–Larkin–Hamilton axis. *Poetry Information* also
reported that Thwaite 'took up cudgels' against Donald Davie's
critical review of Larkin's *Oxford Book of Twentieth-Century English Verse*

and dismissed Horovitz's replying letter in *The Listener*, which did not print his second letter.[22] *Poetry Information* did. In those days, Horovitz stood against intolerance of other forms of poetry and of other publication than your own. There was also the *Axis'* attack on Olson and what they ignorantly summarise as the 'Black Mountain School', as well as their assault on Bunting (even at the celebration Oxford University Press gave for the publication of its edition of his poetry, characteristically without proper acknowledgment of all those presses that published him when he needed the reputation and the money). This kind of record may be considered rather tired stuff now, but it is part of the history of poetry, part of the history of the endless fight against the second-rate. Horovitz was correct: the power of *Axis* opinion, the editing policies of publishing firms, the controls from reviewers did (and still do) contribute to the demise of necessities like Cape Goliard and the ostracising of important sources like *Migrant*, *New Departures* and *Outburst*, three generators he mentions. He quoted Martin Bell's panic in a letter to *The Listener*: 'I was sorry to see the word Ginsberg creep in' and 'you don't need Olson and the whole thing here'. But the Poetry Revival was marked by its willingness to benefit from a wide range of international quality without fear in order to develop the craft of poetics. Even Ted Hughes' mani-festo for the first *Poetry International* in London (1967) evidences this. The variety of poets for that occasion indicated again the inaccuracy of *Axis* narrowness and fear. They included Octavio Paz, Zbigniew Herbert, Amichai, Enzensberger, Bachman, Ungaretti, Neruda, Bonnefoy, John Berryman, Olson, Anne Sexton, Ginsberg, Robert Graves, Auden, Spender.

The British Poetry Revival took place in that context, especially as a number of poets used syntheses of forms they had learned from beyond official British parochialism: open field poetry, concrete and soundtext poetry, surrealism and dada, con-ceptual forms, and the variants of these. But, on the whole, they did not require 'confessional' poetry or the determinacies of that amalgam of Hardy, Edward Thomas and Robert Frost the Move-ment boys serviced themselves with. Only insensitivity and fear would have led an anonymous reviewer of Tom Raworth's *Moving* to dismiss his work as 'spontaneously slapdash . . . pretentiously poetical . . . short-winded jottings (often single words or lines) masquerading as epiphanies' (*Times Literary Supplement*, April 4, 1971). Stephen Spender began his essay 'America and England' (*Partisan Review*, XL, 3, 1973) with a required acknowledgement: 'Just as Americans measured their civilization against the European, so today English literature since 1945 has become provincial – not just in relation to America but in relation also to the English past, perhaps even in relation to Europe.' In particular, he pointed out, the attraction of America lies in 'its being the centre of energies which are entirely contemporary':

> These show themselves in the arts– painting, fiction, and poetry – when these express an American total sum of present-day consciousness, not of a civilization confined to one class or to an élite. The American writer seems open to everything that happens in his country. His attitude is summed up in the idea of 'projectiveness'. He is open to the whole surrounding experience which pours through his senses and realizes itself, almost spontaneously, and in forms mostly free, in his work.

Whether Spender really understood Olson's 'projective verse' ideas is doubtful, but at least he seems to have known something in that direction. The 1930s Oxford poet presumably could not grasp that 'free' could not cover Olson, Duncan, Zukofsky, Ginsberg and the New York Poets, since their forms certainly are not 'free' in any sense which implies they are not composed with clear, conscious ideas of necessary poetics. Perhaps he meant what were roughly called 'confessional' poets, but they were hardly 'open' and certainly did not use Olson's 1950 processes of 'projective verse'. In fact, Spender is critical of the popular confessionals – Lowell, Plath, Sexton, Roethke, Berryman – in a specific way, which the British Poetry Revival would agree to, that related to the public use of their clinical, psychiatric or divorce case materials loosely enclosed in the accusation that America has driven them to suicide, or nearly: 'Confessional poetry represents the democratization of the personal and private, and often the psychotic, inner life. In this it is not religious, nor subjective, but case book material.' So much for the only American poetry favoured by the Axis. Spender is rightly scornful of Lowell's envy of Russian poets because they write under a government which takes them seriously enough to suppress them. Spender also recalls that one of the sources of vitality in American arts since 1946 had been the refugee presence of Europeans. Part of the effect of American poetry on the Revival poets had come through surrealist and dada procedures which were only then, in the early 1970s, being discovered directly. It was that synthesis of experience that attracted the Revival poets. In Spender's terms: 'America now became the centre of the civilization whose main characteristic was the continuous transformation of all lived experience into arts whose values were entirely contemporary.' The reaction of the official British poetry was 'self-conscious provincialism', a blinkered withdrawal (Spender thinks Larkin's work was one good result), a refusal to entertain 'areas of wider consciousness', 'treating the local situation as a special separate case', whereas 'really today it exists within the wider situation of the whole area of the common language, and, beyond that, of the world'.

Tom Raworth, a major poet of the Revival, wrote to the American poet Edward Dorn, who worked at Essex University (one of a short series of American poets there who had a useful effect on British poetry, including Tom Clark and Ted Berrigan), in a manner representative of many young British poets (*Wild Dog*, 3, April 19, 1961), that Ginsberg:

> opened things for me . . . one day I found *Evergreen 2* . . . the San Francisco scene one – with *Howl* and all which started me off reading more and more of the Americans . . . Maybe America some day . . . I don't know. It's the fare . . . there are English poets still, over here, but 'English' and 'poets' . . . you know the sort of thing. It's odd . . . poetry over here is, I think, still a 'class' thing . . . There's no flow: no use of natural language. The whole thing is so artificial and contrived . . . Nothing has the power to *move*.

This situation was partly considered in Jeff Nuttall's 'The Singing Ted' (*Poetry Information*, 9/10, 1974), part of a book intended to be called *Outlaws* and already outlawed by the official presses in spite of the international acknowledgement of his *Bomb Culture*, an impressive account of political and arts engagements in the 1950s and 1960s.[23] Nuttall's essay, given as a talk to the Poetry Society in 1973, concerned the development of language and forms in poetry internationally which had lead to the 'release of the imagination' as against so-called laws and as against the fear of those forms which reject stoic irony, thin obliquity and the stifling wryness of Hardy, so beloved by the English bourgeois poets. He pointed to the achievement of the small presses, and the responses to them of Fulcrum Press, Cape Goliard and the Penguin Modern Poets and Modern European Poets series. He drew attention to the British line of innovation – Sterne and Blake, Joyce and Lawrence – and to the recent effects of Breton and Tzara, and then to 'the competitive academic elitism prevalent among the real Savonarolas of English poetry, Robert Conquest, Kingsley Amis, John Wain, and in these days Alvarez, Donald Davie and the incredible Ian Hamilton.' The latter had, in the *Observer Magazine* for September 9, 1973, reduced all contemporary British poetry to Larkin (and his relation to 'confessional poet' Robert Lowell), Ted Hughes, Ted Walker, Ken Smith, Jon Silkin, Davie and Geoffrey Hill, and his own *Review* magazine stable. (These remain the staple fare of English Department teaching of contemporary poetry in Britain). Nuttall countered with the Revival poets' release of language, release of ambition and risk, the desire for a different inclusiveness and synthesis of materials, and for the evolution rather than the involution of poetry:

> There is nothing particularly wrong with Philip Larkin but it is a perverse and cynical trick to take a poet of modest talents, a veritable apostle of modesty, much of whose poetry not only discards the free imagination but . . . doubts its very existence, and make such a poet a literary doyen of the age. Even the New English Art Club never compared Gwen John with Braque.

Joy and play in free composition are further omissions in the 1950s Axis orthodoxy, or any freedom that risks 'the violation of definition'. Nuttall's example here is Tom Raworth, who edited

Outburst's two issues in the 1960s, and whose understanding of Gertrude Stein helped to release his own particular elegance, which Nuttall related to 'the kind of cool which is the articulation of pride and arrogance that the young of the English working class formulated for themselves in the 1950s' and to the 'tough cool' of Raymond Chandler's style. It was Raworth and the artist Barry Hall who became the executive forces at Cape Goliard Press.

Another access to the Revival is afforded in Nathaniel Tarn, born in France, educated in three countries, an anthropologist with field experience in Central America and the Far East, once general editor of Cape Editions (a remarkable and highly influential series of small books of essential writings issued during the 1960s, including Ponge, Jarry, Günter Eich, Bonnefoy, Nazim Hikmet, Bohumil Hrabal, Nicanor Parra, Michel Leiris, Miroslav Holub, Claude Lévi-Strauss, Neruda, Trakl . . .), and a founding director of Cape Goliard. Tarn translated Neruda, lectured in comparative literature in America and decided to stay there. His poetry draws still on a wide experience, and has always been deeply aware of the forms of American and Latin American writings (*The Beautiful Contradictions*, 1969; *A Nowhere for Vallejo*, 1972).[24] His poems have a complex formal analysis of inventive structures, but their movement has the controlled urgency of a reasoned social analysis. Readers of Raworth and Tarn enjoy new encounters with form rather than a recovery of predetermined forms based on prejudice and habit. Their actions are not conservative but imaginative. Mahler once said, 'To write a symphony means, to me, to construct a world with all the available technique'. That kind of creativity requires breadth of view, openness to the conceptual and the accidental, and an ability to synthesise history and experience into composition. It has the possibilities of excitement and the new rather than the safety of recognition.

Originality combines exploratory behaviour with a cultural accumulation towards the exercise of an ability to make comprehensive and new organisations. Roy Fisher's City (Migrant, 1961) exemplifies how a lengthy, complex work can move between conceptual forms derived from the region of Duchamp and years of living in the city of Birmingham. It is a work with a unique sense of place, but that sense was part of the renewals in the Revival. Bunting's *Briggflatts* (Fulcrum, 1966) has a prosody learned from English renaissance poetics, Wordsworth, Pound and Zukofsky, and to a lesser extent from Ford Madox Ford, from a detailed musical experience from medieval works to Schoenberg, and from local Northumberland historical, geological and linguistic culture – what Chris Torrance calls 'the location of things' in his 'Day-by-Day Poem' (*Acrospirical Meanderings in a Tongue of Time*, Albion Village, 1973). It was Roy Fisher and Michael Shayer's Migrant Press who published Bunting's *The Spoils* in 1965. Jon Silkin's *Stand* published the first considerable essay on Fisher's work in an issue that contained poetry by Raworth, Lautreamont, Max Jacob, Tom Pickard and Vallejo. At Easter 1967, Barry MacSweeney, a major poet of the Revival, organised the Sparty Lea Poetry Festival at Allenheads, Northumberland. In his own words:

> Among those present living in a row of wood and stone cottages overlooking Sparty Lea cemetery and the River Allen: Tom Pickard, Andrew Crozier, Nick Wayte, John James, John Temple, Connie Pickard, Pete Armstrong, Tim Longville, Peter Riley, John Hall, J. H. Prynne, etc., as well as various painters . . . Hours of taped readings taken at all hours of the day and night and now in the possession of J. H. Prynne at Caius College, Cambridge. Two kinds of poet met here, read together, settled somehow to each others' work.

This strong Midlands and North-eastern activity, linked with Cambridge, also brought in Olson's work. (Tom Pickard gained his knowledge of Zukofsky from Bunting). Certainly Prynne and Crozier knew of Olson's exemplification of exploratory open form combined with a maximum intensity of information from location and feeling, history and geography, interest in creativity and creation myths, myth and reality fused in a distinct location; a poetry poised with personal anecdote but never dominated by it, and always politically aware and clear about the responsibilities of inventive form.

In a talk at the Poetry Society in 1973, Roy Fisher distinguished Bunting's achievement as 'sheer closeness of linguistic activity', emphasising the physical qualities of language as well as the events that enter the poem. On MacDiarmid, Fisher spoke of his interface between object and subject towards a 'reconstitution of forms of language after deliquescence', an art of fusing message into formal constructions and inventions of great skill and beauty, an art to be found on a smaller scale in Robert Garioch. Fisher recalled the *Intelligencer* journal of the 1960s (edited by Crozier and Peter Riley, with guidance from Prynne), an art of concentrated precision of language, often located in precise place, operating in such a way as to refuse a sublime which is neither metaphorical nor simply analytical. He characterised Crozier's work as an example of how 'the consciousness is charted' so that it is neither abstract nor autobiographical:

> Getting started is always hardest of all
> for me. The pelicans can float on the water
> in their little raft. The shadow
> of the trees falls from directly overhead
> into the pool, which is
> slowly evaporating.
>
> ('The Zoo in Cairo (ii)', *Neglected Information* 1972)[25]

Precision and logic in poets such as Prynne and Riley moved towards the surreal, but was always deftly conscious and never relied entirely on the formulations of Breton and Freud. The map on the cover and the diagram on the title page of Prynne's *Kitchen Poems* (Cape Goliard, 1968) indicated the kind of continuity and location of discovery with which his poems were concerned[26]. This could be placed with the precision of Greece and classical music in Stuart Montgomery's *Circe* (Fulcrum, 1969); the accurate representation of wartime Britain in Jeff Nuttall's *The Case of Isobel* (Turret, 1973); the combination of the instance of Thomas Chatterton and the landscape of the North East in MacSweeney's *Brother Wolf* (Turret, 1973), and if that sounds conventional, there were also his outstanding inventions in parataxis in *Just Twenty Two – and I Don't Mind Dying* (Turpin 5, Cambridge), his 'official poetical biography of Jim Morrison – rock idol', and *Six Odes* (Ted Kavanagh, 1973), and Eric Mottram's *Shelter Island and the Remaining World* (Turret, 1971).[27] Elaine Feinstein's title poem of *The*

Celebrants (Hutchinson, London, 1973) is imbued with the flatlands of East Anglia, as well as the witchcraft that is part of the history of women's life. It was her letter, written as a student from Cambridge, that Olson replied to in the second part of his 'Projective Verse' essay in 1959.

But the stimulus of American poetry is a constant factor in the new poetry. The series of conversations with poets conducted by the present writer at the Poetry Society between September 1972 and April 1973 confirmed what had been clear in their work: the presence of Zukofsky for Pickard; of Jack Spicer and Barbara Guest for Chris Torrance (and also for Allen Fisher); of Thoreau and Robert Duncan for Jeremy Hilton; of certain New York poets (particularly John Ashbery) for Lee Harwood, and of other American poets for Colin Simms, Ken Smith, Paul Evans (among others). Bob Cobbing, Peter Mayer, Peter Finch, Dom Sylvester Houédard, and other British soundtext poets (then more usually called visual poets or concrete poets) were already part of an international scene stretching from Latin America to Germany. Trevor Winkworth's *Juillard* magazine, Harwood's *Tzarad* and his translations of Tristan Tzara, Paul Buck's *Curtains*, and the work of Ulli McCarthy (later Ulli Freer), Paul Brown, Iain Sinclair, B. Catling, Douglas Oliver all suggest the deepening understanding of dada and surrealism in Britain. But it is impossible to separate out 'influences' in the customary academic exercise techniques. More significant and interesting then was to observe the combinations: the locations of Yorkshire, Exeter and America, and the use of the I Ching, in Ken Smith; the Welsh farms and hills, with the study of alchemy, in Chris Torrance; the effects of a visit to America in the poems of the Yorkshire poet and naturalist Colin Simms; and everywhere the steady lessons of Ezra Pound – of whom even Anthony Burgess said 'He created bloody modern literature. None of us could have written without him' (quoted in *Occident*, 1973) – and Charles Olson. In the same magazine, Hugh Kenner wrote that Olson 'had the sense of the poem as a circulating energy system which could draw anything in', relating that to the Anglo–American vorticists of 1914 to 1919.

The essay 'A prosthetics of poetry: the art of Bob Cobbing'

(*Second Aeon*, 16/17, Cardiff, 1973), later issued as a pamphlet, gave most of what the present writer had to say then on concrete and soundtext poetry. The range and performance abilities of Cobbing, Finch, Fencott, Paula Claire and many others have developed. The trio called jgjgjgjgj – cris cheek, Lawrence Upton and Clive Fencott – was one of the most outstanding performers of this art Britain has heard.

A sense of everyday working life impregnated the work of some first-rate poets of the Revival. Jeremy Hilton's *Ornithology and Ferry* (Joe DiMaggio, 1973) spoke from the daily life of the Border country of Wales and England.[28] *Fox Houses* (*Sesheta*, 6, 1974) contained a poem, out of Hilton's working experience, about a boy found to be 'in need of care and control' (in the jargon of social services), material shaped into a questioning of what we do to each other in the name of 'care'. Elaine Randell's 'Diary of a Working Man' (*Poetry Review*, Winter 1973–74) struck out directly from working-class life. The language, syntax and events of a good deal of Jeff Nuttall's poetry and prose had the authentic sound and sense of working- and lower-middle-class urban people, together with a visceral sense of sex and the body which exorcises the genteel and respectable that infects the weeklies and the academic journals.

Two of the finest achievements of the Revival were by Tom Pickard and Allen Fisher, both working-class poets. Pickard's *Dancing Under Fire* (first printed in *Poetry Review* and in Robert Bly's *The Seventies* magazine, and in book form by Middle Earth Books, Philadelphia, 1973 – not one British publisher could be found for this excellent work in book form) is a long poem which combines a variety of poetics and uses dream experience, the writings of Jung, and the felt life of Newcastle and the North East, day-to-day life known by a working-class man with a developed literary education. Pickard's 'The Devil's Destroying Angel Exploded', first printed in *Stand* and the first poem in *The Order of Chance* (Fulcrum, 1971), became a contemporary classic.[24] In an article for *Lip* (Philadelphia, 1973), the present writer tried to describe something of its value:

The short measures of the opening poem maintain a compassionate exorcism of the past and a recognition of the necessary present movement away from the inevitable conditions of oppression . . . The blackness of coal, industry, railway dirt and coerced labour which was the father's lot and 'moon full above the dole' emerge imaginatively from precise reference: local speech, local ownership of production, and local class justice. Acceptance of degrading conditions of labour is depletion of manhood; the word I heard was slave . . . Political resistance and sensuous warmth of contact are fused values . . . New forms convey the myth and ritual of folk and tribal poetry . . .

In 1978, Pickard's poem was complemented by MacSweeney's excellent book-length poem on the life of the same area, *Black Torch*, a masterly achievement, central to the Revival.[30]

Allen Fisher in those days worked in two different poetic areas, not radically different but enough to make singularisation inappropriate. He was a member of the Fluxshoe group of performers of poetry, happenings and music, involved, as the name intends, in similar actions to the Fluxus group. But *Long Shout to Kernewek* (1971 – a small part appeared in *Poetry Review* in Autumn, 1971) is a collection of topological and topographical poems centred on Cornwall. *Sicily* (1973, Edible Press and Beau Geste) uses cut-ups, random and conceptual procedures in a large book-length work of considerable skill and fascination, perhaps the nearest we have had in this country to Jackson Mac Low's *Stanzas for Iris Lezak*. *Place* (Aloes, 1974), the long first part of a work fulfilled later (parts had appeared in *Sixpack* and *Poetry Review* in 1972 and 1973), is a magnificent development of the methods of *Long Shout to Kernewek* and some of the procedures of *Sicily*, placed at the disposal of the historical topology of South London and parts of the Lake District. The presence of Pound, Olson, Paul Bowles, James Koller, and Gary Snyder is not a question of feeble borrowing, but the usages of a wide range of materials in a large-scale work, itself a development of the idea of open-field poetry – 'a flow of field spiralling out', as Fisher says in one section.

These, then, are some records of a small number of poets in the Revival. Poets have been omitted for space reasons or because it is their later work that requires full treatment. Most of the poets were in their early twenties or early thirties with careers still largely ahead of them. Their promise has in most cases been amply fulfilled. But that is another necessity for account. They have achieved a small but efficient readership, although, of course, the official Arts and British Council, university and press mob ignore or abuse them. The problem was, in 1975, to ascertain and then maintain a possible audience for the Revival poets. Jeff Nuttall put the issues for the visual arts and poetry in 'Why Do We Play To Kids?' (*Time Out*, October 5–11, 1973), to begin with 'the fundamentals that were hammered out by the grand old men of the movement years ago, Picasso and picture object, Schoenberg and the serial form, Breton and automatism, Tzara and anti-art, Jarry and Duchamp and the mythic logic method, Mondrian and proportion, Braque and surface, Max Jacob and the dislocated image'. This programme was not a rehearsal of antiquated modernism, but a listing of a few of the basic requirements in the equipment of any serious artist of the later twentieth century. Nuttall proposed a slender chance that the artists and audience would be ready, and that they would also know about Duncan and Olson and open field forms, the use of music in Zukofsky, the compositional logic in John Ashbery, the multiple forms of William Carlos Williams and Pound, the concentrated political and humanist precisions of George Oppen, and the potentialities of ethnopoetics provided in the poetry, translations and anthologies of Jerome Rothenberg. Such a programme would not, as one pathetic Movement poet believed, be a quisling operation, betraying British national culture to America, but a challenge to the Axis assumptions.

The Movement poets as a whole were scared of the personal confrontations of a poetry reading, a live performance of their poetry. Performance extends to theatre and the theatre of poetry. It was clear from *Live New Departures* in the 1960s, Jeff Nuttall's 'Jack' series, the soundtext performances of Cobbing and the Abana group (the celebration of Writers Forum 100 on October 19, 1973, included poetry read, improvised from texts, and made with sounds of old and new instruments), the entertainments of the

Liverpool Poets, and other actions. Theoretical worries about possible detrimental effects of public readings had proved to be pointless – or Movements poets rightly nervous about their own abilities.

A high proportion of the Revival poets had to publish their own work and that of the colleagues in the battle, and also organised readings. The Revival itself was a performance – the creative presentation of imaginative new work in the public area. Such a movement from private to public was their central concern and a political action. The circulation of printed texts, tapes, LPs augmented by live readings, talks on poetry, conferences, public conversations between poets – this was the action of public demonstration that a new British poetry had emerged and needed support from everyone concerned with the production of a lively culture.

Notes and references

This essay is a revised version of 'The British Poetry Revival 1960–1974', which was issued with the programme book for the Polytechnic of Central London British Poetry Conference of 1974.

1 John Matthias (ed.), *Twenty-three Modern British Poets*. The Swallow Press, Chicago, 1971.

2 Michael Schmidt and Grevel Lindop (eds.), *British Poetry Since 1960*, Carcanet Press, Oxford, 1972.

3 Robert Conquest (ed.), *New Lines*, Macmillan, London, 1956.

4 G. S. Fraser (ed.), *Poetry Now*, Faber & Faber, London, 1956.

5 Charles Tomlinson, *The Necklace*, Fantasy Press, Oxford, 1955.

6 All extracts are quoted from Fraser's introduction to *Poetry Now*.

7 Robin Skelton (ed.), *Poetry of the Thirties*, Penguin, Harmondsworth, 1964.

8 David Gascoyne, *Poems 1937–42*, Nicholson & Watson, London, 1943.

9 F. T. Prince, *The Doors of Stone: Poems 1938–1962*, Rupert Hart Davis, London, 1963.

10 David Wright (ed.), *The Mid-Century: English Poetry, 1940–60*, Penguin, Harmondsworth, 1965.

11 Jon Silkin (ed.), *Poetry of the Committed Individual*, Gollancz, London, 1973.

12 Hugh MacDiarmid, *Collected Poems*, Macmillan & Co., New York, 1962.

13 David Jones, In Parenthesis, Faber & Faber, London, 1937; The Anathemata, Faber & Faber, London, 1952; The Tribune's Visitation, Fulcrum Press, London, 1969.

14 Dylan Thomas, Deaths and Entrances, J. M. Dent, London, 1946.

15 Erich Neumann, Art and the Creative Unconscious, trans. R. Mannheim, Routledge & Kegan Paul, London, 1959, pp. 197–8.

16 Norburt Wiener, The Human Use of Human Beings, Eyre & Spottiswoode, London, 1950, p. 135.

17 Edward Lucie-Smith (ed.), The Liverpool Scene, Rapp & Carroll, London, 1967.

18 J. Z. Young, Doubt and Certainty in Science, Clarendon Press, Oxford, 1951, p. 120.

19 Charles Olson, Human Universe and Other Essays, ed. D. Allen, Auerhahn Society, San Francisco, 1965.

20 William Carlos Williams, 'Against the Weather' in Selected Essays of William Carlos Williams, Random House, New York, 1954, pp. 196–218.

21 Stephen Berg and Robert Mezey (eds.), Naked Poetry: Recent American Poetry in Open Forms, Bobbs–Merrill Co., Indianapolis and New York, 1969.

22 Philip Larkin (ed.), The Oxford Book of Twentieth-Century English Verse, Clarendon Press, Oxford, 1973.

23 Jeff Nuttall, Bomb Culture, MacGibbon & Kee, London, 1968.

24 Nathaniel Tarn, The Beautiful Contradictions, Cape Goliard, London, 1969 and A Nowhere for Vallejo, Cape, London, 1972.

25 Andrew Crozier, 'The Zoo in Cairo (ii)', Neglected Information, Blacksuede Boot Press, Sidcup, 1972.

26 J. H. Prynne, Kitchen Poems, Cape Goliard, London, 1968.

27 Stuart Montgomery, Circe, Fulcrum Press, London, 1969; Jeff Nuttall, The Case of Isobel, Turret Books, London, 1973; Barry MacSweeney, Brother Wolf, Turret Books, London, 1973; Eric Mottram, Shelter Island and the Remaining World, Turret Books, London, 1971.

28 Jeremy Hilton, Ornithology and Ferry, Joe DiMaggio Press, Bexleyheath, 1973.

29 Tom Pickard, The Order of Chance, Fulcrum Press, London, 1971.

30 Barry MacSweeney, Black Torch, New London Pride, London, 1978.

For additional information, see the following publications by the author

'Writers Forum: a successful campaign', Ceolfrith, 26, Sunderland, 1975
'A conversation with Lee Harwood', Poetry Information, 14, 1975–76
'Beware of imitations: Writers Forum poets and British poetry in the 1960s', Poetry Student, 1, Warwick, 1975
'Out Land: Conversation with Basil Bunting', The Listener, August 28, 1975

'Conversation with Roy Fisher', Saturday Morning, 1, 1976

'Inheritance, landscape, location: Data for British poetry 1977', Polytechnic of Central London British Poetry Conference, 1977

'Performances: conversation with Jeff Nuttall', Square One, 1, London, 1977

'Open field poetry', Poetry Information, 17, 1977

'Declaring a behaviour: the poetry of performance', Rawz, 1, London, 1977

'Composition and performance in the work of Bob Cobbing', Kontexts, Amsterdam, 1977

'Conversation with Basil Bunting on the Occasion of his 75th Birthday', Poetry Information, 19, 1978

'An acknowledged land: love and poetry in Bunting's sonatas', Poetry Information, 19, 1978; revised version in Basil Bunting: Man and Poet, ed. Carroll F. Terrell, National Poetry Foundation, Maine, 1980

'Tom Pickard' and 'Three Northeastern Poets: MacSweeney, Pickard, Ken Smith', Poetry Information, 18, 1978

'Foreword to The Catalogue of Little Press Books in Print 1978–79, London, Association of Little Presses, 1979

'The pursuit of innocence: populism and intellect in the poetry of Michael Horovitz and Tom Pickard', Primary Sources, 5 and 6, London, 1980

'Reading Barry MacSweeney's Odes', Maxy's Journal, 3, Arkansas, 1980

' "Every new book hacking on Barz": The Poetry of Bill Griffiths', Reality Studios, V, 1–4, London, 1983

'Bunting in Buffalo', Conjunctions, 8, New York, 1986

Appendix

Poets and the Arts Council of Great Britain
(A 'State of Poetry' supplement issued by Poets Conference, 11 December 1978)

Poets' difficulties and problems with the Arts Council of Great Britain, and specifically with Charles Osborne, its Literature Director, stem from the non-democratic nature of its machinery. The Arts Council was set up by Royal Charter (1946; renewed and amended, 1967) as an independent body (a Qango, or quasi non-governmental organisation). As a result, it is not answerable to anyone for its actions, need take little notice of public protest, and even resists attempts by Members of Parliament to enquire into its operations. The Minister for the Arts himself said, in a letter dated

3 April 1975, that this was 'not a matter on which he should intervene'.

Neither the Officers nor the Council, Panel and Committee members of the Arts Council are elected. They are chosen in consultation with a 'tight little circle' of people already in the business. The advisory panels and committees have become powerless, except to discuss broad questions of policy. Decisions are made, in the case of literature, by the Literature Director in consultation with a small Literature Finance Committee; but applications for grant-aid are first vetted by the Literature Director himself, and only those approved by him go before the Literature Finance Committee.

In practice, Charles Osborne has absolute control over every decision made on how to allocate public money in the field of literature. This absolute control has resulted in a narrow and personally-biased policy, to the exclusion of vast areas of literature not approved of by the Director himself.

Many writers, publishers, administrators, and literary figures are hesitant to come forward with criticisms. They know that their livelihood, or an important part of it, depends on not being on bad terms with the man who holds the power. For example, *Index* magazine, which deals with censorship, seemed interested in including an article on literary bias and censorship by the Arts Council of Great Britain, but, realising its own grant came from the Arts Council, it got cold feet and the promised article was not proceeded with.

Despite the difficulty in obtaining evidence, and despite the reluctance of the Arts Council or anyone else to take any action as a result of evidence submitted, the case against Charles Osborne is clear and precise: he has used his position to further a small group of associates and practitioners, and to exclude those categories of literature and those individuals of whom he does not personally approve.

New Departures magazine and its editor, Michael Horovitz, are typical examples of activity and an individual of which the Arts Council doesn't approve. In the *Times Literary Supplement* 'Changing Guard' issue (6 August, 1964) *New Departures* was described as 'the most substantial avant-garde magazine in Great Britain'. An editorial in the same issue held that 'the difficulties encountered by so stimulating a magazine as *New Departures* are lamentable, and would hardly be so severe in any other Western country'. The editorial went on to prescribe the obvious remedy: 'What is really needed is a more open-minded attitude on the part of the literary establishment'. Since when, the situation, rather than improving, has deteriorated. Magazines and presses which 'adhere to existing standards' are generously financed; those which do not set out to do so get virtually nothing.

Poetry Information, edited by Peter Hodgkiss, is another case in point. Like New Departures, Poetry Information has consistently had its applications for grant-aid turned down. The last grant application did not reach the literature panel or its financial committee; a secretary took it upon herself to state that she saw no point in Peter Hodgkiss applying for a grant in the near future unless 'you have radically changed the style and content of the magazine'. 'Again', says Peter Hodgkiss, 'the Arts Council of Great Britain demonstrates its unwillingness to accept that poetry appears in many shapes and guises different from those favoured by our cultural mandarins. The result is that areas of choice are limited and important channels of information stifled.'

In contrast, The New Review, the archetypal establishment magazine, received £12,500 ('towards the launching cost') in the year before it began to publish, when the total grant that year (1973–74) to little presses was £8,550, and to all other literary magazines only £11,050. Since then, The New Review has consistently received grants of up to £35,200 annually. Magazines receiving grants obtain additional assistance as they are included in an Arts Council free distribution scheme to libraries. In the case of The Poetry Society's magazine Poetry Review, the Arts Council refused any grant whatsoever while Eric Mottram was editor, but promised 'a special grant – at the end of the present editor's tenure' – an example of the non-democratic Arts Council's attempting to dictate to a democratically elected body, The Poetry Society Council.

The Poetry Society fell foul of Charles Osborne when it cast off its Victorian image and attracted poets to its Council who reformed its policy, its programme and its magazine. Osborne insisted on trying to nominate three members to The Poetry Society's Council in order to redress the balance of power. When it was pointed out that this was contrary to The Poetry Society's constitution and probably to the Arts Council's Charter as well, Osborne climbed down, but not before he had threatened to cut off The Poetry Society's grant in mid-year. At that stage, he announced an investigation into The Poetry Society to be led by Professor Cox. However, he had apparently not consulted his Literature Panel nor the Arts Council itself, so another announcement had to be made saying that no enquiry had been ordered and that no invitation had been extended to Professor Cox. (See The Times, 28 May 1976.) Not long after, an internal Arts Council Committee, led by the Arts Council's vice-chairman, Sir John Witt, investigated the Society and its report by coincidence confirmed all Charles Osborne's worst fears. The report remarks that the Arts Council's nomination of three members to the General Council of The Poetry Society 'has worked badly in practice' and 'has failed to achieve any satisfactory measure of control'. It recommends Arts

Council 'control through an effective Assessorship carried out by the Literature Director'.

When The Poetry Society adopted the Witt report and when its Council found out that control meant control, more than a dozen poets resigned from the General Council, stating: 'The Council is no longer in control of Society policy. Policy is being controlled by the Arts Council of Great Britain and the Society's paid staff.' (Press Release, 26 March 1977.) The Arts Council's Charter states that it is the object of the Council 'to develop and improve the knowledge, understanding and practice of the arts' and 'to increase their accessibility to the public'. There is nothing about control. Indeed, the Arts Council report for 1973–74 speaks of policy as being the provision of 'public money combined with autonomy and independence', which has 'often (though not always) saved us from the dullness and conformity of 'Establishment' art', Yet an exclusive 'Establishment' poetry seems to be exactly what the Literature Director is working to achieve.

Examples abound. Britain has a flourishing group of concrete and sound poets whose work is consistently recognised abroad. They have been represented in the 1969 and 1978 Venice Biennale exhibitions, at the 1977 Berlin festival and at festivals in Stockholm, Amsterdam, Toronto and Glasgow, among others. Yet when they put on an exhibition and festival at The Poetry Society's National Poetry Centre in 1974, Charles Osborne described them in the press as 'those rag-bags down in Earls Court', (The Times, May 1974) later corrected by Charles Osborne himself in a phone-call to The Poetry Society as 'those rat-bags down in Earls Court'. An application for funds to organise the 11th International Sound-Poetry Festival in London in 1978 received the reply that the Arts Council's Literature Panel feels 'that it is outside the field of literature which they should recommend for support'. Prior to that, Osborne had himself intimated that there were no funds available for such a purpose.

The two hundred or more little presses and the scores of little magazines, described by Geoffrey Soar, a librarian at University College London, as 'the growing points of literature' receive minute recognition from the Arts Council (apart from a handful of 'establishment'-minded magazines and presses). In fact, Charles Osborne has written in the *Guardian* that they 'make no useful contribution to literature' and 'generally are not worth supporting'. Yet the little presses produce three-quarters of the new poetry published each year in Great Britain.

Oasis Books have been refused a grant because their programme has insufficient literary merit. Yet their forthcoming list includes translations of poems by Anna Akhmatova. When Pirate Press approached Charles Osborne for a contribution towards the production of a new version of Beowulf, they were turned down because 'the thought of another Beowulf fills me with gloom and dismay'. Yet this edition is the only parallel text in old and modern English available and is now approaching its third edition. Ceolfrith Press and Arts Centre met similar opposition when they wished to put on an exhibition and publish a book entitled: 'All My Eyes See: The Visual World of Gerard Manley Hopkins'. If Akhmatova, Beowulf and G. M. Hopkins are too avant-garde or of insufficient literary merit to be supported, what hope is there for the writer today who is genuinely breaking new ground? As Eric Mottram has written in the foreword to the 1978–79 *Catalogue of Little Press Books in Print*: 'if Eliot, Pound, David Jones, MacDiarmid, Bunting or Dylan Thomas turned up today with their unknown works . . . the chances of publication would be nil'. No British big publisher would be courageous enough to publish them, and a little press could count on no financial support from the Arts Council.

The above are only a fraction of the instances which might be quoted in support of our case. It will be obvious that if literature in all its forms is to be supported adequately, rather than on the narrow and biased basis applied at the moment, much more money will have to be available for grants. It is significant that in England only 1.5 per cent (nearer 1 per cent in most previous years) of the total Arts Council grant-in-aid is spent on literature; this contrasts with 3¼ per cent in Scotland and over 9 per cent in Wales. That the proportion, at least for poetry, is so low may well reflect Charles Osborne's opinion that 'Poetry receives a large slice (of grant-aid), in relationship to its readership and what other people might think of its general importance in the literary world as a whole'.

Poets Conference has consistently called for an increase in the amount of grant-aid to poetry. An improvement in this field would do a lot to ease the present meanness in the way grants are spread around. However, it is difficult to escape the need for serious revision of the machinery of the Literature Department of the Arts Council of Great Britain. It is necessary for all grant applications to be considered by the Literature Panel, but it is equally important that the Literature Panel should be fully representative of trends in literature today. Many poets would feel that there isn't a single person on the Literature Panel of the Arts Council at present capable of exercising any expert opinion on what Geoffrey Soar calls 'the growing points of literature'. But even these reforms would be meaningless unless it was the Literature Director's responsibility to take note of what his advisers advise. Only in this way can grants reflect contemporary directions in literature, rather than the present practice of aiming to impose an established policy on its development.

Poets Conference calls for an independent enquiry into the workings of the Arts Council's Literature Department to ensure that critical standards are applied by people best qualified to do so, that the whole span of present day literature is properly represented, and that poets and writers themselves are enabled to play a full democratic role in the formation of Arts Council policy.

Fred D'Aguiar

2

Have you been here long?
Black poetry in Britain

Introduction

Black poetry in Britain began with the publication of Phyllis
Wheatley's *Poems on Various Subjects, Religious and Moral* (London,
1773).[1] Phyllis Wheatley was an American slave educated by her
owners then given her freedom. The publication of her book
coincided with a short stay in London. After she returned to the
States her poems sold steadily in both countries as the abolitionist
cause gained momentum, and her book was posited as an
example of black achievement. The achievement is remarkable
when held up against her personal circumstances and the condition of her race as slaves forcibly relocated in strange lands. In
literary terms, the poems are straightforward elegies or else serve
up exhortations to her fellow citizens to follow the example of
Christ. The poems lack any commentary about her personal
condition and the morality is mostly stated in terms of a general
upliftment through an acceptance of Christ, with the movement
from Africa to America seen in conventional terms as a movement
from darkness to light.

> While an intrinsic ardor prompts to write,
> The Muses promise to assist my pen.
> 'T was not long since I left my native shore,

The land of errors and Egyptian gloom:
Father of mercy! 't was thy gracious hand
Brought me in saftey from those dark abodes.

('To The University of Cambridge, In New England',
lines 1 to 6)

It is easy to understand Phyllis Wheatley's dilemma. There were no positive images or opinions of Africa around her. As far as she could see she had left a simple world for one more scientifically and materially advanced. She places her destiny in God's hand, thereby neatly sidestepping any awkward questions about her capture and subsequent purchase which she might have entertained asking her owners. We should marvel that she was literate at all. The material reality of each poem she produced would serve as an indictment against slavery. But even in these lines there are nuances of a brooding discontent with her saviours. Her use of 'native shore' is a mark of her identification with Africa. This is by no means cancelled out by her subsequent criticism of the place. She appears to be thanking God for her safe delivery from Africa. In fact, the 'dark abodes' is ambiguous. On one level it refers to Africa. On a deeper, more caustic level it points to the hold of the slave ship and the many holding places where she would have been corralled with other slaves as they were herded towards their market. Wheatley is thanking God for her fortunate condition within the parameters of the status of a slave who knows her place, but has enough insight to outwit her owners by writing a poem that uses irony in as sophisticated a manner as her favourite poet, Pope.

Black poetry in Britain subsequently took second place to various documents in the form of essays and autobiographies by former slaves (for example, that of Olaudah Equiano),[2] or else narratives transcribed by white liberals in close contact with slaves. Work songs and songs about the Africa left behind and the struggle to live on earth until some future salvation came were the order of the day. These belong to Caribbean poetry or Black American poetry, as opposed to an original act of creativity generated on British soil as a result of residence here or a wish to connect recent British involvement in the former colonies, or an amalgamation of the two

The definition of Black Britishness according to birth or residence narrows down the poems to a handful of writers active in Britain after the end of World War II. The writers are in roughly two groups. The first are those writers who were born in the Caribbean and came to Britain as teenagers or young adults. The second group consists of poets born and bred in Britain with one or both parents from Africa, India or the Caribbean. Poets from South Asia in Britain, who operate in their native languages such as Urdu or Gujerati, are excluded for the simple reason that the work is not widely available in translation and deserves treatment in its own right. Exceptions are Iftikhar Arif, Tariq Latif, Saqi Farooqi, Rukhsana Ahmad and Mahmood Jamal, all of whom write in English and have at least one book to their name, if not a clutch of poems seen in periodocals.

Although there are about sixty black poets currently writing,[3] recording or performing in Britain, of that group only a handful will be examined here to show the themes, techniques, forms and language of the poetry as a whole. The focus will be on James Berry, Linton Kwesi Johnson, Grace Nichols, John Agard, and Jackie Kay. The work of other poets such as E. A. Markham, David Dabydeen, Amryl Johnson, John Lyons, Jean Binta Breeze, Merle Collins, Lynford French, Lemn Sissay, Levi Tafari, Benjamin Zephaniah, Gabriel Gbadamosi, and Valerie Bloom will be touched on. What should become clear are the ways in which black poetry has re-invigorated poetry in Britain and legitimised its contemporary nature.

II
The seventies

The most important poetry book published in Britain by a black poet living in Britain in the seventies (the decade in which recent black poetry established itself) came from Linton Kwesi Johnson. His *Dread Beat and Blood*, (1975) appeared when he was 23.[4] By that time Edward Brathwaite's ground-breaking trilogy had been issued together as *The Arrivants* (1973)[5] As a pointer to the dogged lack of opportunity for black poets among the white publishing houses in Britain, only two Caribbean poets, Brathwaite and Walcott, had books published here during the sixties by established houses. It would be left to the black presses (New Beacon Books, Bogle-L'Ouverture, and later Black Ink and Akira) and to smaller, specialist poetry presses to help the work of black poets to see daylight.

Jazz and blues rhythms and T. S. Eliot were templates for Brathwaite. Jazz and blues were also popularised by Amiri Baraka (formerly Leroy Jones). Both poets would have been well known to Johnson. Among the black poets in London, Johnson included, not jazz and blues, but the newer music of reggae (which grew out of ska, and ruled the dance houses frequented by blacks then) proved to be the single, most important influence on their work. Brathwaite's and Baraka's influence on the generation of poets following them in Britain was massive too. The late Lynford French mixed jazz rhythms (Gil Scott-Heron's included) with reggae and was moving towards a fusion of the two forms when he died. Lynton Kwesi Johnson would learn from Brathwaite and Baraka but pick up more from reggae, as would so many other younger poets coming after him, such as Desmond Johnson and Benjamin Zephaniah and, from Jamaica, Jean Binta Breeze, and the late Michael Smith, probably the most talented of all the dub poets.

With the exception of Brathwaite's three books, Johnson's *Dread Beat and Blood* was therefore a departure from anything that had ever been published in Britain as poetry in terms of the kind of English used. (From Robert Burns to MacDiarmid to Sorley Maclean there had already existed within British culture a healthy departure from the standard English vernacular.) More particularly, its innovation lay in its deployment of reggae-based rhythms. In addition, the poems had startling resemblances in their social concerns to the best of the Liverpool poets of the decade before, making them anti-establishment in their appeal and popular – qualities unfamiliar to most poets operating in Britain at the time.

> Shock-black bubble-down-beat bouncing
> rock-wise tumble-down sound music;
> foot-drop find drum, blood story,
> bass history is a moving
>   is a hurting black story.
>   ('Reggae Sounds', *Dread Beat and Blood*, p. 56)

The rhythm of the poem is demonstrated and locked into the lines which are working like a bass guitar and drum combined. Reading the lines aloud should yield a rhythm akin to reggae music, that is, a regular bass line with its double beat-pause-double beat timing from the rhythm section with all the usual sophistication of a medley to break up the monody. Johnson's claim here is that the music, its very rhythms, are founded on black history.

1
muzik of blood
black reared
pain rooted
heart geared;

all tensed up
in the bubble and the bounce
an the leap an the weight-drop.

it is the beat of the heart,
this pulsing of blood
that is a bubblin bass,
and bad bad beat
pushin gainst the wall
whey bar black blood.
          ('Bass Culture', *Dread Beat and Blood*, p. 57)

The extract has three movements which roughly define where the music originates, how it is enjoyed, and in section three, a definition of it is attempted drawing on the two earlier sections but with the added ambiguity of 'wall' at the end and the apparently contradictory reference to 'blood' as 'black'. The early short lines create a slow, stomping effect. Though short, the lines are loaded with nouns working as adjectives and vice versa, adding to their heavy or weighted feel. The punctuation is more in the line breaks and the double spaces than in the actual commas, semi-colons and full stops we see. The spaces inform the breath where to pause and add emphasis. This creates the effect of a poem which is scored rather than punctuated, or at least punctuation works to make it a score.

The poet's claim is a big one: listen to the 'muzik' (the spelling forms an integral part of the poem's language which will be looked at later) and you will hear something of the hurt of recent black history. Few listeners to reggae and its dub derivative, with the DJ voice laid on top of the rhythm, will deny the high tension and brooding nature of the rhythms and beat. We are told that the music is made in the blood, that it is 'black reared' or invented and fostered by blacks, that pain is the principle reason for its invention or the need to articulate pain and that the engine for the music, what drives it, is the heart, 'heart geared'. Even the response to it, the poem's argument continues, the way people who know about the music dance to it, is seen as similarly propelled by an inner hurt (slavery, colonialism, racism) and need for self-expression. The 'wall' in the penultimate line is the system that needs to be bucked or overcome, namely the oppression that has given rise to the 'rebel' music, making the music a form of protest as opposed to simply an expression of protest.

The roots of the music are Jamican. 'Bass Culture' is dedicated to Big Yout, a Jamaican pioneer of the DJ system of 'chatting' or speaking in roughly iambic, end-rhymed, Jamaican creole, pentameter lines, to a bass rhythm. This form of entertainment characterised the so-called 'blues parties' in the early to mid-seventies, that is, a cross between a private party and a club since it was held at a private residence but with an admission charge and a bar. These were the only places where the music could be heard. The DJ chat format still features today as the leading form of reggae in the dance halls. The records from this period had an underlying rasta ideology placing them outside the system and antithetical to it. The form of the protest appeared home-made, homegrown, that is, 'black reared', not another imported solution. The image of the rasta with his set of ethics re-fashioned from the Bible with a black viewpoint, and with a rationale for everything from his hair-style to his diet meant that rastafarianism offered an alternative to everything white and from the west. Through music the ideology got to the youths whose minds were hitherto being fought for and won by a second invasion of US culture in the Caribbean or in Britain, and by experiences of rejection in the form of British racism.

Linton's poems gave vent to that underground cultural experience which existed outside of British culture at the time. Apart form Bob Marley and the Wailers and the odd Top Thirty hit from the occasional reggae artist, reggae was hardly heard. (Two-tone groups such as UB 40 and The Specials would follow a few years later.) After all, the music had to be purchased from special shops, the records never made the charts, the DJ's did not appear on national radio but were confined to pirate radio stations. To all intents and purposes this was a subterranean and youth culture growing beyond the confines of the few clubs and sound systems propagating it as the numbers of those enjoying the music grew. Inevitably, Linton Kwesi Johnson's work broke into the youth scene as other forms of protest in British culture such as punk, the anti-Nazi league and gay rights activism formed coalitions to fight what were perceived as common problems and a common enemy. Linton Kwesi Johnson would go on to give a joint concert with the punk poet and fellow recording artist John Cooper Clarke. I labour the social and political dimension because the poetry had aligned itself to campaigns and issues of importance to the black community. Linton Kwesi Johnson's involvement with the Race Today Collective, a publishing and community-based pressure group with headquarters in Brixton, and his involvement in campaigns such as the one to free George Lindo (allegedly framed by the police for armed robbery) made his work both a literary and political document in a way not seen since the early poetry of Adrian Mitchell and Adrian Henri and more akin to Peter Porter's 'bomb culture' poem, 'Your Attention Please'. A poem by Johnson wasn't simply a record of an event but formed a part of the history surrounding it. In addition to his book, his albums could be bought. This immediately made his work widely available in a form which confirmed the oral basis of his creativity, rooted as it was and still is in black culture and the black experience in Britain, but with implications for the wider youth culture and other groups opposed to the establishment.

The criticism, however, was not always directed outwards. Johnson's poem 'Five Nights of Bleeding' charts the enemy within the culture (that is, the self-oppression of senseless in-fighting) and those caught up in it as seen and heard (if you can get hold of the album from Virgin Records) in the refrain,

> it's war amongst the rebels:
> madness . . . madness . . . war.
> ('Five Nights of Bleeding', *Dread Beat and Blood*, p. 17)

The war is also with the police whose singular claim to fame in black letters is the alarming regularity with which they feature as the state's main agent of black oppression, whether in the seventies, eighties or today. There were also books in the seventies by James Berry, such as *Bluefoot Traveller* (Harrap, 1976) and *Fractured Circles* (New Beacon Books, 1979) and E. A. Markham's *Cross-Fire* (1972), *Mad* (1973) and *Love Poems* (1978), with similar themes to Johnson's and seemingly more literary, but it was not until 1982, with the publication of James Berry's *Lucy's Letters and Loving*,[6] that a viable alternative to Johnson was registered.

III
The eighties

Some background is crucial if the literature produced during this period is to make sense. 1981 saw the first of the big inner-city riots, centred around the black communities, that would characterise the early to mid-eighties. In January of that year the New Cross Massacre occurred, the death by fire under suspicious circumstances of thirteen black youths. March saw the biggest demonstration ever held by black people in Britain in what was dubbed the Black People's Day of Action and in April things exploded in Brixton. A generation of British-born and bred blacks had come of age only to find that Britishness did not include them. Jobs were not open to them, the police harrassed them, there was an increase in racist violence, and subtler forms of racism, such as discrimination in the classroom, meant that black youths were underachieving in school and getting pushed into sport, or else signing on for the dole. This bleak picture fed back into the arts as poets tried to find ways of expressing this experience and articulating creative solutions to it. Writing and music workshops blossomed during this period, so the riots cannot be viewed simply as destructiveness by mindless youths but must be seen as one form of protest and collective action among many. Both the April riots and the New Cross Fire are commemorated by two Linton Kwesi Johnson poems,[7] confirming his status as the leading poet of protest in the black community and in the 'dub poetry' format widely popularised by him.

What is absent in Johnson and abundant in Berry's book is humour. Johnson's earnestness is entirely fitting to his subject matter; his celebration is assertive and affirming, never playful or comic. It takes Berry's character Lucy, writing (from England) home (to Jamaica) to Leela, to gently satirise black and white lifestyles in Britain and to show a gentle home-sickness and love of the home that is lost but not forgotten in Lucy's Letters. Like Johnson's book, the language is a mixture of Standard English and the creole vernacular derived from it. Otherwise known as Nation Language (a term coined by Edward Kamau Brathwaite, the Barbadian poet and historian), creole can most conveniently be viewed on a continuum, with Standard English at one end and the most countrified creoles at the other and all the city-speak in between, that is, Manchester, London, Bristol or Glasgow-based. This includes the 'all-Islands' creole spoken by black youths in Britain, which is really an amalgam of every particular island creole picked up by black children in British schools and youth clubs and melted down as the children mixed together, adding local dialect words, and even Americanisms. A healthy state of affairs for any language wishing to self-perpetuate itself instead of stagnate and perish! There is a residue of African terms and grammar in creole but a predominance of English words and grammar; the former is outweighed by the the latter in its influence on creole. The incomprehensible nature of some spoken creole is no more than that of some British regional dialects when they land on an untrained ear.

James Berry remains as loyal as is possible to the phonetics of Jamaican creole but even in his poems we see a wide-ranging creole emerging, at once closely affiliated to the English spoken here and to the more radical forms of creole associated with the Jamaican countryside (to the extent that English translations are necessary!). As we move from one poem to the next linguistic continents are crossed! I don't just mean that an English regional dialect is seen in opposition to Standard English, as in a Tony Harrison poem, but that within the creole itself we see movements and revisions which highlight differences in the location and perspective of black people, movements typical of several regional dialects in Britain put together!

Caribbean Proverb Poems 1

Dog mornin prayer is, Laard,
wha today, a bone or a blow?

Tiger wahn to eat a child, tiger sey
he could-a swear it was a puss.

If yu cahn mek plenty eyewater
fo funeral, start a-bawl early mornin.
(News For Babylon, Chatto, 1984, p. 181)

If the dropped last letters of words are replaced and minor adjustments made to the creole phonetic spellings of 'wahn' for the English 'want' and 'could-a' for 'could have' then only the grammar remains. Even in this department there isn't much to do. Some of the economy is peculiar to poetry and desirable. The poem published one year later is more marked in its attempt to capture the creole sound of the proverbs,

Caribbean Proverb Poems 1

Dog mornin prayer is, Laard
wha teday, a bone or a blow?

tiger wahn fi nyam pickney, tiger sey
he could-a swear e woz puss.

If yu cahn mek plenty yeyewater
fi funeral, start a-bawl early mornin.

(*Chain of Days*, Oxford, 1985, p. 3)

The spellings are pushed further along the road of a creole register. For instance, 'yeye' for 'eye' safeguards both the sense of the
word and its most likely pronunciation. 'Nyam' for 'eat' uses a
Ghanian word which survived the middle passage and three
hundred years of slavery. Of course Berry could have gone even
further. For example 'Laard' for 'Lord' would logically mean that
'daag' would stand for 'dog'. The issue is not about spelling
though. If the tone of the poem is true and the sense is intact then
the language is working.

Most of these language issues are satirised by John Agard in
his poem 'Listen Mr Oxford Don':

Me not no Oxford don
me a simple immigrant
from Clapham Common
I didn't graduate
I immigrate

But listen Mr Oxford don
I'm a man on de run
and a man on de run
is a dangerous one

I ent have no gun
I ent have no knife
but mugging de Queen's English
is the story if my life

I dont need no axe
to split/up yu syntax
I dont need no hammer
to mash/up yu grammer

. . . .
Dem accuse me of assault
on de Oxford dictionary/
imagine a concise peaceful man like me/
dem want me serve time
for inciting rhyme to riot

. . . .
I'm not a violent man Mr Oxford don
I only armed wit mih human breath

. . . .
I ent serving no jail sentence
I slashing suffix in self-defence
I bashing future wit present tense
and if necessary

I making de Queen's English accessory/to my offence.

(*Mangoes and Bullets*)[8]

The immigrant narrator from Clapham Common is someone
who has lived here a very long time but still cannot shake off the
immigrant label. Immigration is a university if the syllabus is seen
as centred around the language of the immigrant. The don is a
figure of authority, policing the English language. The outlaw is
the immigrant who breaks all the rules of English grammar to say
what is on his/her mind. What Agard does is incorporate his
argument into the form of the poem through a use of lower case,
obliques and an absence of any conventional punctuation. His
brand of creole is close to the Standard English he practices his
piracy on. Perhaps the don would give him full marks for his use
of metaphor. And with precursors such as e. e. cummings's
poetry and Sam Selvon's prose, Agard's immigrant is in good
company. His role as experimentalist is to disturb the peace
where peace means stasis and stagnancy. The weapon is 'human
breath'. It is also the use of calypso rhythms, as opposed to reggae
ones, which distinguishes Agard's work. The claim made for the
oral in preference to a donnish notion of the literary is pivotal to
the argument made for creole as a legitimate language for literature. It is spoken and alive, enough grounds for its validity. The
dominant irony of the poem is that the assult on the Oxford

dictionary is a necessary one if the creative energy of the language is to continue. As the poem demonstrates, the evolution of the language is better safeguarded at Clapham Common where it is breathed, than it is at Oxford where it is likely to become extinct or frozen in time between hard covers.

A similar oral desiderata is stated by Levi Tafari in his poem, 'De Tongue'. Levi Tafari gives us an example of the verbal gymnastics his tongue can perform,

> it will get yuh inna muddle
> and you will get trouble
> pon de double
> Nuh bother trouble, trouble
> weh nuh trouble yuh
>
> ('De Tongue', from *The Liverpool Experience*)[9]

The pace of the poem is indicated by a rhyme scheme which he explains at the end and a rhythm which is tied to a drum beat akin to rap and funk music, BUM BUH BUM CHA, BUH BUH BUM BUM BAH CHA (twice). This beat is a part of the poem, part of what the tongue does. It defines too the poem's pace, confirming its oral basis and its composition for performance, though not exclusively so. Agard, Tafari and Berry show a preoccupation with language, geography and history typical also of Irish poetry since Patrick Kavanagh's 'The Great Hunger'. In Berry's poetry this is less epic, relying more on local and personal effects.

> Things harness me here. I long
> for we labrish bad. Doors
> not fixed open here.
> No Leela either. No cousin
> Lil, Miss Lottie or Bro'-Uncle.
> Dayclean doesn't bring
> Cousin-Maa with her naseberry tray.
> Afternoon doesn' give a ragged
> Manwell, strung with fish
> like bright leaves. Seven days
> play same note in London, chile.
> But Leela, money-rustle regular.
>
> ('Lucy's Letter', lines 1–13, *Lucy's Letter and Loving*, p. 39)

The scene which Lucy describes is a country setting. This is contrasted with the metropolis. London brings money but it is lonely for her. Lucy feels hemmed in; her country code cannot be found anywhere in London. 'Labrish' means talk or friendly gossip in Jamaica; in Guyana the word for the same activity is 'gaff'; in Trinidad people 'liming' would be engaged in this particular type of conversation. Lucy does not mean that she is mute in London. She longs for talk that is not always linked to a purpose. She tells us why she had to swap the country ideal for the lone-liness of the city in that reference to money. The letter format is used as straightforward reportage with some lyrical moments *secreted* there. The rhythm of the piece established by the line breaks distinguishes it from prose, along with powerful lines such as 'strung with fish like bright leaves', a Standard English line as terse as any in the language. Many of the Lucy poems end with a Jamaican proverb drawing on folk wisdom to make sense of the city and showing that the past is far from redundant.

The two dialects in question here both pertain to English. Both are working to clarify a complex world with two poles, one in the Caribbean and the other in Britain. John Lyons dramatises this duality as an existential condition.

> Exiled under silver birch and conifers
> see the poui and immortelles blooming;
>
> the mistle-thrush sings
> but I hear the kiskadee,
>   'Qu'est ce qu'il dit,
>   qu'est ce qu'il dit.'

('Lure of the Casadura')[10]

The tension of one world forever being substituted by another, coupled with the feelings of loss, is acute, verging on nostalgia. Another form which this dualism takes is a portrayal of the two worlds in terms of outright conflict. E. A. Markham's classic poem 'Don't Talk to Me About Bread' replays a post-colonial revenge from the standpoint of the colonised,

> she kneads
> deep into the night
> and the whey-coloured dough

springy and easy and yielding to her will

is revenge.

(Human Rites)[11]

The Caribbean-British nexus is also seen in David Dabydeen's wry tribute to the movement of Indians to the Caribbean as indentured labourers, from around 1850, and to post-World War II Britain.

> Now that peasantry is in vogue,
> Poetry bubbles from peat bogs,
> People strain for the old folk's fatal gobs
> Coughed up in grates North or North East
> 'Tween bouts o' livin dialect,
> It should be time to hymn your own wreck,

('Coolie Odyssey')[12]

The 'vogue' is sardonically referred to and perhaps the finger is pointed at Heaney's 'North' and Tony Harrison's poems about his working-class background. Nothing is wrong with the dialect except when it becomes a trend. And as Tom Wolfe warned in his T. S. Eliot lectures, 'Beware of the trend that walks like a man'. The fashion permits one or two genuine 'hymns' to be sung. The last stage of the Odyssey, to Britain, lacks dignity, Harilall ends up 'known as the local Paki/ Doing slow trade in his Balham cornershop', ('Coolie Odyssey'). The elegy to the woman whose life of sacrifice propels her children to a better material existence through migration and education appears to have been in vain, with the exception that some of them might turn their learning towards making that life into art:

> We mark your memory in songs
> Fleshed in the emptiness of folk,
> Poems that scrape bowl and bone
> In English basements far from home,

('Coolie Odyssey')

From these complex dualities a third possible world surfaces: that of the unifying poetic mind. This will to synthesis means that a James Berry or John Lyons poem must always be viewed in terms of these two geographies. The link with the Caribbean is seen not in terms of 'fracture' but as continuity and dialogue. In the Lucy poems a kind of 'labrish of geographies' occurs over the fence of the Atlantic! Whereas for Dabydeen and Berry, England and home are two different places, in Jackie Kay's poetry Britishness and notions of home as elsewhere are unified. The loss is parental because she was adopted and her base is Scotland, not such a faraway land. Her language is Scots and English yet tied in with this is a complex notion of her blackness, her sexuality and her gender. Her book, *The Adoption Papers*,[13] recreates a past she mostly intuits by presenting three voices, her birth, her adoptive mother and the point of view of the poet herself. Together they create an imaginative narrative account for what were real absences. The cross-racial adoption is funnily retold through social agencies vetting the left-wing parents, including one visit where they try to disguise their politics in order to qualify as parents,

> I thought I'd hid everything
> that there wasnie wan
> giveaway sign left
>
> I put Marx Engels Lenin (no Trotsky)
> in the airing cupboard – she'll no be
> checking out the towels surely
> ('The Waiting Lists', *The Adoption Papers*, p. 14)

What is absent from the book are the perspectives of the fathers, both biological and adoptive fathers. The feeling is that a similar journey of recreation by the poet is necessary. The use of Scots is something that Jackie Kay comes up against when she is sceptically seen as an anomaly, namely a black Scotswoman. In an early anthologised poem, 'So You Think I'm a Mule' printed in *A Dangerous Knowing* (Sheba Feminist Publications 1989)[14] but not included in *The Adoption Papers*, the poet has to assert her blackness and her right to be Scots. Comparisions with Liz Lochhead are inevitable but should not obscure what is surely a new and distinctive voice on the British literary scene.

Kay's interracial concerns are shared by Gabriel Gbadamosi. His Irish and Nigerian parentage has resulted in an exploration of Nigerian myths and Irish folklore in a strict and consciously literary genre. All this does not make his poetry anything other than English,

> The sky's blue lapels flap open,
> the cloud makes a fine herring-bone fossil.
>
> I am an Englishman motoring to the airport
> for my mother's funeral.
> >   (from 'Flying Home' *The New British Poetry*, p. 36)[15]

The visualisation is typical of poetry written in England, leaning heavily towards the lyric and burying feeling into sensuous detail which collectively should stand for what the poet thinks and feels. Gbadamosi's sense of being English is total and we should not doubt him. Presumably all things Nigerian and Irish not picked up in the home will have to be researched. The poet will have to deliberately chase those roots if he wishes to know them since his base is first and foremost English. It is as strong a claim as Kay's Scots defence if taken on the level of language alone.

The celebration of womanhood which features in Jackie Kay's work forms part of an extended historical exploration of black women in history begun by Grace Nichols in her long poem *I is a Long Memoried Woman*.[16] Modelled closely on Brathwaite's epic trilogy *The Arrivants*, Nichols's poem offers a female perspective of the middle passage.

> Child of the middle passage womb
> push
> daughter of a vengeful Chi
> she came
>   into the new world
> birth aching her pain
> from one continent/to another
> >   (*I is a Long Memoried Woman*, p. 5.)

The pain of history is felt again in the course of her poem. The idea is twofold, firstly, to redress an imbalance which has to date worked in favour of male representations of that past at the expense of the female experience and equal participation in the making of that past; and secondly, by the poet immersing herself in an historical hurt of that magnitude it is hoped that the process of re-imagining, recreation and re-visioning will itself offer up solutions for overcoming that hurt and solving some of the problems facing black people today.

> Face up
> they hold her naked body
> to the ground
> arms and legs spread-eagle
> each tie with rope to stake
>
> then they coat her in sweet
> molasses and call us out
> to see . . . the rebel woman
>
> who with a pin
> stick the soft mound
> of her own child's head
>
> sending the little-new-born
> soul winging its way back to Africa – free
>
> they call us out to see
> the fate for all us rebel
> women
>
> the slow and painful
> picking away of the flesh
> by red and pitiless ants
>
> ('Ala' *I is a Long Memoried Woman*, p.23)

Rebellion entails murder if the baby is to be saved from a life as a slave. Her punishment for an act which must have taken a degree of courage impossible to postulate is a slow and painful death. What is clear is that the flame of rebellion is fuelled by the witnessing of this act, rather than extinguished as it is intended to do. Grace Nichols' work includes satires of what a beautiful woman should be, by celebrating fatness in *Fat Black Women's Poems* (Virago, 1984), and a humanity lived without always having to keep an eye on an agenda of how that life should be lived if the person happens to be black and a woman (*Lazy Thoughts of a Lazy Woman*, Virago, 1989). The personal tone struck in these poems is reminiscent of Amryl Johnson's work.[17] Amryl Johnson mixes a public responsibility to a black community with fiercely private moments in her poems where she seems to be working something out for herself to do with love, loss and loneliness,

> I sensed you by my side
> As ancient as the trees
> Your eyes
>   like ice
>   like fire
> There were times when
> I could not
> look into them
> You would lean
>   on my arm
> and on days when nothing
> made much sense
> I would lean
>   on your wisdom
>
> ('Hole in the Wind', *Tread Carefully*, p. 54)

There is here a vulnerability, a fragility and a lyricism; a knowledge of the world and of life. The feelings are intense but strictly mediated through the physical world. The brittleness and tension are almost tangible. Balancing a loyalty to the tribe with a loyalty to the craft and to the self can seem at times contradictory and destructive, but it is the test of good poetry when a poet is able to meet the requirements of all three. I'm not sure how much mileage is to be had out of seeing this wellspring of black women's writing as so different from what black men are writing that it merits separate treatment. The female chorus constructed by Jackie Kay's three women's voices and the women in Amryl Johnson's new collection, *Gorgons* (Cofa, Coventry, 1991), appear to make a case for such an approach; the idea being that black women have more in common with women of other races living here than they do with black men.

IV
Conclusion

This writing places the work of black poets at the centre of what is happening in poetry in Britain. In fact it is impossible to account for British poetry without taking on board the work of black poets living and working here. With the regional loyalties which a poet like Jackie Kay or Levi Tafari carry alongside their concerns about race and sex and gender, surely critical attempts to isolate their work and group them together will look more and more absurd. It is important to state categorically that it is a nonsense to pretend that what black writers are doing in Britain is so unlike what their white compatriates in craft are practising that it merits a category entirely of its own. That brand of reasoning isolates black poets from their white contemporaries and makes their art inferior by difference. The reality is that poets of a particular age, class, and locality, often have more in common in terms of their craft and themes, whatever racial differences may obtain, than poets of the same race who belong to a different generation and class and live at opposite ends of the country. This complicates the approach somewhat. What it adds up to is this: the category 'black' must confine itself to a particular geography if it is to mean anything. Black as a political term has tended to spread its net widely in order to present a broad and unified, if diverse, front to a hostile public and to what the rap group *Public Enemy* calls 'the power'. It has included anyone of African descent including people from the Caribbean or of Caribbean parentage and Asians from South Asia. But it excludes people from the Far East. It is a definition which is political; this means it does not necessarily hold for a definition of who writes what. The major benefactor out of all this activity is the language itself. Dub poetry, poetry influenced by calypso, reggae, jazz and blues rhythm, creole language and Standard English articulating for the first time the black experience in Britain have all changed what it means to be British; deepened it in fact, making it more sophisticated, giving it a new lease of life. Black prose in Britain, well, that's another story.

Notes

1 Phyllis Wheatley, *Poems on Various Subjects, Religious and Moral*, London, 1773.

2 Olaudah Equiano, *The Life of Olaudah Equiano, or Gustavus Vassa, the African*, London, 1789.

3 For a complete list check the anthologies, James Berry (ed.), *News for Babylon*, Chatto and Windus, London, 1984; Fred D'Aguiar *et al.* (eds.), *The New British Poetry*, Paladin, London, 1988; Jackie Kay *et al.* (eds.), *Charting the Journey*, Sheba, London, 1988.

4 Linton Kwesi Johnson, *Dread Beat and Blood*, Bogle-L'Ouverture, London, 1975.

5 Edward Brathwaite, *The Arrivants*, OUP, Oxford, 1973.

6 James Berry, *Lucy's Letters and Loving*, New Beacon Books, 1982.

7 Linton Kwesi Johnson *et al.*, cassette, *An Evening of International Poetry*, Bogle-L'Ouverture and New Beacon Books, 1983.

8 John Agard, *Mangoes and Bullets*, Pluto, London, 1985.

9 Levi Tafari, *The Liverpool Experience*, book and cassette, London, 1988 and 1989.

10 John Lyons, *Lure of the Casadura*, Bogle-L'Ouverture, London, 1989.

11 E. A. Markham, *Human Rites*, Ambit, London, 1984.

12 David Dabydeen, *Coolie Odyssey*, Dangaroo Press, Coventry, 1988.

13 Jackie Kay, *The Adoption Papers*, Bloodaxe, Newcastle upon Tyne, 1991.

14 Jackie Kay, *Bluefoot Cassettes*, The British Library National Sound Archive, 1990.

15 Gabriel Gbadomosi, 'Flying Home', *The New British Poetry*, p. 36.

16 Grace Nichols, *I is a Long Memoried Woman*, Karnak House, London 1983.

17 Amryl Johnson, *Tread Carefully in Paradise*, Cofa Press, Coventry, 1991.

R. J. Ellis

3

Mapping the United Kingdom
little magazine field

> where our present is, is, strictly speaking,
> irredeemable. terms jostle. within
> the elastic limits speeches slide collide
> bumping against the steel skull-cap it's
> undeniable the step is gone
>
> Wendy Mulford from 'Valentine'[1]

I

The field of United Kingdom little magazine publishing is large and varied: *International Directory of Little Magazines and Small Presses* lists over 100 titles in production in the United Kingdom during 1990–91 that could be reasonably described as 'little magazines', and almost certainly at least as many more exist which remain unlisted.[2] Eventually I will become compelled to search for a definition of the term 'little magazine', but pretending for the moment that the term is self-explanatory, I will begin by making the self-evident assertion that a field which regularly in the last three decades has consisted of between one and two hundred more or less regular serial publication titles cannot be adequately described, let alone analysed, in one short article. This is why I have taken the decision to focus my attention on analysis rather than description, though acknowledging that this analysis will be both partial (incomplete) and partial (biased). What I am seeking is an analytical over-view – a species of 'mapping' which will depend on my perspective but, I hope, will not be entirely reliant on it. To this end, I wrote to twenty-four little magazine editors in 1990, enclosing a questionnaire,[3] which I will make free use of in my analysis – to provide both reinforcement of and counterpoint to my views.

I anticipated a low response rate, and that is what I got. I anticipated this for three reasons: firstly, some of the little magazines would have ceased to exist, in a field which is notoriously volatile as editors run out of cash, or patience, or interest – as they themselves report (self-deprecating humour recurrently appeared in the questionnaire replies);[4] secondly, the editors would have moved on and the questionnaires would not have reached them – this a product (in a different but complementary way to the first) of the non-commercial status of the great majority of little magazines; thirdly, and most revealingly (though already we have learned some fundamental things about the field), I believed that the editors would find filling in questionnaires about their 'aims and objectives' disconcerting, difficult or even distateful, and would not wish to conform to my request. Some measure of validation for this belief resides in the fact that almost all of the editors who did reply declined to answer several of my questions, and many declined to answer over one-third of them. Anthony Linick, carrying out a much more comprehensive, yet not unrelated survey in the United States in 1963,[5] experienced similar problems about getting survey replies, and advanced a related set of reasons, including my third one – that editors chose deliberately to decline to conform.

The grounds on which I base my belief that this third reason is the most revealing are, to some extent, ones that derive directly from the central proposition of my analysis. I estimate that editors might find my request disconcerting because they are functioning very often, but not always, in a discursive matrix that does not encourage a systematic questioning of the rationale behind the act of (editorial) creation – a matrix representing creativity as a product of imagination, inspiration, genius or the like, which establishes a virtually tautologous, hermetic argument and one which, since it is advanced recurrently by practising poets, bears comparison with a hermeneutic circle, excluding analysis. This also accounts in large part for why I feel some editors might find answering the questionnaire difficult: trapped in such a circle, explanations or analyses of an activity that seems 'natural' become difficult. Finally, and again relatedly, the task might seem distasteful to some editors because, precisely, assumptions about their editing activities are in some ways being affronted by the questions posed merely because the questions are posed – in a sense, because they can be posed about what seems to them to be self-explanatory.

Let me offset this by offering one other explanation for non-reply: busy-ness, perhaps related to a surfeit of surveys/ questionnaires, an argument advanced by, amongst others, Martin Bax (Ambit).[6] Certainly, my questionnaire's demands on their time were clear, and any response would go unrewarded. In a sense, though, I could turn this excuse around on the editors: the real demand on time was perhaps made greater precisely by the lack of a framework of arguments and theories to which they could refer about the processes of little magazine production, a lack precisely stemming from my hypothesised tautologous matrix.[7]

That hardly anyone has written concertedly about little magazines in the UK (despite the expansion of the field since World War II and the acceleration in activity generated by the introduction of affordable off-set lithographic printing processes could, with a touch of irony, be attributed to the same problem – of busy-ness amongst those critics and academics who otherwise one might have expected to show at least an interest in, if not a concern about, little magazines. The few who have engaged with it have generally had a finger in the pie – as poets, as editors, or as both – and as such were often bound by the genre's convention of (almost at times a conspiracy of) critical silence: 'there are certainly some magazines which have slightly modelled themselves on Ambit around now, but it would embarrass them if I stated who'.[8] Here, I feel sure, Martin Bax is influenced by a sense of solidarity generated by participating in little magazine publishing and stemming from the constant disheartening sense that no one out there is actually reading what you produce – another recurrent (but not omnipresent) theme in questionnaire returns, and one which can give way to an elitist, resigned acquiescence, centreing on the idea that those who care and who, in return, need to be cared about are the ones who do, indeed, subscribe.[9] My questions asking editors to relate their magazine's position to that of others in the field were frequently avoided.[10] This is not to say some reviewing of other little magazines does not occur, and that some of this is highly critical. But it is equally true that the 'reviews' section in a little magazine is usually last to come and first to go, and many little magazines avoid it altogether; furthermore, reviews of other little magazines are, overall, surprisingly rare.

II

Thus, faced with the question, 'How would you attempt to "map out" the "landscape" of little magazine activity in the UK at present?' editors, like critics and academics, mostly fell silent. Commentators and commentaries are plainly rare, and, I am maintaining, this lack is produced by the discursive matrix investing the field. Those commentaries that do appear, in this sense, tend to be descriptive rather than analytic, following in the footsteps of Denys Val Baker, who in 1943 was almost resolutely descriptive in approach.[11] Since even such descriptive accounts are rare, they can be of real interest and value, but I try to eschew this approach because other articles I have published (mostly with Geoffrey Soar of University College, London) have described this field, not comprehenisively, of course, but in some breadth.[12] These articles have also attempted to offer some analysis, but rather than use these, I will turn to an attempt at 'mapping' offered by one of the editors responding to my questionnaire, Ken Edwards (*Reality Studios*). His necessarily brief outline of how he would map the little magazine field ran as follows: 'Mainstream/ Establishment/Funded on the one hand; Independent/

Marginalised on the other. The latter category is very heterogeneous'.[13] In fact, it could be claimed that this apparently simple binary opposition is quite conceptually daring, linking as it does apparently disparate categorisations under the same grouping on either side of his binary divide. Thus for a little magazine to be funded (an economic distinction), is to ally it with the mainstream/establishment (a distinction based on what might be loosely described as the politics of poetry publishing), and this, by implication at least, means that if a little magazine is financially independent it is more likely be part of the heterogeneous complex 'independent/marginalised', which also includes 'the avant-garde/experimental'.[14]

A lot of issues are thus raised by Ken Edwards, and in pursuing these I shall be led steadily away from what has so far been my main argument concerning a constricting discursive matrix. But, importantly, the lines of analysis which will now develop will also come to constitute a critique of what I have so far said. The dialectic thus established will, better than anything, I believe, establish the contradictoriness of the little magazine publishing field, rendering it unstable both financially and (not coincidentally) in terms of its constituent titles' survival. In other words, I will start to argue that the grip of the discourse of artistic creativity, with its insistence on individual genius, is rendered inherently incomplete by the very dynamics and economics of the field: little magazines stand in an inherently contradictory relationship to commercial publishing.

A way of approaching Edwards' points which will lead me in this direction, I think, is to return to the problem of defining the little magazine genre: what is a 'little magazine', especially if one element of Edwards' binary divide alone can be described as 'very heterogeneous'? The simple consequence is that all generalisations about the field are going to be false, and my failure will only be one of many other, at best only partially successful, previous attempts.[15] My approach will hinge on an inclusive/ exclusive system thickly hedged by a set of qualificatory conditions. To some extent, however, what follows is intended to be rank-ordered:

1. *Little magazines are generally not commercial* in terms of viability or intent, but to be a commercial success cannot in itself be sufficient to be a disqualification. A classic case to point to here is that of Bill Buford's *Granta* which, all said and done, 'evolved from a student magazine',[16] and which was, in 1982, still edited in 'the same unheated attic' as when founded in 1979,[17] however much a distribution agreement with Penguin and consequent visibility might complicate an assessment. Even if the disease most rife among little magazines is low circulation, terminally enhanced by distribution problems, little magazine editors are happy to confess that they are 'trying to get th[e] poetry [they publish] an audience',[18] and Martin Bax is happy to recognise that 'some little magazines have of course been enormous'.[19] *Granta* really should not be excluded, not least because 'we [at *Granta*] need cash', despite a print run of 10,000 as at December 1990.

2. *Little magazines primarily, or only, publish poetry and/or fiction and/or other forms of imaginative writing*, and most usually primarily publish poetry in their pages (though a significant number deliberately seek to bring the arts together). Again, a qualification must be erected to some extent, for a number of serial publications exist with very small publication runs, acute circulation problems, precarious finances, non-commercial in approach whilst seeking as many readers as possible, which rarely if ever publish imaginative writing, fiction, or poetry. These are frequently attached to pressure or single-issue groups, or seek to disseminate the ideas of groups outside of the cultural mainstream (e.g. the 'New Age' proponents of humanity's possession of sixth sense faculties or those seeking to promote or sustain the beliefs of the counter-culture). It would be easy to simply rule these exceptions out, and this essay will, indeed, entirely neglect them, but the qualification needs to be drawn up: many publish imaginative writing, fiction and poetry, if to limited extents. Thus, for example, *Writing Women*, and *Spare Rib* (the latter publishing a deal of creative writing) are not entirely unrelated, particularly if their early histories are compared.

3. *Little magazines are oriented towards publication of the experimental, and/or the avant-garde, and/or the emergent/new*, classically, they should claim to be doing at least two of the above. In practice, when surveying the little magazine field, it has to be said that many, or even most, little magazines do no such thing, unless the adjectives 'new' and 'emergent' are taken merely to refer to

previously unnoticed or unpublished poets and writers, or those just beginning to write (a classic role of little magazines, and one frequently and correctly emphasised, is that they provide forums for new young writers' work). This qualification, that the 'emergent' or 'new' may rarely or never also be experimental or avant-garde in some little magazines, is of critical importance, of course, and feeds directly into one element of Ken Edwards' binary system's dividing line. It is a point to which this essay will return.

4. *Little magazines are prepared to take risks.* This assertion is closely linked to my first, and also bears fundamentally on my third proposed characteristic. Recurrently non-commercial, frequently experimental in approach, little magazines can potentially enjoy an enormous flexibility in terms of format, production processes, even the medium used; *Alembic*, *Curtains*, Allen Fisher's *Spanner* and David Mayor's *Schmuck* spring to mind here, but one could also even name *Poetry Review* at the other extreme, for this Poetry Society organ has shown a preparedness to change format to some extent, as part of a limited recognition of the need to adapt to encompass the growing degree of formal experimentation in UK verse. This last example will seem pretty thin to some, even if I point out that the review's format change incorporated page enlargement, by which the magazine grew to a size where 'open field' compositional approaches stood more chance of adequate deployment (a point made by Peter Hodgkiss, when emphasising that, after all, most poets compose on A4 sheets of paper).[20] But this, I suppose, is my point, for one could also enter into a debate about to what extent *Poetry Review* is, really, a 'little magazine' in the sense emerging here, underpinned and limited as it is by its institutional identity. Which is why, perhaps, this point deserves some emphasis; for example, the 'risk' taken may be to endeavour to marry, merge or otherwise bring together artistic forms usually regarded as somehow distinct. Just eight editorial examples would be: Stuart Mills, in *Aggie Weston's* interest in concrete poetry, particularly that of Ian Hamilton Finlay, Finlay's own *Poor, Old, Tired, Horse.*, 1983's (unsuccessful) attempt to establish itself as a series of performance poetry audio-cassettes, Jake Tilson and Stephen Whitaker in *Cipher's* use of colour xeroxes, stickers, hand-tinting and rubber stamps, Stephen Willats in *Control's* use of photography linked to texts, George Maciunas in *Fluxus 1's* use of mail art, and, less ambi-

tiously, Martin Bax in *Ambit*'s interest in existing as a 'magazine . . . where artists appeared together, complemented each other'.[21] 'Risk' is, quite simply, here to be understood in the broadest meaning of the word but *Poetry Review* hardly qualifies.

III

By now, I believe, something of a pattern has emerged to the recurrence of cautionings built up around my definition of the term 'little magazine'. For the pattern seems to me repeatedly one concerned with the degree of risk, or let us call it radicalism, built into any little magazine publishing project. And this, I think, is precisely what systematises, conceptually, Ken Edwards' mapping, for all of its apparent categorial inconsistencies. What he is postulating is the existence of two 'camps', both of them in fact large and heterogeneous; the inherent danger, of course, is of some sort of combat between them.

Recurrently, this is in fact what commentators have claimed has existed over the last four decades or so. It is, anyway, a 'split' that could be said to pre-date this period – a split ultimately emanating from the impact of modernism upon the late Victorians and, in a different way, upon the Georgians' reactions to late Victorianism, and the unceasing variety of responses to these collisions in the United Kingdom (in poetry, via the imagists, Wyndham Lewis, Ezra Pound, David Jones, and, later, Basil Bunting, Hugh MacDiarmid and many others on the one hand and those figuring in the lineage of the Movement poets, and to a lesser extent also the Group, in their reactions against the Apocalypse, on the other; in prose, via James Joyce, Virginia Woolf, Malcolm Lowry etc., – summary here is quite impossible) and in America (in poetry, via Pound [again], William Carlos Williams, Louis Zukofsky, George Oppen, Charles Reznikoff, Marianne Moore, H. D. and many more on the one hand and those whose lineage needs to make close reference to the Fugitives on the other; in prose, via Gertrude Stein, John Dos Passos, William Faulkner etc., – summary again is quite impossible). It must quickly be conceded that this rapid sketch is over-schematic; the one hand/other hand divisions set up here are not simple. This can well be illustrated by mentioning a few other poetry practitioners: T. S. Eliot, W. H. Auden and the left-wing Louis MacNeice, for example, whose locations are more problematic.

However, it supplies us both with a way of illustrating *en passant* the importance of little magazines, which served throughout this period as forums for debate and definition, and, more central to my argument, with one method of understanding how I resolve my dilemmas over *Granta*'s status, for Bill Buford, despite the scale of his enterprise, has been concerned when publishing to 'develop . . . a writing that started to satisfy an appetite for a literature that engaged actively with the culture'. Thus he turns to writing of the sort which leads him to list, as his 'especially significant/representative contributors' the writers 'Richard Ford, Raymond Carver, James Fenton . . . Ian Jack . . . John Berger, Seamus Deane and Salman Rushdie' (amongst others).[22] And yet, in the same questionnaire, Buford writes that he possesses a 'loathing for the traditional little magazine that no one buys and fewer people read'.[23] Buford is here, I believe, collapsing several issues into one statement, and a fundamental conceptual confusion exists. On the one hand, certainly, the shades of the 'split' are invoked: the adjective 'traditional' carries within it an implication that little magazines that operate within conservative parameters in terms of form and content warrant neglect and are deservedly small circulation ones. But this implication is undercut by an ambiguity lacing the statement, for another reading of his words would understand them as asserting that small circulation is a vice of little magazines – a tradition to be broken – and that what the genre needs are innovatory serials deliberately seeking large audiences. After all, almost all of the authors' names that Buford regards as being of special significance to *Granta* are ones that one could count on as also appearing on the spines of book covers in any branch of the large bookshop chains. In a sense, 'risk' in one (economic) sense is limited here, but I do not believe that Buford would wish therefore to ally himself with the sentiments of Charles Osborne, who, in a not unrelated way, attacked the whole terrain of little magazine publishing in 1975 (and in successive years) '[. . . little magazines] make no useful contribution to literature [and] generally are not worth supporting'.[24] Here, any apparent consanguinity is not real; Buford's averred intent of featuring literature that 'engaged actively in the culture' carries within it, in sharp contrast to Osborne's predilections, an implied radicalism that *Granta* recurrently bears out in its pages.

It is precisely these discursive instabilities that I am interested in, for I believe they permeate the whole level of debate concerning the field of little magazine activity and its characteristics, whenever descriptive accounts of it advance towards analysis. I find related instablities, for example, in the discussion of the 'split' in the field of poetry production in the United Kingdom, even within my own minor contributions to this debate. Osborne's astringent dismissal of little magazines, voiced when he was Director of the Arts Council's Literature Panel, ensured hard financial times for UK little magazines in the second half of the seventies (from which they have never really recovered), and well introduces the note of acerbity that was extant in a battle commencing in the fifties and sixties, raging in the seventies and lingering on into the eighties and nineties still. It proved to be a battle with a more or less clear winner emerging in economic and mainstream cultural terms, at least for a while; how else can one account for the otherwise extraordinary statement in Blake Morrison's and Andrew Motion's *The Penguin Book of Contemporary British Poetry*, that '[for] much of the sixties and seventies very little . . . seemed to be happening . . . in British poetry'.[25] The fact is that this was precisely the period when the groundwork laid down in the late Fifties in the terrain of modernist re-engagement, after the (not complete but noticeable) hiatus created by the war years and their immediate aftermath, began to bloom quite copiously within the inter-related little magazine and small press fields, as the influence of such figures as MacDiarmid, Bunting, Wyndham Lewis and Pound revived, and Surrealism, in Britain and America, attracted new practitioners. It would quite plainly be wrong to pretend that the little magazine field in this period was wholly or even on balance dominated by the avant-garde and experimental in poetry writing, since a large number of more or less institutionally-linked serial titles continued to appear, and perhaps found main expression in the regular publication of Howard Sergeant's *Outposts*, the model to which, one could argue, many local poetry society publications or college poetry magazines aspired, consciously or not.

Nevertheless, set against the general lack of interest in little magazines as outlets amongst the Movement poets and their fellow travellers (since, as Edward Lucie-Smith put it in 1970, speaking perhaps on their behalf, 'the network of little presses and little magazines ... has always existed ... encouraging writers who were for some reason unfashionable'),[26] the United Kingdom modernist revival had a clear and contrasting regard for little magazines. These they saw as the correct medium for experimental development. This meant that, quite visibly, the cutting edge of little magazine activity in the fifties and sixties became dominated by writers working with new forms. These frequently were American, also, to a lesser extent, from Europe: Peter Russell's *Nine* (1949–58) and William Cookson's *Agenda* (1959–) brought together, amongst others, Ezra Pound and Basil Bunting; William Carlos Williams' influence showed clearly in the pages of *The Window* (1951–55?) and *Artisan* (1953–55); Black Mountain poetics were important to Gael Turnbulls' and Michael Shayer's *Migrant* (1959–60) amongst others; Michael Horovitz's *New Departures* (1959–?] paid close attention to US activity in general, particularly the Beats' writings, but also to European activities; Bob Cobbing's *And* (1954–?) moved towards exploring visual poetry's possibilities, and Jon Silkin's *Stand* (1952–) consistently published European poetry. This list is very partial, and only begins to usher in the Sixties (well signposted, anyway, by magazines like *New Departures* and *And*), when the list extends itself very rapidly; to name but a few, Tina Morris' and Dave Cunliffe's *Poetmeat*, *PM Newsletter* and *Global Tapestry Journal*, Finlay's *Poor. Old. Tired. Horse*, Jeff Nuttall's *My Own Mag*, Tom Pickard's *King Ida's Watch Chain*, Andrew Crozier's *Wivenhoe Park Review*, Lee Harwood's *Horde*, *Soho*, and *Tzarad*, Peter Riley's

The English Intelligencer, Kris Hemensley's *Earthship*, and Pierre Joris' *Sixpack*, all started up in the period 1960 to 1970. This burst of activity I want to relate to the recovery of modernism, but also, of course, to the impetus provided to Sixties writers by the arguments of the counter-culture following in the wake of the decisive advances in cheap reproduction processes.

Thus it is that Eric Mottram formulated, in his essay for the 1974 Modern British Poetry Conference at the Polytechnic of Central London, the idea of a 'British Poetry Revival' during the period 1960–74. This, of course, was the very period when, for Morrison and Motion, 'very little' was happening.[27] Mottram's use of the phrase becomes exact, and the contradiction between him and Morrison and Motion becomes largely alleviated, if we take the words of his essay title as ones that are carefully weighed: 'modern' here does not mean 'contemporary', but modernist-inspired. Whilst it cannot be said that the Morrison and Motion anthology consists of poets completely uninterested in the modernist revolution of the word, it is true to say that not one of the poet-editors of the titles listed above, and virtually no one from the long list of their little magazine's contributors, were anthologised by Morrison and Motion. The division this implies was one Mottram was precisely intent on describing, and five years later Barry MacSweeney was concerned to extend it on to 1979, in the process re-confirming that a sense of a split existed.[28] Both their positions were openly partisan, but even slightly less committed commentators, such as Douglas Dunn, showed a sharp awareness of some sort of divide.[29] By 1981, Stephen Pereira (*Angel Exhaust*), in trying to put together as exhaustive as possible a survey of contemporary United Kingdom poetry, was to speak of a total breakdown: 'The radicals have nothing to do with the Establishment and vice versa'.[30] His was one of the relatively few attempts to bridge the gap, others perhaps being made by *Palantir*, *Slow Dancer*, *Little Word Machine* and *The Wide Skirt*. That such mainstream serial titles as *Poetry Review* and, in a different, more mixed way, *PN Review* have become over the years a little more receptive to living as well as dead modernists might be in part taken as a tribute to their efforts.

All this may sound extreme, but an extraordinary, illustrative anecdote will intimate the degree of breakdown as well as anything: significantly, it returns us to the history of *Poetry Review*, the creative-writing organ of that 'establishment' institution, the Poetry Society. In 1969 *Poetry Review*'s editor, Derek Parker, chose to feature the work of a number of avant-garde/experimental post-war UK modernists and in 1970 some of these (Allen Fisher, Lee Harwood, Peter Hodgkiss, Pete Morgan, Tom Pickard, Elaine Randell, Ken Smith and Barry MacSweeney) were elected to the society's general council, Hugh MacDiarmid and Basil Bunting to the presidency and Eric Mottram took over the editing of *Poetry Review* from Parker. Mottram set about deliberately to transform it from 'a mansion of grandmotherly amateurism into the outpost of American and European modernism'.[31] To do this, however, he had to upset the sensibilities of a number of Poetry Society luminaries, not least through his use of rejection slips to make room for the work of such poets as Tom Pickard, Michael Horovitz, Andrew Crozier, F.T. Prince, and the Americans Robert Kelly and Joel Oppenheimer. What next happened is well described by Mottram in *Poetry Information*, Number 20/21 (Winter 1979/80).[32] In brief, Charles Osborne of the Arts Council was called in to restore a 'balance' and in a heated public meeting in 1974 the Arts Council assumed effective control of the Poetry Society; subsequently, Mottram was squeezed out of the editorship of *Poetry Review*.

It would, I believe, not be much of an exaggeration to suggest that this battle, and the defeat, had long-lasting repercussions, as well as injecting a degree of rancour. For, during the coming decade, the Arts Council was fundamentally to re-assess the amount of financial subsidy it was prepared to give to 'little magazines'. Dunn's belief in 1977 that 'a little magazine's . . . prayers . . . are likely to be answered by the Arts Council' was already almost anachronistic;[33] on the contrary, in the period 1975 to 1985, and ever since, re-assessments of policy were under way that ensured that right through the Eighties grants were sharply reduced or withered away (depending on which Regional Arts organisation was involved). Whether this withdrawal of support is a good or bad thing is a matter of unresolved debate: Graham Sykes of *Kudos* sees subsidy as meretricious, since arts grants shield little magazines from their primary *raison d'être* – to get themselves out to as wide an audience as possible through 'actual grass roots sales'.[34] More fundamentally, Paul Buck argues, in typically outspoken fashion, that: 'Subsidy is the death of art. I discovered that more and more as the magazine developed. Do anything but give yourself over to government control'.[35] It perhaps needs to be recalled here that Buck is speaking from experience: his May 1978 issue of *Curtains*, named *bal:le:d curtains*, contains a labyrinthine account of a censorship intervention by Yorkshire Arts, which (predictably) centrally involved Charles Osborne and ended in the axing of *Curtain's* grant: '. . . the prime villainy of the Osborne Mafia, with its operations room in the Arts Council Literature Department is working . . . effectively to undermine the energy of the new contemporary writing', Buck went on to claim he was 'turning [his] back' on English literature' by moving to Paris.[36]

In fact, *Curtains* virtually ceased publication from that moment, which is one way of reminding us that loss of subsidy can cut both ways for a little magazine. The real risk is of marginalisation in economic as well as literary terms, and their interaction, here quite apparent, needs always to be borne in mind. It is true to say of little magazines that their potential role is well illustrated by reference to past achievements: James Joyce's *Portrait of the Artist* was at first published serially in *The Egoist*, much of *Ulysses* in *The Egoist* and *The Little Review* and *Finnegans Wake* in *transition*; little magazines were important to the development of William Carlos Williams, Ezra Pound, T. S. Eliot, Wallace Stevens and W. B. Yeats. Pound's editing of *The Exile* and Williams' editing of *Contact* were part and parcel of their development as poets and Pound's *Cantos* and Williams' *Paterson* at least partly evolved in little magazine publication; much of Wyndham Lewis's development was enabled via his editing of *Blast*, and Robert Duncan's and Charles Olson's moves towards achieving their long-poem projects were enabled via experimentation in little magazines in

America.

But the risk in adopting this approach when specifying the merits of the little magazine genre is that it looks backwards anachronistically, by failing to take account of the fundamental transformations which have beset publishing in the intervening decades. The risk of stressing the past as a means of understanding the significance of the little magazine field is that this implicitly accepts somehow the very limited audience that little magazines in particular and poetry in general commands at present. I believe that the very decision to edit and publish a little magazine carries within it an implicit (perhaps even unrecognised) or an express desire to direct more people's attention to what poetry can do in terms of producing an alertness to meaning and language, and their interaction, for poet, poets and readers. Donald Davie writes in a recent *PN Review* that 'poetry which should speak to all men at present speaks to few' and that the poets in *A Various Art* (a 1987 anthology edited by Tim Longville and Andrew Crozier and publishing such avant-garde experimentalists as J. H. Prynne, David Chaloner, Nick Totton, Roy Fisher, Veronica Forrest-Thomson, Douglas Oliver, Anthony Barnett and Peter Riley) are an 'antidote' to an 'abyss of self-regarding and cynical frivolity' into which 'English literary culture' has sunk. In saying this he is precisely, I think, legitimating my concern over the problems posed by Arts Council subsidy withdrawals.[37] Ironically, earlier in his article Davie had, quite inconsistently, argued that the poets anthologised in *A Various Art* had 'never tried' to be 'generally "on offer" ',[38] a statement completely disregarding the actual struggles enacted around the split between the institutional establishment and the experiemental/ avant garde that the little magazine field accurately maps out – as complex, shifting, unstable but very real. The poets featured in *A Various Art*, and their fellow experimentalists, have in fact been 'on offer' in the Seventies and Eighties, in such magazines as *Spanner*, *Figs*, *And*, *Reality Studios*, *Grosseteste Review*, *Alembic*, *Ninth Decade*, and *Rock Drill*, but, quite simply, this offer has not been taken up. The evidence provided by *A Various Art* is quite plainly that, as its title implies, a very varied set of poetic practices are in full flood in the

United Kingdom, though their emergence into the 'customary institutions of British poetry' is at best spasmodic and usually incomplete.[39] This can be attributed, as it is by Gavin Selerie, to attempts by the 'critical establishment ... to reject or simply ignore the vitality of the new British poetry in its various forms', but Selerie also goes on, correctly to my mind, to stress how 'the current policies of many grant-giving authorities [such as the] Arts Council of Great Britain ... [by] shift[ing] the emphasis of its support away from writers in favour of secondary aid, meaning channels of distribution and direct bookselling', has meant favouring 'authors "of merit" (in some cases those who are already dead)',[40] with the result that the existing contemporary establishment 'canon' is reinforced. Selerie censoriously quotes from a Greater London Arts Council Policy Paper which suggests that: 'Publishing grants ... have become lower and lower priorities ... for a variety of reasons ... [including] the constant doubt about whether such grants do more than provide a little clotted cream for the heavily jammed scones of the printing industry',[41] a policy suggestion that displays an appalling ignorance about the processes of little magazine and small press production; if an editor goes along with the maintenance of economic independence, it is precisely because of 'distrust ... [of] the big houses' media-hype and show-casing of personalities', as Donald Davie correctly points out.[42]

IV

It is perhaps a good idea to temporarily focus here on anthology-publishing to provide some specific focus for these generalisations. In this respect A Various Art is plainly almost diametrically opposed to the collection edited by Morrison and Motion, The Penguin Book of Contemporary British Poetry, published five years earlier; they do not, nor could they, have any poets in common. An anthology following soon after A Various Art, and one perhaps to a minor extent capitalising on the space created by Longville's and Crozier's anthology, was The New British Poetry (1988), divided into four sections – black (edited by Fred

D'Aguiar), feminist (edited by Gillian Allnutt) and two experimental, one edited by Eric Mottram and one ('Some Younger
Poets') by Ken Edwards.[43] That it followed so closely behind *A
Various Art* is in itself encouraging, as is the breadth it achieves by
bringing together four different sets of poets. Less encouraging
was the pasting this Paladin anthology received in many reviews.
Robert Sheppard's defence of it in *Pages*, against a Peter Porter
attack, clarifies well the discouraging gulf that still exists:

> So many aggressive terms in Peter Porter's review for *The Observer*
> could be translated from the sneering of the well-anthologised
> into the language of the neglected. For 'whingeing' read 'angry';
> for 'Sixties Old Boys' Society' read 'poets who, since the flash
> of publicity in the 1960s, have been forced further underground
> than the "Underground" ever was'; for 'ageing experimentalist'
> read 'senior formalists'; for 'self-referring hagiography' read
> 'axiomatic reference points not normally associated with British
> poetry'.[44]

These 'axiomatic reference points' are mainly American, as
the title 'New British Poetry' implies, with its oblique reference to
The New American Poetry anthology edited by Donald M. Allen and
published in 1960.[45] This association would have been eased by
the more recent publication of a follow-up US anthology. *The
Postmoderns: The New American Poetry Revisited* in 1982.[46] Thus Michael
Horovitz, in a review published in *PN Review*,[47] makes the link back
to the 1960 anthology, and specifically, in turn, relates the Paladin
anthology to his own Penguin anthology, *Children of Albion*,
published in 1969, itself intended as a UK reponse to Allen's first
anthology.[48] This US orientation can in turn be reinforced by
reference to Gavin Selerie's guest editing of a forty-eight page
'Selection of Contemporary British Poetry' section in *North Dakota
Quarterly*.[49] This transatlantic link is mostly a matter of influence,
though it has not, especially recently, been solely a one-way affair,
and it has to be understood that the influence has been multi-
faceted: the Beats influencing Michael Horovitz's endeavours in
New Departures and Jim Burn's in *Palantir* to some extent; Black
Mountain poets (and the earlier Objectivists) having a recurrent

influence, for example on *Grosseteste Review* (especially before it developed its interest in the Cambridge school of poets) and on *Spectacular Diseases*; the New York poets (particularly Ashbery and O'Hara) proving similarly recurrent as a reference point; the $L=A=N=G=U=A=G=E$ school interacting with amongst others, *Lobby Press Newsletter* and *Reality Studios*; and *Alembic 7* (*Assemblic*, Spring 1978) borrowing Richard Kostelanetz's 'assemblage' technique.[50] If one takes these cross-seminations in sum, it is possible to see that the Beats' demand for a reappraisal of the social role of creative writing, the Black Mountain poets' insistence on open form, proprioceptive verse forms to liberate meaning from the constraints of conventional forms, and the subversions of language and syntax erected in different ways by the New York school and the $L=A=N=G=U=A=G=E$ poets can all interact with the modernist practices of Bunting, MacDiarmid, Jones and their progeny (which were in part re-discovered via the impact of US activities in Britain), particularly as these were taken up in the Fifties, to constitute a sustained, versatile and various interrogation of the politics of signification.

Indeed, if one reads back over the last several paragraphs an undercurrent of political dissent is plainly present: Buck's concern to stay clear of 'govenment control' interacts complexly with the Arts Council's progressive withdrawal from any preparedness to subsidise little magazine publishing activities, for example, since, as Selerie points out, the 'aim ... of the present [Thatcher] government ... [is] to remove support from all but the most "essential" services.[51] The interaction is complex because Donald Davie's accurate identification of the distrust the avant-garde has for the hype and personality-vaunting of the commercial publishing arena is plainly allied to unease about the discursive representations of the subject – as self-reliantly able to make his (patriarchal) own way – erected by bourgeois individualism. Davie in fact goes on to value most the romantic strain he detects in the work of some of the contributors to *A Various Art*,[52] thereby confirming my initial contention that activity within the little magazine field constantly tends to risk collapsing the debate back into the terms of individual creativity offering transcendent insight (here by not specifying what he understands by 'romantic'), rather than setting up the possibilities of negotiated re-definition – poet to poets to reader. In this respect I believe that the best little magazines are those which seek out interactive positions through sustained critical debate (rather than short reviews), through a sense of continuity and fraternal/sororial endeavour. Choosing more or less at random, but from (unfortunately) a readily exhaustible list, one could point out the continuity set up by *Poetmeat*, *PM Newsletter* and *Global Tapestry*, and the way in which the newsletter served, in incidental combination with Cavan McCarthy's *Loc-Sheet*, as a composite information bank about little magazine/small press activity; how *Reality Studios* first set out to be a 'monthly newssheet . . . a supplement to *Alembic*',[53] how at first *Poetry Information*, and then subsequently *Poetry and Little Press Information* sought to function as information exchanges and debating forums for the experimental/avant-garde wing of little magazine activity, and how *Ninth Decade* brought together the editors of *Shearsman* (Tony Frazer), *The Atlantic Review* (Robert Vas Dias), and *Oasis* and *Telegram* (Ian Robinson).

This co-operative spirit suggests how the writer and reader as subjects might break out of the powerlessness of individualised subjectivity, into re-formulation – an already implicitly disruptive possibility, I would wish to maintain, set up by a little magazine's establishment of a non-commercial community in its pages. As Eric Mottram put it: 'There's a whole hidden etymological environment in the word 'private' . . . in which we are held'.[54] The little magazine field has the potential to erode this grip, but it is only a potential. It can be seen to be emergent in this statement by Allen Fisher that '. . . much of my work has included the need to carry the work process across into book production . . . partly out of a wish to *make* for oneself – to have autonomy in production – and partly to engage with the 'communities' of artists similarly involved. . . . The overall activity complex can be seen as a political one – against an established norm.'[55]

If we ally this potential to the view of the poet as someone seeking, in this sort of communal endeavour, to fracture, loosen and re-formulate the referential structure of language and language-forms, to liberate meaning for the producer (poet/ poets/readers), then Kris Hemensley's apparently large claims make sense:

> In order to be a big press in a liberal-capitalist-consumer society, you have to have availed yourself of the wherewithal of the existing value system, economic political cultural. There is a point to the littleness of the little press . . . .
> It is not turned out for a market . . . .
> The point is to devolve control . . . to decentralize the creative capacity of society.[56]

V

This potential, which can exist for a group of poets nationally, locally or regionally, I am therefore claiming as a specifically political one, and it is here, perhaps, that the pervasive discursive representation of creativity as essentially personal, inspirational and private, draws the 'terrain' of the little magazine into most obvious incoherence. Thus Gavin Selerie, in attempting to map out contemporary British poetry in a way akin to mine, through identifying a modernist-derived tradition which seeks to recognise the dimensions of the referent ('the crucial issues here, I think, are language and the scope of reference'), also quotes approvingly Alan Halsey's unresolved contention that 'The demand for "political" or "committed" poetry is betrayal of poetic as mode . . . Yet it is true that poetic cannot fail to be political . . . the Political completely embedded in the word'. The more than residual oscillations of meaning here are, for me, symptomatic of a mistrust of the political as being, somehow, in its essence incompatible with the sort of poetic practice that Robert Sheppard calls 'the poetry . . . of unproblematic experience'.[57] The point is that Halsey's position is itself not uncontentious, and a recurrent debate in the eighties has been, I think, the extent to which it is possible to sustain political commitment within contemporary modernist practices; this problem is one, of course, infusing debates about post-modernism as a concept and as an aesthetic, and poets and writers have been debating this as actively as critics and academics.[58] My point here will merely be that for poets and writers this debate has been one of raw necessity and often therefore of real intensity; Glenda George's guest editing of *Reality Studios* No. 7 (1985), 'The Inseam', is just one successfully provocative outcome, and as such an implicit answer to Gavin Selerie's reservations about how feminism operates within UK poetry activity.[59] Elsewhere, too, exploration predominates; Bob Perelman perhaps best sums up one dilemma these poets face: that any poetry which is alert to the referential treachery of words can become what, for him, some L=A=N-=G=U=A=G=E poetry becomes: so burdened by 'large supplies of surplus meaning' that it can have 'little political effect' (except, I would add, that which is contained within its consequent self-referential interrogation of language's relationship to meaning).[60] It would seem to be the belief of some poets moving within this field of poetic practice that this last – let us call it formal – mode of political engagement is in itself enough. This would seem, for example, to be both the grounds for Gavin Selerie's unease with poetry adopting specifically feminist positions, and instructively, from my point of view, to lie behind Michelene Wandor's defence of feminist poetry by attacking Ken Edwards for what she sees as his belief that one can be 'uncommitted', a position which she feels gives rise to 'a deep-rooted philistinism across the board in British poetry, in which one must be seen either in "art" or in "politics" '.[61]

To my mind this is reminiscent of an earlier debate, in the sixties and seventies, fought out mostly in the pages of *Stand*, when Jon Silkin (primarily) and others (including Terry Eagleton, Raymond Williams, E. P. Thompson, Cairns Craig and Jim Wyatt), in argument with P. N. *Review* stalwarts Michael Schmidt, A. R. Simmons, Donald Davie, and a Movement alumnus, Robert Conquest, took up the position that in a pluralist society the search for 'common values' was a search for that hoary old ideological illusion, the apolitical, and that instead, all writing activity had to be seen as necessarily 'committed', either implicitly or explicitly.[62] I think it can be argued that this perspective of Silkin's *Stand* was assisted by the pronouncedly European orientation of its editorial attentions (in contrast to the already-noted US emphasis apparent in some other modernist-oriented little magazines' interests). Certainly, it is incorrect to over-stress this American/European divide; *Ecuatorial*, *Curtains*, *Granta*, *Prospice*, Buck's guest-edited issue of *Spectacular Diseases* (No. 5, 1980) and earlier on, *Soho*, *Tzarad*, *Schmuck*, *Adam* and *New Departures* are just a few examples of modernist-oriented little magazines with a European orientation. Thus Eric Mottram, in attempting to speak of the fields of interest of contemporary avant-garde modernist activity in Britain, does indeed name Olson, Duncan, Zukofsky, William Carlos Williams, Pound, Oppen and Jerome Rothenberg, but he also approvingly quotes Jeff Nuttall's nomination of 'Picasso and the picture-object, Schoenberg and the serial form, Breton and automatism, Tzara and anti-art, Jarry and Duchamp and the mythic logic method, Mondrian and proportion, Braque and surface, Max Jacob and the dislocated image . . .'[63] These interactions are seminal, but there is, nevertheless, more than a trace of a not un-American political confusion reverberating through the more recent debates about modernism and post-modernism, which cannot be readily resolved, or reconciled with the interrogation of language that otherwise is quite plainly fore-grounded, in theory and in the writing produced. The important thing that *Stand* did in the middle decades of the twentieth century was attend to events in Eastern Europe, to the writing activity generated there and the censorship suffered; to drive home my point, I recall David Mayors' and Felipe Ehrenberg's production of 'The Czech *Schmuck*' in January 1974, an issue that went unchecked by its contributors because of censorship fears so real that the arrest, shortly afterwards, of many of the contributing Czechs was almost predictable. As the Iron Curtain draws back in the nineties we are, perhaps ironically, in danger of losing this simple reminder of the political potential of radical art practices evidenced by this sort of oppression. Poetry and prose at their best are able to remind us of the repressive potential of language arranged as hegemonic discourse; I find it hard to disagree, therefore, with Nicki Jackowska when (to return to the debate about the desirability of subsidising little magazines) she attacks the arguments of opponents of subsidy for recurrently reminding her of 'so much of Thatcher's peculiar and unpleasant mixture of naive philosophising and materialistic moralising'.[64] To swerve rather violently in my argument yet again, I would propose that, in the 'discourse' of poetry writing, the inherent resistance provided by the publication of little magazines (and small presses) in all parts of the British Isles to the centripetal, cosmopolitanising tendencies of commercial London publishing is, in itself, political, as the recurrent neglect of these activities in the mainstream (London) cultural debate illustrates. I am conscious here of how I have had to pass over in this essay the regional roles of the little magazines, itself another complex debate in which the 'discourse' set up by such diverse magazines as *Akros, Cencrastus, Lines Review, Poetry Wales, Anglo-Welsh Review, The Honest Ulsterman* etc. would have to be analysed.[65] John Crick is precisely right in suggesting that contemporary British poets, and I would add, their little magazines, are at their most exciting in their 'involvement with history, class, feminism and "nation" '.[66] But Crick's mistrust of contemporary modernism is less helpful; better, I feel, to stress that, as Peter Middleton puts it, 'formal experiment is not necessarily politically radical',[67] though once again with the qualification added that to recognise that the politics centreing on the lapses between signifier, signified and referent is both political and a space that the dominant ideology, or rather ideologies, seek to fill: radicalism is the remaining constituent. Perhaps an appropriate note to end on, then, is to quote a poem that cuts to the heart of the debate I am entering into here from the direction my essay has overall assumed (the politics of signification). The point of the little magazine, potentially, is to teach us how not to 'shut up'. If a little magazine (to risk a pun) *realises* this, it has succeeded:

> this is thi
> six a clock
> news thi
> man said n
> thi reason
> a talk wia
> BBC accent

iz coz yi
widny wahnt
mi ti talk
aboot thi
trooth wia
voice lik
wanna yoo
scruff. if
a toktaboot
thi trooth
lik wanna yoo
scruff yi
widny thingk
it wuz troo.
jist wanna yoo
scruff tokn.
thirza right
way ti spell
ana right way
ti tok it. this
is me tokn yir
right way a
spellin. this
is ma trooth.
yooz doant no
thi trooth
yirsellz cawz
yi canny talk
right. this is
thi six a clock
nyooz. belt up.[68]

Little magazine select bibliography

For ease of reference, and to provide some sort of over-view, the following list incorporates all the UK little magazines mentioned in my article
and footnotes, their dates of duration (so far as they are known; often no
definitive termination date exists), and their chief/main/significant/
indicative editor's or editors' name(s) – in this case, an intervening
comma indicates editorial collaboration, a semi-colon sequential editing.
The obvious omissions that show up will indicate how partial my 'map'

of the little magazine field has had to be. Ultimately, to understand the role of little magazines they have to be read, for their sense of immediacy and vitality; University College London's justifiably famous little magazine library collection is, I think, the place to do this, and there my omissions will become apparent.

1983 Robert G. Sheppard, Supranormal cassettes. 1975–78
Adam Miron Grindea. 1929–?
Agenda William Cookson. 1959–
Aggie Weston's Stuart Mills. (Superseded *Tarasque*) 1973–?
Alembic Robert Hampson, Ken Edwards, Peter Barry. 1973–79
Akros Duncan Glen. 1965–82
Ambit Martin Bax. 1959–
And Bob Cobbing. 1954–?
Anglo-Welsh Review Raymond Garlick; Roland Mathias; Gillian Clark. (Superseded *Dock Leaves*) 1958?–
Angel Exhaust Stephen Pereira. 1980?–81?
Artisan Robert Cooper. 1951–55
The Atlantic Review Robert Vas Dias. 1979–80
Cencrastus Sheila Hern. 1979–
Cipher Jake Tilson, Stephen Whitaker. 1979–?
Control Stephen Willats. 1966–82
Curtains Paul Buck. 1971–78?
Dock Leaves Raymond Garlick. (Superseded by *Anglo-Welsh Review*) 1949–58?
Earth Ship Kris Hemensley, Colin T. Symes. 1970–72
Ecuatorial William Rowe, Jason Wilson, Juan A. Masoliver, Anthony Edkins. 1978–
The English Intelligencer Andrew Crozier, Peter Riley. 1966–67
Figs Tony Baker. 1980?–?
Fluxus 1 George Maciunas. 1964
Global Tapestry Journal Dave Cunliffe, Tina Morris. (Incorporated PM Newsletter) 1970–?
Granta Bill Buford. 1979–
Grosseteste Review Tim Longville. 1968–84?
The Honest Ulsterman Frank Ormsby. 1968–
Horde Johnny Byrne, Lee Harwood, Roger Jones. 1964
IRON Peter Mortimer. 1975–
joe soap's canoe Martin Stannard. 1978–
King Ida's Watch-Chain Tom Pickard. 1965–?
Kudos Graham Sykes. 1979–
Lines Review Alan Riddell; Robert Calder; Robin Fulton; William

Montgomerie; Trevor Royale. 1952–
Little Word Machine Nick Toczek, Yann Lovelock. 1972–80
Lobby Press Newsletter Richard Tabor. 1978–82
Loc-Sheet Cavan McCarthy. 1966–68
Migrant Gael Turnbull, Michael Shayer. 1959–60
My Own Mag Jeff Nuttall. 1964?–66
New Departures Michael Horovitz. 1959–?
Nine Peter Russell. 1949–56
Ninth Decade Tony Frazer, Ian Robinson, Robert Vas Dias. (Superseded by *Tenth Decade* for the obvious reason) 1978–
Oasis Ian Robinson. (Superseded by *Telegram*) 1969–80
Outposts Howard Sergeant. 1944–
Pages Robert Sheppard. 1987–
Palantir Jim Burns, Stuart Brown. 1973–83
The Park Andrew Crozier, (Superseded *Wivenhoe Park Review*) 1968–?
PM Newsletter David Cunliffe, Tina Morris. (Superseded *Poetmeat*; superseded by *Global Tapestry Journal*) 1967–69
Poetmeat Tina Morris and David Cunliffe. (Superseded by *PM Newsletter*) 1964–67
Poetry Information Peter Hodgkiss. (Superseded by *Poetry and Little Press Information*) 1970–79
Poetry and Little Press Information Peter Hodgkiss, Bob Cobbing. (Superseded *Poetry Information*) 1980–?
Poetry Review Harold Monro; Stephen Phillips; Galloway Kyle; Muriel Spark; John Gawsworth; Thomas Moult; John Smith; Derek Parker; Eric Mottram; Roger Garfitt; Andrew Motion; Mick Imlah, Tracey Warr; Peter Forbes. 1912–
Poetry Nation (Superseded by *PN Review*) 1973–76
Poetry Wales Meic Stephens; Sam Adams; J. P. Ward; Cary Archard. 1965–
Poor. Old. Tired. Horse. Ian Hamilton Finlay. 1962–67
PN Review C. B. Cox, C. H. Sisson, Donald Davie, Michael Schmidt. (Superseded *Poetry Nation*) 1976–
Prospice J. C. R. Green, Michael Edwards. 1973–?
Reality Studios Ken Edwards. 1978–
Rock Drill Penelope Bailey, Robert G. Sheppard. 1980–
Schmuck Felipe Ehrenberg, David Mayor. 1972–76
Shearsman Tony Frazer. 1981–82
Sixpack Pierre Joris. 1972–76
Slow Dancer John Harvey. 1977–
Soho Lee Harwood, Claude Royet-Journoud. 1964–?
Spanner Allen Fisher. 1974–
Spectacular Diseases Paul Green. 1976–

Stand Jon Silkin. 1952–

Sunk Island Review Michael Blackburn. 1989–

Tarasque Stuart Mills. (Superseded by *Aggie Weston's*) 1965–71

Telegram Ian Robinson, John Stathatos. (Superseded *Oasis*) 1980–82

Tenth Decade Superseded *Ninth Decade*.

Tzarad Lee Harwood. 1965–67

The Window John Sankey. 1951–55

Wivenhoe Park Review Andrew Crozier; Thomas Clark. (Superseded by *The Park*) 1965–67

The Wide Skirt Geoff Hattersley. 1987–

Writing Women Eileen Aird, Linda Anderson, Gay Clifford, Sheila Whitaker. 1981–

Notes

1 Wendy Mulford, from 'Valentine', in G. Allnutt, F. D'Aguiar, K. Edwards and E. Mottram (eds.), *The New British Poetry*, Paladin, London, 1988, p. 207.

2 Len Fulton (ed.), *The International Directory of Little Magazines and Small Presses: 26th Edition, 1990–1991* Dustbooks, Paradise, California, 1990. I should perhaps add that this *International Directory* also lists many, but not all, of the small presses active in Britain, and that some of these run in conjuction with little magazines. In this article it has not been possible to survey both the little magazine and the small press fields, even though these are inextricably linked. Arbitrarily, but necessarily, I have therefore determined to focus solely on little magazine publishing activities. If readers are interested in exploring the small press field, they will rapidly find that hunting down the little magazines listed at the end of my article will lead them to discovery of the small press publishing universe. The annual *Small Press Yearbook*, now in its third edition, provides some details, as well as being another source of information on little magazines: E. Baxter (ed.), *Small Press Yearbook: 1991*, Small Press Group, London, 1991. Peter Finch's 'The Small Press Scene', *ARLIS Newsletter*, 11, July 1972, was, in its day, comprehensive.

3 The questionnaire was sent out to twenty-four little magazine editors in late 1990 and was answered by nine of them. The text takes care to identify, where applicable or important, which editor in particular is referred to. The eight editors who replied were Paul Buck (*Curtains*), Bill Buford (*Granta*), Martin Bax (*Ambit*), Ken Edwards (*Reality Studios*), John Harvey (*Slow Dancer*), Peter Mortimer (*IRON*), Jon Silkin (*Stand*), Martin Stannard (*joe soap's canoe*). To make reference easy for the reader, an editor's name is usually immediately followed by his current or main little magazine's title, in brackets. The questionnaire asked seventeen interrelated questions about the editor's views concerning little magazine publishing, and was accompanied by a basic bibliographic data sheet.

4 For example Martin Stannard: 'Q: What were your aims in setting up a little magazine?/A: No idea. I guess I thought there was a gap to fill. . . . Q: Why

and when did your aims evolve/change (if at all)? A: I got older. Learned more. Forgot a lot, too. The forgetting was probably more important. Now I think I'm getting younger. That means remembering a lot' (questionnaire response, December, 1990).

5 Anthony Linick, 'A History of the American Literary Avant-Garde Since World War II', unpublished dissertation, University of California, Los Angeles, 1965 Ann Arbor, Michigan, University Microfilms, 1965).

6 'Thanks for your questionnaires. I must confess I do seem to get lots of these at the moment and what I've done is filled in the short one [the bibliographic data sheet]'. Martin Bax, questionnaire response (7 Dec. 1990).

7 The allusion to Pierre Macherey's *Theory of Literary Production*, trans. G. Wall (Routledge and Kegan Paul, London, 1978) is deliberate. An argument this essay develops is that editors' magazine production is produced – in the sense that the 'story' ['fable'] editors tell about contemporary poetry is constrained inextricably by the ideological 'project' – constraints of language as a social product, of generic conventions, and of their magazine's ['texts'] problematic. However, my allusion to Macherey will also turn out to be revisionary in two critical respects: firstly, 'production' here also alludes to the production process of publishing the magazine; secondly, I do not subscribe to a prevalent interpretation of Macherey that describes him as situating the author as passive in the face of ideology. Macherey's Althusserian view of ideology sees it as complex and contradictory, a terrain of conflict where 'ideology' encounters 'ideologies', where subjectivity is both produced and destabilised, and where, therefore, space exists for the interrogative to emerge in disturbances to the trajectory of the (in this case) little magazine publishing field – not only in gaps, lapses and silences, but also fissures, incompletenesses and, significantly, divisions of meaning. Macherey, fortunately, does not insistently follow Althusser down scientificity-loaded paths. Compare, for example, Louis Althusser's arguments in 'Ideology and the ideological state apparatuses', in *Lenin and Philosophy and Other Essays*, trans. B. Brewster, Monthly Review Press, London, 1971, pp. 127–86 and *For Marx*, trans. B. Brewster, Penguin Books, Harmondsworth, 1969. My revisionary reading, as you can see, has looming over it the shadow of Michel Foucault; see for example, his 'The order of discourse' in R. Young (ed.), *Untying the Text: A Post-Structuralist Reader*, Routledge and Kegan Paul, London, 1981.

8 Bax, questionnaire response.

9 The tendency towards elitism I will leave unillustrated; the sense of a limited readership comes across in these quotes: '. . . you won't get a very large audience through little magazines', Bax, questionnaire response; 'I started to see the magazine as a research project, not necessarily something to attract readers', Paul Buck, questionnaire response, (9 Dec 1990).

10 Martin Stannard sums up this reluctance when he baldly states that he would only attempt such a mapping 'after several drinks' (Stannard, questionnaire response).

11 Denys Val Baker, *Little Reviews 1914–1943*, Allen and Unwin, London, 1943. In contrast, Remy de Gourmont, in the preface to his bibliography, *Les Petits Revues*, Mercure de France, Paris, 1900, Ezra Pound, in his essay, *Small magazines*', *English Journal*, XIX, Nov. 1930, pp. 689–704 and Cyril Connolly, 'Fifty years of little magazines', *Art and Literature*, 1, August 1974, pp. 28–30 have attempted analysis; see Geoffrey Soar and David Miller, 'Little magazines and how they got that way', exhibition catalogue, Festival Hall, London, 1990, n.p. [p.4].

12 Geoffrey Soar and R. J. Ellis, 'UK little magazines: an introductory survey', *Serials Review*, VIII, 1, Spring 1982, pp. 15–28; G. Soar and R. J. Ellis, 'Little magazines in the British Isles today', *British Book News*, Dec 1983, pp. 728–33; R. J. Ellis, 'Producing the poem: UK little magazines – a second survey (Part 1)', *Serials Review*, X, 4, Winter 1984, pp. 15–23; R. J. Ellis, 'Producing the poem: UK little magazines – a second survey (Part 2)', *Serials Review*, X, 1, Spring 1985, pp. 35–44. My debts to Geoffrey Soar are substantial; the assistance of David Miller also needs acknowledgement. Any errors that appear are all my responsibility, however.

13 Ken Edwards, questionnaire response (1 Dec 1990).

14 Ibid.

15 See, for example, explicit or implicit attempts in M. Bradbury, 'Literary Periodicals and Little Reviews and Their Relation to Modern English Literature', unpublished Ph.D. dissertation, London University, May 1955; Anthony Linick, 'History of the American Literary Avant-Garde'; Frederick J. Hoffman, Charles Allen and Carolyn F. Ulrich, *The Little Magazine: A History and a Bibliography*, Princeton University Press, Princeton, 1967; I. Hamilton, *The Little Magazines: A Study of Six Editors*, Weidenfeld and Nicholson, London, 1976; Geoffrey Soar and R. J. Ellis, 'Little Magazines in the British Isles Today'. Other attempts to depict the little magazine field include A. Sullivan (ed.), *British Literary Magazines: The Victorian and Edwardian Age, 1837–1911*, Greenwood Press, Westport, 1984, *British Literary Magazines: The Modern Age, 1914–1984*, Greenwood Press, Westport, 1986; J. Burns, 'Little magazines', *Palantir*, 2, 1974, pp. 63–9; Thalia Knight, 'An Examination of the Bibliographical Problems Posed by the Alternative Publication of Fiction and Poetry', unpublished M.A. dissertation, University College, London, 1981; E. Stevens, 'A Study of British Literary Little Magazines 1960–1980 together with a critical analysis of their bibliographical control', unpublished Ph.D. dissertation, Polytechnic of North London, 1982; Jacob Korg, 'Language, change and experimental magazines, 1910–1930', *Contemporary Literature*, XIII, 1972, pp. 144–61; A. Wall, 'Little magazines: notes towards a methodology', Francis Barker *et. al.* (eds.), *Literature, Sociology, and the Sociology of Literature: Proceedings of the Conference held at the University of Essex, July 1976*, University of Essex, Colchester, 1976, pp. 105–117. Wall's approach is of real interest; in a sense, I have adopted his approach of regarding a little magazine as a 'composite text'. I have also adapted it, however, by regarding little magazines, taken together, in groups, and as a generic whole, as both composite texts and *a* composite text, or, more exactly, as a composite 'discourse' about 'writing'.

16 Bill Buford, undated questionnaire response [December 1990].

17 Buford, quoted in R. J. Ellis, 'Producing the poem (Part 1)', p. 17.

18 Stannard, questionnaire response.

19 Bax, questionnaire response.

20 P. Hodgkiss, 'Editorial', *Poetry and Little Press Information*, 7, Dec 1981, p. 7.

21 Bax, questionnaire response.

22 Buford, questionnaire response.

23 *Ibid*.

24 Charles Osborne, quoted by Richard Tabor in *Lobby Press Newsletter*, 6, Feb 1979, reprinted in R. J. Ellis, 'Producing the Poem' (Part 2), p. 36.

25 Blake Morrison and Andrew Motion, *The Penguin Book of Contemporary British Poetry*, Penguin Books, Harmondsworth, 1982, p. 11. Geoffrey Soar and R. J. Ellis have also raised this point in their 'Little magazines in the British Isles Today'. Some of the following discussion follows the tracks laid down there. An acerbic review of the Morrison and Motion anthology is by John Ash, in *Rock Drill*, 4, 1983, p. 32.

26 Edward Lucie-Smith, *British Poetry Since 1945*, Penguin, Harmondsworth, 1970, p. 31.

27 Eric Mottram, 'The British Poetry Revival, 1960–1974', *Modern British Poetry Conference*, Polytechnic of Central London, 1974, pp. 86–117; see pp. 15–45 (above).

28 Barry MacSweeney, 'The British poetry revival, 1965–1979', *South East Arts Review*, 9, Spring 1979, pp. 33–46.

29 Douglas Dunn, 'Coteries and commitments: little magazines', *Encounter*, XXXXVIII, 6, June, 1977, pp. 58–65.

30 Stephen Pereira, untitled, *Angel Exhaust* 4, 1981.

31 Dunn, 'Coteries', p. 62.

32 Eric Mottram, 'Editing *Poetry Review*', *Poetry Information*, 20/21, Winter 1979/80, pp. 154–55. See also my account in B. Katz (ed.), *Magazines for Libraries: 5th Edition*, 1986, Bowker, New York, 1986, pp. 202–3.

33 Dunn, 'Coteries', p. 58.

34 G. Sykes, 'The state of affairs', *Kudos*, 8, 1981, p. 4.

35 Buck, questionnaire response.

36 Paul Buck, [untitled], *bal:le:d curtains*, May, 1978, p. 17.

37 D. Davie, review of *A Various Art*, *PN Review* XVI, 2, 1989, p. 58; A. Crozier and T. Longville (eds.), *A Various Art* Carcanet Press, Manchester, 1987.

38 Davie, p. 57.

39 Anon., publicity flier for *A Various Art*, Carcanet Press, Manchester, n.d. [1987].

40 G. Selerie, 'Introduction [to 'A selection of contemporary British poetry'], *North Dakota Quarterly*, LI 4, Fall 1983, pp. 6–7.

41 *Greater London Arts Council Policy Paper: 1982*, Greater London Arts Council, London 1982, quoted in Selerie, p. 7.

42 Davie, p. 57.

43 G. Allnutt, F. D'Aguiar, K. Edwards and E. Mottram (eds.), The New British Poetry; the four sections are headed, respectively, 'Black British Poetry', 'Quote Feminist Unquote Poetry', 'A Treacherous Assault on British Poetry', 'Some Younger Poets'.

44 Robert Sheppard, 'Poor fuckers: the New British Poets', Pages, (n.d.) [May, 1989], p. 161–63.

45 Donald M. Allen (ed.), The New American Poetry 1945–1960, Grove Press, New York, 1960.

46 Donald M. Allen and G. F. Butterick, The Postmoderns; The New American Poetry Revisited, Grove Press, New York, 1982.

47 M. Horovitz, 'More New Brits', PN Review, LXXVIII, Winter 1988/9, pp. 64–7.

48 M. Horovitz, Children of Albion: Poetry of the 'Underground' in Britain, Penguin, Harmondsworth, 1969.

49 G. Selerie (ed.), 'A selection of contemporary British poetry', North Dakota Quarterly, LT, 4, Fall 1983, pp. 5–67.

50 See R. J. Ellis, 'Assembling', in id. 'Accessing US little magazines', Sow's Ear, 1, Summer 1983, pp. 10–11.

51 Selerie, p. 7.

52 Davie, p. 58.

53 Ken Edwards, quoted in R. J. Ellis, 'Producing the poem (Part 2)', p. 39.

54 Eric Mottram, quoted by B. Morton, 'At the edge of darkness', The Times Higher Education Supplement, 24 March 1989, p. 13.

55 Allen Fisher, quoted in G. Soar and R. J. Ellis, 'Little Magazines' p. 732.

56 K. Hemensley, 'Up the Merri Creek or Nero', Poetry and Little Press Information, 3, Dec 1980, pp. 7–8.

57 G. Selerie, 'Introduction', p. 17; Alan Halsey, 'On poetics: notes in the blackout', Rock Drill, 4, 1983, p. 13, quoted in Gavin Selerie, p. 167; R. Sheppard, 'Poor fuckers', p. 163.

58 See, for example, successive issues of Reality Studios and Rock Drill, or, more specifically, the special issue of Poetics Journal, 'Postmodern?', 7, Sept 1987.

59 Selerie, pp. 16–17.

60 Bob Perelman, quoted in a review of his Face Value, Roof Books, New York, 1989 by Robert Sheppard, 'Meet me outside the Daily Planet', Pages, n.d. [1989], p. 201.

61 M. Wandor, letter to Ken Edwards, Reality Studios, VI 1984, p. 83.

62 See, in particular, the symposium 'Common values? An argument' in Stand, XX, 2, pp. 11–42 and XX, 33, 1973, pp. 8–48. See also for example interview with Anthony Thwaite in Stand, VI, 2, 1963, pp. 7–24 and J. Silkin, 'Introduction', Poetry of the Committed Individual, Gollancz, London, 1973, pp. 16ff. The title of this last anthology demonstrates, perhaps, how broadly my hypothesised 'disarray' resonates throughout the field of little magazine activity.

63 J. Nuttall, 'Why do we play to kids?', Time Out, 189, 5–12 Oct 1973, p. 24; Eric Mottram, 'Editing Poetry Review', Poetry Information, 20/21, Winter 1979–80, pp. 154–55.

64 Nicki Jackowska, letter to the editor, Poetry and Little Press Information, 6, Sept 1981, p. 6.

65 John Harvey (Slow Dancer) makes this point, in his own way, as well as I, when he writes: '... there's Huddersfield, then there's Tyneside, then there's Nottingham and somewhere else there's London (and in some miasma of his own making, there's Michael Blackburn's Sunk Island) ... Huddersfield happened. Newcastle on Tyne continued to happen, but in a more lively way. Whatever was going on down in London or up in Manchester became even less relevant, which is a shame since they don't know that yet' (questionnaire response, 19 Dec 1990). Peter Mortimer (IRON) makes a related point when, like Harvey, he chooses to 'map' the little magazine field geographically, and describes 'the South' as 'pretty dull' (questionnaire response, 26 Nov 1990).

66 J. Crick, 'Spitting Image', PN Review, XVI, 6, 1990, p. 55.

67 P. Middleton, review of B. Andrews and C. Bernstein, The L=A=N-=G=U=A=G=E Book, Southern Illinois University Press, Urbana 1983, Poetics Journal, 7, Sept 1987, p. 85.

68 T. Leonard, from Unrelated Incidents, in The New British Poetry, p. 191.

Poetics: politics: procedures

Peter Middleton

4

Who am I to speak?
The politics of subjectivity
in recent British poetry

I

Contemporary British poetry is as stratified as the class system.
At times the divisions between poetic schools reproduce the
class system almost exactly (and the same is true of gender and
ethnic divisions), but neither class, race nor gender can be completely correlated with these divisions. This is particularly evident
in the case of poets who have published work aligned with
different schools of poetry. J. H. Prynne, Denise Levertov,
Nathaniel Tarn, and Thom Gunn all fit this pattern. They have
each belonged to at least two very different schools of poetry,
with very different authority and legitimacy. Levertov, Tarn and
Gunn emigrated to the United States, but that alone is not enough
to explain the changed status of their poetries. J. H. Prynne's
history is even harder to explain. Why was Prynne's first book
Force of Circumstance (1962) acceptable to the establishment and *The
White Stones* (1969) not? In all four cases (which deserve a
detailed discussion outside the scope of this essay), it is clear that
the social identity of the author is not the only determinant of
their poetry's social position. The divisions in contemporary
British poetry, and the often relentless exclusion of certain poets

from the public sphere, remain puzzling if we only look at the politics of identity. Why are poets as internationally known as Tom Raworth barely acknowledged in this country? What makes the poets in recent anthologies like *The New British Poetry, A Various Art* and *Floating Capital*[1] largely unpublishable by 'mainstream' publishers, and on what principles other than their membership of a network of poets are these writers distinguished from one another (few appear in more than one of these anthologies)? What is wrong with this poetry in the eyes of the establishment? Plenty of answers have been offered. The poets are said to be too political, too left wing, too much aesthetic extremists, uninterested in and perhaps incapable of good metrical form. Their new, floating variousness is said to be too burdened with theoretical discourse to be truly poetic. Such explanations are offered by all sides. In this essay I shall examine these explanations and argue that a politics of subjectivity is also at work. The different schools of poetry do map onto contemporary political and social divisions, if we recognise that the different poetries represent different relations between subjectivity and the public sphere. It is not the cultural identity of the author alone which is significant but also the politics of subjectivity encoded in the poetry.

Consider first one of the most successful, yet politically explicit, poets in the establishment, Seamus Heaney. Heaney's success as a poet is part of a widespread phenomenon in recent British literature. A surrogate political culture has developed in which the representations of political struggles within South Africa, Eastern Europe, India and Ireland provide the primary media for much of the politically conscious cultural argument widely disseminated within the public sphere in England. The Hector Petersen playground near my house in Cambridge typifies this culture. A plaque dedicates this tiny blacktop playground for small children (it only has a slide, a swing and a horse) to the memory of a thirteen-year-old pupil of a South African high school who was shot in the back by police. To anyone familiar with recent British politics it will be immediately evident that ours is a stable Labour council. Such use of council property to celebrate South African struggles is characteristic of council activities that have provoked a whole series of Conservative government repressions and threats.

Why has the council chosen to honour this murdered South African schoolboy? The plaque is a way for the council to say, as a collective public body in a public space, that it opposes racism, and especially the use of public institutions (in this case the police) to enforce racist policies. The South African struggle is available as a signifying code for this assertion in a way no local struggle or local figure (whether from Cambridge or England) appears to be, because the meanings of the South African struggle are already established, whereas the local struggles have not had access to the public spaces where political discourse becomes symbolically coded, and thus available for memorial plaques. There are no local legitimate symbols of black heroism in the face of white oppression. The memorial plaque is an instance of the problem. It is actually trying to create what is missing, a political collective subject, the 'we' who are safe (and ought to recognise our safety as a possibly temporary achievement . . . we will not be shot in the back as we use the playground), and morally outraged at what happens elsewhere. We can then unite in our affirmation of moral and political principles. But why are there no indigenous political symbols for our anti-racist struggles? There's no lack of heroism and martyrdom in England, and there is a vigorous black culture, which does provide a public space for political debate within that community. It is the dominant public sphere which is the problem. Even opposition parties and groups have not understood the importance of innovative art as a form of political debate. The general failure to develop a political culture which could produce symbols, discourses and narratives adequate to our political conditions, continues to marginalise all those arts which lack the kind of institutional support that can provide the entry into public debate (the alliance of institutions and practitioners in the theatre is a notable example of what does not happen in poetry).

Cambridge City council is behaving no differently than the wider political culture in Britain. In many fields our political culture is mediated through a kind of safely distanced surrogate, usually South Africa, Eastern Europe (this is already a less attractive option since the end of Communist Party rule) or Ireland. Political issues from those countries, mediated through literary modes, can provide safe, inexplicit means of referring to internal British political affairs, similar to the use of historical parallels in literary works published under totalitarian regimes (historical novels in Poland, for example). In recent poetry this has been especially evident. Acceptable Irish political verse is published by the mainstream publishers, and has given its authors canonical status, while British political verse has only survived through the efforts of small press publication. These foreign political struggles are important, and they need both our support and our recognition of historical and economic complicity as a nation, but if they are also used as the *sole* means of our own political articulation then the result is an impoverishment. The hard work of finding ways of representing political purposes, struggles, values and events in the public sphere goes largely undone or unregarded, even by those who are wholly supportive of the politics themselves. I don't want to go as far as Constantin, the Romanian would-be art dealer in Timberlake Wertenbaker's play, *Three Birds Alighting On A Field* (1991), who says to a socialist painter, 'the trouble for us is we have to carry your dreams, your ideals, always', but there is some truth in his anger.[2] Radical intellectuals and the institutions to which they are attached (The Labour Party, *The New Statesman*, *Marxism Today*, or universities and colleges, for example), have largely failed to support innovative, politically radical British writers. They are not responsible for its exclusion from the public sphere. Exclusion is a repressive measure of the establishment that has made a culture of political surrogacy appear the only option to many in radical politics. For political writing to be acceptable to the public sphere policed by the establishment, it must be possible to repackage it as an easily decodable work about universal human issues like the resistance to tyranny or the dangers of bigotry. Work that constructs its relation to the public sphere through an investigation of subjectivity in language, as most innovative writing does, especially poetry, does not lend itself to such appropriation, especially if it is committed to an emancipatory discourse close to home. New poetry about politics in London is much too dangerous. These prohibitions affect work by black, white, gay, heterosexual, men and women writers, but the precise degree of exclusion will depend on the politics of subjectivity in their work.

Sometimes even an establishment figure like Heaney has to prove his credentials to the authorities, when his Irishness itself becomes too much of a British political issue. Then what shows up under the searchlights are the repressive agents of the state, demanding your identity papers, and ready to arrest or kill you if that identity proves unacceptable. Under such conditions what happens to the self? Seamus Heaney has recurred again and again to this dilemma while he comfortably occupies a central role in the English poetic establishment. In his poem 'From the frontier of writing' Heaney recounts two encounters with British troops in Ireland.[3] The first is a moment of 'pure interrogation,' a moment where nothing is substantive, nothing asserted, but everything the poet says or is, is questioned. As a result the self is 'a little emptier, a little spent', as if it lost some part of its substance once questions were asked of it. Reflexivity, or the problem of self-consciousness, results in the effacement of some part of the self in the dizzying paradoxes of self as both subject and object (for the soldiers the self is an object ready for annihilation if necessary). The second encounter with the troops is framed with a metaphor, the border as 'frontier of writing'. Is this a Wittgensteinian limit of language where what lies beyond can only be gestured at and never spoken? Or is it the frontier where linguistic pioneers go to clear the ground of language and start new settlements? It is certainly a limit to the British state's power, where that power is made violently visible. Are the troops guarding the limits of language?

Once through the road-block the poetic faculty sighs with relief and gets to work on its Romantic pastoral metaphors again, letting the car's windscreen turn the soldiers into images of trees, and transforming sniper into hawk, road-block into waterfall, and border checkpoint into the antipodes of language. Throughout the poem the subject is 'you' rather than 'I' in order to emphasise that there is a people whose identity is formed by such questionings of their identity. Nevertheless the poem narrates its events from an unmoved subject position outside this interrogation, a position from which the self narrates both the story of itself, and generic self of the people, at once. The concluding poetic facility depends on a clear, logical sequence of sentences, and a rational control unaffected by interrogations. It is as if without the road-blocks neither the frontier of writing nor the reflexive self would be manifest. The familiar transcendental self invulnerable to language or power, so evident in Heaney's poetry, would drive on along the highway of despair.

Heaney's poetry exemplifies a familiar phenomenon: conservative poetics linked with a mildly radical content. His border checkpoint poem manages to negotiate these requirements by cleverly implying that it is the unnatural intrusion of soldiers into the pastoral of poetic tradition which unsettles the self. Without them poetry would never need to resort to fragmentation, experiment and challenges to limpid relexivity. Heaney's poem is also a fine example of the Janus quality of such writing once subjected to the repackaging of the English poetic establishment. For the Irish reader the road-blocks are British imperialism or British security maintenance, but whatever their politics, they are manifestations of the state. For the English reader the road-blocks are a modernist excess, part of that cultural terrorism that destroys the orderly suburban self.

II

The virtual suppression of politically conscious poetry in England, achieved by its systematic exclusion from the establishment institutions, has occurred not because the arbiters of these institutions think radical poetry is worthless, but the reverse, because those institutions fear its effectiveness. Poetry in post-war England signifies cultural heritage. It sustains continuities with the past, with orderly class relations, and with the rationality (reasonableness) that finds its outward symbols in the monarchy, the church, the country estate and the educated voice. Poets who tamper with these orders might raise forces the establishment cannot control. You can be a shaman as long as you only talk to crows and other denizens of rural life.

One of the most complex engagements with the political and philosophical difficulties of producing a political poetry in Britain can be found in the volume I mentioned earlier, J. H. Prynne's *The White Stones*, his first major collection after *The Force of Circumstances* (the small volume *Kitchen Poems* (1968) published a year earlier, forms a prelude to *The White Stones*). *The White Stones* belongs to 1968 and its aftermath. Prynne, like many of his contemporaries, influenced by the political ambitions of Charles Olson and Allen Ginsberg, wants to address the collective with political advice, and to use the pronoun of collective self-membership, 'we'. *The White Stones* registers everywhere the problem of forming a political discourse in the British situation. In place of a linear, realist argument culminating in a strong use of the collective pronoun to speak of the political experience of the author, Prynne signals the opening of arguments and then traverses unfinished syntaxes, telescoping metaphors and non-linearity. The poetry of *The White Stones* is highly conscious of the political rhetoric of sudden social change, and deconstructs it. Not however like Charles Tomlinson's poems 'Against extremity' or 'Prometheus' ('We have lived through apocalypse too long'),[4] which conventionally deplore the alleged results of extremism, but by questioning the current state of social order and its internal dynamics of change.

Like several of the poems in *The White Stones*,[5] 'In the long run, to be stranded', makes explicit a resistance to the left-wing idea of vanguardist revolution: 'there's no/good in the brittle effort, to snap the pace/into some more sudden glitter of light' (p. 47). Another poem, 'Questions for the time being', takes up the issue more extensively, mocking the 'scout-camp idea of revolution', and insisting that there was no 'underground' as was claimed in the sixties because 'it would re-/quire a constant effort to keep below the surface' (p. 111). Revolutionaries dream of a moment that will never happen:

And expectancy is equally silly when what we think/of is delay, or
gangsterism of the moment, some/Micawberish fantasy that we
can snatch the controls/when the really crucial moment turns up.
Not with/out asbestos gloves we can't, the wheel is permanently/
red-hot, no one on a new course sits back and/switches on the
automatic pilot.   (p. 112)

The poems don't oppose revolution on the grounds that all is
well or that change will only worsen things (the Tomlinson view),
but because that kind of dramatic vanguardism won't work. The
White Stones is a political text aiming at a grand synthesis of linguistics, ethics, science and history necessary to foster emancipatory
social change. Its syncretic optimisms are held in check by a
humanism at odds with the authority of knowledges that enabled
such theorising to gain dominant legitimacy in the seventies and
eighties. I can best illustrate this point by making a comparison
with another ambitious project of political synthesis from the
same historical moment.

The White Stones may affect an intellectual superiority over its
activist contemporaries, but it actually shares its ambitions with
that very underground it finds superficial, and with new socialist
initiatives of the time, notably the May Day Manifesto 1968 edited by
Raymond Williams (others involved included Stuart Hall, Terry
Eagleton and E. P. Thompson).[6] This was not the manifesto of an
existing political institution but a call for new socialist institutions
to be formed: 'It is intended to have not only theoretical but
practical consequences' (p. 11). The 'new left' has been more
successful 'in communicating a new current of thought, which
has indeed been widely recognised, than in finding the self-
sustaining institutions, the widening contacts, the effective con-
frontation with official politics, which were so urgently needed'
(p. 10). The irony of this statement made just before the events of
May 1968 is palpable. Instead of institutions there was an uprising
against them, an uprising that even dismissed the institutional left.
Nevertheless, the manifesto was a useful analysis of the current
situation, especially for its recognition of the role of finance
in modern British life, something it shares with Prynne. Its
conclusion did to an extent anticipate May 1968, because the

manifesto argues for the value of more heterogenous political organisations capable of recognising the common, but not identical, interests of trade union, CP, Labour Party and anti-nuclear activists: 'We want then to connect with what is still strong in Britain: a democratic practice, a determined humanity, an active critical intelligence' (p.189). Democracy, humanism and theory: the seventies used the third to call the other two into question in the name of semiotics and the search for a perfect trinity of Althusser, Lacan and Barthes – Ideology, Unconscious and Language. That development also might be seen as the outcome of the programme of the manifesto: 'This is then our own immediate political decision: that the first thing to do, against a discontinuous experience, is to make and insist on connexions: a break and development in consciousness, before we can solve the problem of organization' (p. 183). And this work assumes that words and actions go hand in hand:

> Our orthodox culture continually prompts this response: 'action not words' are the first obligatory words, from many apparently different men. But we reject this separation of thought and action, or of language and reality. If you are conscious in certain ways, you will act in certain ways and when you are not conscious you will fail to act. (p.183)

In Britain in the seventies, the left largely committed itself to post-structuralist social theories, and argued that action and meaning were determined in unconscious ways, because not only was language not separate from reality, but it helped constitute reality. Consciousness lost its constitutive role. Connections were made and insisted upon in *theoretical* discourse, but the discontinuity of experience was argued as the consequence of entry into language, not as a contingent result of contemporary history. The subject could not make connections unless they were already made, and the possibility that consciousness could develop (be educated) was largely superseded by the idea of liberating existing potential by clearing up ideological misprisions. Critical intelligence was all that could prevent the complete paralysis of actions by ideology, and therefore no appeal to humanity or democracy would do any good. Humanity was an ideological fiction and democracy certain to fail in the face of unconsciously operative determinations.

The White Stones holds to a position very close to the manifesto on these issues. Against 'discontinuous experience' it insists on making connections, 'the concentration/ of intersect' (p. 69) ('First notes on daylight'), and indeed does so to the extent of an often echoichally unreadable allusiveness. It insistently works with breaks and developments in consciousness, and explores the possibilities of speaking or acting collectively. The differences lie in the means of presenting what the manifesto ambitiously calls 'an alternative view of our world' and The White Stones calls 'our own/ level contemplation of the world' (p.70) ('Frost and snow, falling'). The use of poetry rests on certain assumptions about language that are evident both in the larger forms of the poetry and in explicit characterisations of language throughout the book.

The White Stones does not offer one uncontradictory account of language. Several concepts are visible. In 'Star damage at home', 'We live here and must mean it, the last person we are' is the poem's answer to its earlier, despairing question: 'And what is the chance for survival, in this/fertile calm, that we could mean what/ we say, and hold to it?' (pp. 107–08). Integrity of utterance means careful naming (an idea central to Pound and Olson): 'What the name has in its charge, being not deceived'. This ethical call for a unity of word and meaning does more than repeat the time-worn ethical demand for truthful plain speaking. It also implies a doubt about the *logical* possibility of such adherence. Bob Perelman has observed that 'the first person is actually the last person',[7] meaning that the first person is really the end of a series of linguistic determinations, not the first. Prynne's formulation seems to hold both ideas in suspension. Similarly, when the poem says that 'we desire what we mean/and we must mean that', this can be read as saying that we must mean what we say, but it also implies that desire engages with what is meant by the saying, and therefore language in use is an energetics of desire. This almost Lacanian idea is opposed by the moral injuction – 'we must mean that', where the world 'must' has the force of both 'ought' and 'have to'.

Prynne calls into question the relation between ethics and expressivism in poetry. The poem objects to the ethical appeal based on deserving:

> the noble fiction is to have
> a few good moments, which represent what we know
> ought to be ours. Ought to be, that makes me
> wince with facetiousness: we/you/they, all the
> pronouns know by now how to make a sentence
> work with *ought to*, and the stoic at least saves
> himself that extremity of false vigilance. (p. 112)

Like the false reassurance that thinking of 'the charity of the hard moments as they are doled out' gives in John Ashbery's poem 'Soonest mended',[8] this outburst of frustration in Prynne's poem arises from a deeper frustration than the arrogance of great expectations. The expressive first person, and its disguises, the second person of Heaney's poem, and the third person of so much safe verse, are intolerable not so much because they presume on some objective ontological stability for the rational ego, but because they presuppose an existent moral order in which they are flatteringly hegemonic.

Yet everywhere in *The White Stones* are appeals to the collectivity that uses just these pronouns. The implicit appeal of these pronouns is a feature that distinguishes the book from later ones. In recognition of the difficulties presented by pronominal rhetoric, the poem finally puts its conclusions about the rhetoric of political change numerically, in a deliberately anti-rhetorical list. The third conclusion is that language is not just a semiotic medium determining subjectivity. Language is an achievement:

> 3. What goes on in a
> language is the corporate & prolonged action
> of worked self-transcendence – other minor verbal
> delays have their uses but the scheme of such
> motives is at best ambiguous. (p. 112)

Language isn't just a limitation on what we can say, or a restrictive,

ideological construction of the speaking subject, it is the collective embodied achievement of human labour going beyond
what is already known and made. Language pulls the individual
along but is not therefore wholly external. Individuals have to
work at it too. The poem insists on the differences between
people, differences which make collectivity, when represented as
a collective singular subject, a grotesque misrepresentation. This
leads to an emphasis on the uniqueness of desire: 'our desires/ are
so separate, not part of any mode or con-/ dition except language
& there they rest on/ the false mantelpiece, like ornaments of
style' (p. 112). No collective description functioning as a unitary
agent of social process is sufficient to other than misrepresent
such heterogeneity of desire. The contempt for 'ornament of
style' is significant for a poet whose work is so insistently rhetorical. The falsely unified desires or homogenous wishes issue in
rhetoric that is ornamental. As the poem concludes, 'not even
elegance will come/of the temporary nothing in which life goes
on' (p. 113). The only alternative is what the poem calls
'luminous/take-off' which 'shows through in language forced into
any/compact with the historical shift' (p. 113). Prynne's style in The
White Stones is a 'luminous take-off', a brilliant and revealing
imitation of contemporary forms of ethical and political
explanation.

III

Politics becomes a problem of pronouns, an ethical linguistics,
and in doing so moves further and further into questions of
subjectivity, of expression and its authority. This has been the area
most identified by linguistically innovative poets as the disputed
territory of poetics. Their aesthetic extremism in the eyes of the
establishment is a radical overhaul of available public forms of
linguistically produced subjectivity. Most poets who have commented on their exclusion from the mainstream, both here and in
the United States, locate the unassimilable element in their poetry
as the disrespectful junking of the expressive self that dominates
establishment poetries both in Britain and in America. Most

mainstream poetry (see, for example, Helen Vendler's anthology of modern American poetry, or Andrew Motion and Blake Morrison's anthology of recent British Poetry, or the anthology *Poetry With An Edge*[9]) assumes that a poem is the record of an 'I' speaking its loves and losses. This self expresses its feelings, narrates its history, and makes judgements, as if its right and ability to do so were beyond question. It is a self untouched by post-modernism. Each poem is a tiny resistance to theory (to echo Paul de Man) and testifies to a general rule. Poetry is self-expression. Anything else is not poetry. Burton Hatlen neatly summarises this conviction by summarising the kind of poem that meets no suspicion from those policing the boundaries of taste, as one which is:

> the invocation of a series of sensory images that claim to encode universal human feelings. This gesture is Romantic in that it locates the unifying personal consciousness at the center of the pheno-menal world. In the pages of the *American Poetry Review* or of Dave Smith's massive new anthology of poets under forty, we see the final outcome of this Romantic aesthetic: a poetry almost entirely controlled by the first person pronoun, which claims to name the one fixed point in an unstable world – a poetry, therefore, of nostalgia, for in the end it turns out that in such poems the self is constituted largely by its longing for a lost homeland.[10]

The unanswered question is then why do readers and poets want to wallow in these delusory longings, and why do they so dislike poetries which don't share it? Nostalgia is a desire to re-experience earlier emotions of harmony. Societies that indulge it are diverting attention from present day political circumstances by making it appear that our difficulties are the result of some kind of inevitable decline. Hatlen's formulation reminds us that the expressive self in dominant poetries is not a bouncy self-satisfied subject but a self locked into a regression that undermines any power to act in the present. The difference between dominant poetries and those where subjectivity is put into question, is not between a happy and a decentred self, but between a paralysed self-division and an engagement with contemporary event by a participant subjectivity. A reading of recent British poetry excluded from the public sphere shows that far from rejecting the expressive self it actually gives it much play, negotiating complex tensions between the pronouns of self, community and state. The exclusions are political, and they are made possible by the identification of refusals of the right kind of poetic authority.

Poets who don't write expressivist poetry are excluded. This causes confusion because these poets are deeply interested in expressivism and subjectivity, and at times are as resistant to theory as the establishment. The difference lies in the scope of their engagement. The readership may be small, resources limited, and the public sphere closed off, but nevertheless ambitions are large and the range of poetic resource wide. This range of poetic resource results in divisions which I want to consider now in relation to the criteria of inclusion and exclusion. A recent accidental example of this division occurred in July 1991 when two poetic conferences were held on the same day. Poets associated with *The New British Poetry* (the sections edited by Eric Mottram and Ken Edwards), and *Floating Capital*, gathered in London for a day of talks and discussions, organised by Gilbert Adair under the informal rubric of Jack Spicer's ironic line, 'No one listens to poetry', with the aim of discussing the current state of poetry.

Once gathered together for a whole day the London-based poets discussed the problem of post-structuralist literary theory. A couple of speakers talked about more pragmatic issues like performance, but most questions of audience, publishing, reviewing, funding, teaching, and opening the way for younger writers, were passed over. Theory was the issue that eveyone was excited by. Some poets believe Lyotard and Derrida essential for an understanding of current poetic projects, others find them a major obstacle. Almost everyone shares the conviction that this is the disputed territory. Why should this be? Are we in the same situation Robert Creeley found himself in at the start of his poetic career, in the forties?

> In the forties there was so much talk *about* the poem, about levels of meaning, ambiguities, symbols, allusions. It was even felt that criticism itself would prove the most significant literary activity of

the time . . . Pound in contrast, spoke of the literal condition of the writing, and it was he I used as a guide . . . What Olson made evident to me was that writing could be an intensely specific revelation of one's own content and of the world the fact of any life must engage . . . what emerges in the writing I most value is a content which cannot be anticipated . . . poems are not referential.[11]

Literal condition is opposed to the secondary talk about it, and revelation of one's own content (with the pun on contentment surely unintended but significant of a resistance to the presumption of the confessional school of poets that only anguish is poetic) is opposed to outward reference to prior content. Criticism would be a mixture of both secondary commentary and reference. At the recent colloquium Adrian Clarke took what might seem a directly opposite stance, saying: 'vague ideas of 'total theory' prevent us recognising the strategic interventions of what, following Randolph Starn, one might characterise as *petite théorie*'.[12] Like many linguistically innovative poets, Clarke is sceptical of recent attempts at a 'biographical approach to literature' by politically radical poets tempted by the deceptive empowerments of connected, undisrupted sentence-making, when in fact such attempted biographising, as Hatlen says, can be disempowering. This goes to the heart of the problem. Such a claim applies to the poets at the colloquium, but not necessarily (as Clarke would agree) to poets writing for and within disenfranchised communities where what may read like an affirmation of the universal, fixed self to the dominant culture, is also a radical strategy for creating collective actions within the marginalised social group. What we can say about such poetic strategies is that they can be mobilised for different ends by the dominant culture, and made to represent quite different moralities and political principles.

That same day a group of poets mostly represented by *A Various Art*, were talking about shamanism in their own colloquium. In an article appearing simultaneously in *Modern Painters*,[13] one of the organisers of the event, Iain Sinclair, revealed a distrust of the establishment similar to the mood of the other colloquium. He celebrates the sculptors Steve Dilworth and Brian Catling for their indifference to the cultural centres (Dilworth living in the Hebrides), and for going 'in search of some depiction of our deepest fears . . . challenging the darkness' (p. 46). Sinclair makes no mention of theory or theorists. His excitable language is tense with allusions to imminent revelations; events are miraculous, ghosts hover, objects are about to speak. Catling's writing (he is a poet as well as a sculptor) is said to use 'a language that could be formulated and inscribed, but never spoken' (p. 50). Catling is engaged in 'the mapping of an unknowable field of consciousness' (p. 49); consciousness, but *unknowable* consciousness, not that by convention biographical, expressive, transparent consciousness Clarke wants to avoid.

An almost identical phrase, 'the mapping of consciousness', was used by the 'language' poet, Charles Bernstein, to describe one of the most significant, and now, he claims, outmoded features of modernist writing. In this passage he sums up the limitations of such mapping in terms of its blocking of political interaction:

> The pecularities that form the trace of consciousness and make it specific or individual demonstrate the *partialness* of any construction of mind or reality, in sharp contrast to the universality of claim in the tone of many conventional writing modes. This acknowledging the charting of partialness does in fact break the monologic spell of writing seen as a transparent medium to the world beyond it, but it does so only by making a projection of self central to its methodology. In the end, this practice leaves the reader as sealed-off from the self enacted within it as conventional writing does from the world pictured within it; while the trace may frame the reader, it also exteriorizes him/her; while it critiques the suprapersonal transcendental projection, it creates its own metaphysical fiction of the person. The experience is of a self bound off from me in its autonomy, enclosed in its self-sufficiency.[14]

The work of Projective verse or Beat poets may have a liberating sense of first-hand, uninhibited talk aiming to bring together the underground opponents of hegemonic culture, but it actually achieves this beguiling voice by suppressing the intersubjectivity which could be politically radical. The end result is 'an uncanny mimicry of my own experience of otherness'. (p. 232). Is this the uncanny which Sinclair actively conjures up? For Bernstein, such ghosts can be laid by producing a writing in which the reader is 'actively involved in the process of constitution of meaning'. There is no already constituted knowledge, only the knowledge formed in specific acts of knowing in specific contexts. Does Sinclair's 'unknowable field of consciousness' overlap with the fields Olson, and other of his contemporaries, were mapping, according to Bernstein, or is the qualification of unconsciousness a key distinction? And isn't Sinclair's claim, despite its terminology, a familiar Romantic claim about the priority of unknowable feelings in poetry, feelings that reason can only reduce to a shadow of their true numinosity?

IV

Invitations and resistances to theory seem definitive of the poetics of linguistically innovative poets. One theorist argued that this was inevitable. Paul de Man claimed that theory necessarily produced resistance, in his essay 'The Resistance to Theory'.[15] The focus of resistance is rhetoric because 'tropes, unlike grammar, pertain primordially to language. They are text-producing functions that are not necessarily patterned on a non-verbal entity, whereas grammar is by definition capable of extra-linquistic generalization' (p. 15). Grammar, which is 'extra-linguistic', and logic, are used to underpin a 'general science of man and of the phenomenal world' and to form a 'stable cognitive field'. Rhetoric upsets the apple cart: 'Rhetoric, by its actively negative relationship to grammar and to logic, certainly undoes the claims of the trivium (and by extension, of language) to be an epistemologically stable construct' (p. 17). De Man explains that the trivium was the medieval curriculum linking rhetoric, grammar and logic in a fashion quite alien to modern thought. In his argument, rhetoric becomes an active subject busy undoing others' claims. Language is also active, making claims on its behalf (but what is the 'it' that makes the claims?). Therefore primordial rhetoric can overturn, by its very presence, language's claim to epistemological foundationalism. De Man writes as if language were a material entity able somehow to make claims, because its instances, its actual usages, can always be read as exemplary. It is theorists, however, who make claims. De Man shifts the blame for obstacles to the poet's ranging imagination onto the theoretical activities of grammar and logic. Get rid of them, he seems to say, and all will be well.

Paul de Man's attribution of subjectivity to language as an entity, carries over into his description of reading. The rhetorical weave of language 'can be revealed in any verbal event when it is read textually. Since grammar as well as figuration is an integral part of reading, it follows that reading will be a negative process in which the grammatical cognition is undone, at all times, by its rhetorical displacement' (p. 17). Why isn't rhetoric undone by grammar? Grammar is extrinsic, something outside the bounds of the text, whereas rhetoric is happily primordial. This is an odd way to think of reading. We readers start with a fixed set of grammatical categories, categories as constitutive of experience as Kant's *a priori* fixed structures, and these are then teased mercilessly by the playful tropes until we realise that our initial certainties, our epistemology, have become unstable. But how do we realise this, with what intellectual capacity if that has been destabilised? And what after all is a verbal event, except a human project considered entirely in terms of one dimension of its activities, their verbal trace? For de Man, truth and tropes don't mix but surely what he actually shows is that truth tropes, a less surprising discovery. More importantly, the irreducibly plural relations between readers and texts, like those Bernstein is so much concerned to make actively intersubjective, are reduced to a collectivity, a 'we' external to the animate process of language. The theorist becomes the shaman through his/her metacritical engagement with tropic discourses like poetry.

Bernstein and de Man both want to sweep away the image of a self able to master knowledge, make claims and form relations, without itself being subject to those processes. De Man's way out is to transfer these processes across to language. Bernstein wants to re-situate them in the relations between subjects, between writers and readers, between verbal events. Theory challenges the sovereign self, and de Man names this challenge rhetoric. Creeley's remark in the interview suggests that the claims of theory are claims about the authority of literary writing, claims that challenge the writer's right to certain kinds of subjectivity as content. Poets can respond by claiming access to deeper, more mysterious fields of inner psychic activity that mysteriously manifests itself in the material world, helping objects speak, or by pushing back theory and claiming that some linguistic process is so tropic, contains such phrasal energies that theory cannot but recognise its force, and the authority of the poet who channels it. Theory turns its searchlights on the poet, reading his papers to see who s/he is.

Against this our best poets have struggled to articulate the relations between self, language and power, by either going deeper into those shamanic realms, or liberating rhetoric from its positioning by the authorities of grammar, order and the state. Sometimes their poetic self is 'inside', as in the first poem in Bill Griffiths's sequence *Cycles* 'Cycle 1: On Dover Borstal'.[16] Prison is at once the manifestation of state power, the prison-house of language, and the sovereign self. From the opening line a tension develops that illuminates the authoritarian limitations of the dramatic monologue, without having recourse to an innocent or self-watchful I, nor the safeties of language's anonymities. Opening with 'Ictus!' is a brilliant move. Derived from the Latin *icere*, to strike (and in later use, wounded, from which its modern use to mean apoplexy derives), it merges poetry and anger, in what is both command and a summary of the situation. Life is rhythm, yes, but the rhythm of violence is part of it: 'At running in the sun/ I thought/ this serious, my world is'. There is an exactness of expression here that says both that he recognises that his predicament is serious, *and* that it was his. This is now his world. The effect of putting the verb last is to leave the thought incomplete. He does not know what his world is, he just knows that *this* is it. He also confuses himself and this world: 'Sky's lead's closed low of fear'. It is hard to have an identity in Borstal: 'You're you/ and I aint anyone but you'. Under prison conditions the warder's cry is 'you' . . . objectifying the prisoner as the addressee of the commands, but an addressee without the dignity of name and social position. This is also a bootstrapping project to turn oneself into a 'you', to deny the expressive I that cries, and become the other, the 'you' that is the addressee of commands. The result is violence:

> Got trumpet you
> screaming as an elephant
> dog, fist, ground
> god of an hiding.

The 'you' may scream but he gets beaten up. The ground of this is a god in hiding as well as a god of such hidings, beatings, rhythms. Or is god simply the dirty Borstal ground? The only resolution is to rethink verse and violence:

> drumming
> losing all the words, the shapes and
> circles part
>
> I think on the pattern of an action
> till the gold of the answer I can beat anyway.

The regular ictus becomes a drumming and the distinction of words is lost. This entails the loss of 'the shapes and circles part', the visual lettering that may well be difficult for the boy if he is also semi-literate. He needs to focus on the pattern, the 'pattern of an action', whether writing or not, until 'the gold of an answer I can beat anyway.' Out of the rhythm comes the answer he can create, like the goldsmith beating shape into gold, and which he can control like nothing else. There is a suggestion of more than control here. 'I can beat' suggests that he will use violence to win. He can defeat this answer, this poesis. But the penultimate section questions such answers: 'Kid stood stretched like a unicorn like poster/ as who anywhy wants?' This shift into the third person of 'kid', into the objectivity of seeing himself, allows an explicit simile, but one that introduces a mythical creature, as if the kid is a myth, who then recedes into art and representations (the poster). The possibility of poetic self-possession may be as fabulous as the unicorn. Griffiths' poem shows that the rationality of the 'I' has not only to be learned, but to be struggled for.

V

One reason that self-possession, the use of the 'I' as anything more than a repetition of bourgeois ideology, has to be struggled for, is that our culture commonly presents subjectivity as a form of self-confession. Eric Mottram explores the suspicion of expressive selves this has provoked in much recent British radical poetry in his 'Elegy 24: Wittgenstein'.[17] At first sight the poem is a series of laconic assertions about Wittgenstein strung together paratactically, whose style imitates the intellectual asceticism of its subject. The opening lines describe the complete intellectual control Wittgenstein needed to achieve 'a rout of masked rubbish'. This military metaphor overlays the idea of setting fire to waste, and implies both victory over stupidity and the disposal of what is of no use.

The next section makes explicit the issue of expression and confessionalism:

> Without self-exposure or glib
> hints of interesting insides
> the confession riddle mob indulges

This criticism of self-expression produces a central tension in the poem as a whole. It is attributed to Wittgenstein, but is also endorsed implicitly by the poem. It occurs immediately after the poem has told us that the Wittgenstein family had seven pianos, as if to restrain itself more from colourful revelations of interesting insides to the Wittgenstein household. The elision of verbal connectives in this laconic mode not only conveys a sense of no-nonsense clarity, but also displaces issues of authority and feeling. If the lines had read: '[he was] without [the desire for] self-exposure or glib hints of interesting insides [of the kind of] confession [that the] riddle mob indulges' – then the authority or ground of these statements would have been fixed. To say 'he was without the desire for self-exposure' is to not only locate a specified desire in the subject, but also to place the statement as one whose veracity is being asserted by its author, the poem's poet, as it were. It says that there is such a desire and Wittgenstein possessed it; the subject existed in this way and not another. Such assertions draw attention back to the place from which they are asserted. Moreover the phrases in the final two brackets identify forms of 'confession' and 'riddle mob' with their use of the definite article. To be able to use the definite article, the subject of the énoncé has to be able to make some claim to their validity. The missing syntax is a form of claim to legitimise these descriptions of Wittgenstein and the people who value representations of interesting insides. Leaving out the formal markers of such legitimation, markers which explicitly identify the making of a judgement, yet leave the judgement itself intact, has the effect of suspending the poem between the poet's assertiveness and the subject's, in a space in which the reader operates. The poem avoids any suggestions that these are the poet's insides. These are not judgements that can be read backwards into the poet as signs of his interests, signs of his interesting insides. Yet the interests remain in the poem, both in the heavily emotive lexical items like 'glib' and 'mob', and in the very form of the syntax which is still assertive despite its dispersed space of operation.

The poem has a great deal to offer about Wittgenstein's insides despite the strictures. The poem's Wittgenstein says he is 'forty and a fool', and experiences 'surprise' (a strong emotional reaction) 'that a man could do that' [we are not told what this refers to]. Active beneath this surprise is 'the ageing nervous muscle' which 'youth must control until death'. The inside is made of 'nervous muscle', or in other words, of fearful muscle (a muscle full of emotion), and of a unity of mind and body (nerves and muscles). Such a description emphasises the material character of the insides, but other references pick up moral and psychological terminologies:

Liberty in him uncomplacent
the id will down
the open not a place to sit down in

Liberty becomes both political freedom and the concept of free will. The id echoes Freud and presumably implies Wittgenstein's mistrust of psychoanalytic representation of internal processes. The id is just another name for will – 'the id is will' – and such concepts 'down' or undermine people's liberty. Sitting down in the open is an image of endorsing the idea of an id that is a descent down into the trenches of human perversity.

The interesting insides speak of their dilemma in a direct quotation from Wittgenstein: 'I'm always afraid I shall die before I've finished it', to which the poem's response is 'discussion finished him'. The 'I' that is afraid is a different 'I' to the one that will die before that I is finished. There are at least two selves here, one which is doing the work and one which is acknowledging it. The 'I' that confesses to fear is the 'interesting insides' of the earlier section. The mortal 'I' is the agent which carries out the work of the self. The I which works depends on the 'I' inside. This is why 'discussions finished him'. Discussions are not under the complete command of the one self; they can change the expressions of both participants. Legitimation of what is social cannot be controlled by one self alone, except by force or 'metallic weaponry'.

The poem ends with an attempt to formulate an epistemology, an attempt precisely because the line breaks under the weight of its final assertions about the nature of truth, and the methods for achieving it:

If I do
not serve
it properly
it breaks
or it breaks
me.

The breaks in the lines are the trace of a dispersal of broken Truth. Now we can see that the quotation from Wittgenstein which uses 'finished' twice, the second time to mean 'killed' or 'destroyed', reads as if Wittgenstein's aim is to kill or destroy 'it'. 'It' becomes the work, truth, the id, and death itself. His aim is to destroy the work of truth or the id, before it destroys him. Eric Mottram's poem subtly maintains the tension of its attempt to eschew the traditional idea of poetry as a form of emotional self-expression by showing that this attempt undoes itself. Self-expression returns – 'it breaks/ me' The insides break open, break me open, indeed I *am* the breaking open process. That final 'me' forlornly on its own is both poet and philosopher.

Eric Mottram's poem confronts the self through the mask of another man speaking. cris cheek, much of whose work is in the style of the New York Language poets, and eschews extended narrative, expressivism and lyric form altogether (as in *A Present*), has also written from within the political complexities of the first persons offered to him. His poem, 'By committee', from *Mud*, is one of the most direct engagements with the problem of what the poem calls 'I aversion' amongst the poets of *The New British Poetry*.[18] The published poem reproduces the poet's own handwritten upper-case letters. The poem moves between 'I', and the 'we' which would apparently give the 'I' a response, a community, and an authority, while uneasily recognising the evasions of both positions. Allowing the self to be a position where discourses speak, turns self into medium:

> That is
> the voices the opinions the arguments
> flow thru you separating
> with pressure
> as thru a sieve
> become distinct
> for a moment
> by force of circumstance.

The poem begins with the second person, admonished about the danger of 'loosing yourself on the wind' or giving up the power of decision making. Separating out all the opinions and theories into their distinct components makes the constituents clear but also breaks up into such tiny fragments that they blow away.

'Speaking your mind' may only be the provision of a persona fit for the occasion, a mere familiarity with the arguments, or
at the worst, simply conditioning. This dilemma results in the
tendency to think of authentic commitment as the taking up of a
position, but doing so results in mutual abrasion and even
destruction:

> speaking is easier whilst 'saying' what you 'feel'
> becomes hard i.e. 'it' is simpler to be fluid
> and soft to be pliable and amenable
> than 'it' is to take up 'a' position on 'the'
> spectrum
> and stand your ground.
> It is exactly this problem
> upon which we are ground.

The two lines that begin this section produce an internal
contradiction across the line break. Either it is easier to speak
when you say what you feel, or it is not. The lines begin asserting
that it is, and then switch to the opposite. The effect is to transform the initial proposal that speech is made easier by emotional
honesty into the more complex assertion that these are different
forms of speech, and that 'saying what you feel' is the more
difficult. This leads into the possibility that it is the 'saying' that
becomes 'hard', that is, harsh and intractable. The proliferation
of quotation marks has the effect of putting the words into
escrow. These words, 'saying', 'feel' and 'it', begin the process.
'Saying' in quotation marks becomes a question about the nature
and process of speech. What is such a saying? The word 'feel' in
quotation marks also has the effect of reminding us of its possible
departures from the literal into metaphoric and analogic implications. 'It', 'a' and 'the' remind us that these simple elements of
syntax also presuppose fixities, like one spectrum of opinion. The
result of the dilemma is that 'some come to pray'. The innocent
word for prayer alters under pressure into its sinister counterpart
'prey', and the subsequent reference to 'fires of anger' visible on
the London skyline is not so surprising.

The resistance to theory Paul de Man diagnosed in contemporary thought turned out to be a resistance to rhetoric, but he found it necessary to play the shaman with language and its own mysterious subjectivity. Theory functions then as a powerful sign of the legitimising role of the academy, able not only to explain what poets are doing, but to usurp their very creative subjectivity. Arguing about theory is a way of arguing about the authority of subjectivity claimed by the poet, and for this reason we do need to argue with and within theory. Theory notoriously would deny the position of the subject in possession of his or her own originating meanings. Recent British poetry shows that there are complexities to subjectivity, especially political complexities, which are not fully accounted for by mainsteam theory. The right to speak from a position is one of those rights which have no bill behind them, a right all too easily abrogated. The poet speaks for and to subjectivities, which are not wholly reducible to either emotion, language or actual persons. The poets I have discussed are part of a wider movement in recent poetry that recognises the political importance of subjectivity and is prepared to accept marginality to speak for it.

This is a poetry able to address the scale of England's virtuality, its monochrome overlay images of empire, class positioned people, and pyschic traces of war damage. England has a lot to answer for, and many contemporary poets are doing that, writing poetries which make its unknown a wider language than it has been. Every utterance has many replies. The poems can only mean as much as the discourse where we give them attention.

Notes

1 Fred D'Aguiar, Gillian Allnutt, Eric Mottram and Ken Edwards, eds., *The New British Poetry 1968–1988*, Paladin, London, 1988; Andrew Crozier and Tim Longville (eds.), *A Various Art*, Carcanet, Manchester, 1987; Adrian Clarke and Robert Sheppard (eds.), *Floating Capital: New Poets from London*, Elmwood, Potes and Poets Press, Elmwood, Connecticut, 1991.

2 Timberlake Wertenbaker, *Three Birds Alighting on a Field*, Royal Court Theatre and Faber, London, 1991, p. 30.

3 Seamus Heaney, *The Haw Lantern*, Faber, London, 1987, p. 6.

4 Charles Tomlinson, *Collected Poems*, Oxford University Press, Oxford, 1987, pp. 163, 156.

5 All page references to J. H. Prynne, *Poems* Agneau 2, Edinburgh and London.

6 Raymond Williams (ed.), *May Day Manifesto 1968*, Penguin, Harmondsworth, 1968.

7 Bob Perelman, 'The First Person', *Hills: Talks*, 6/7, Spring 1980, p. 148.

8 John Ashbery, *Selected Poems*, Paladin/Grafton, London, 1987, p. 93.

9 Helen Vendler (ed.), *The Faber Book of Contemporary American Poetry*, Faber, London, 1986; Blake Morrison and Andrew Motion (eds.), *The Penguin Book of Contemporary British Poetry*, Penguin, Harmondsworth, 1983; Neil Astley, *Poetry With An Edge*, Bloodaxe, Newcastle, 1988.

10 Burton Hatlen, 'Crawling into bed with sorrow: Jack Spicer's *After Lorca*', *Ironwood*, 28, 1986, p. 118.

11 Robert Creeley – I have been unable to trace the source of this quotation.

12 Adrian Clarke 'Listening to the Differences', talk given 20 July 1991, at the Sub-Voicive One-Day Colloquium, Institute of United States Studies, London. It has been published as an RWC Extra, available from 16 Southview Avenue, Caversham, Reading, RG4 0AD.

13 Iain Sinclair, 'A new vortex: the shamanism of intent', *Modern Painters*, IV, 2, 1991.

14 Charles Bernstein, 'Writing and Method', *Content's Dream: Essays 1975–1984*, Sun & Moon, Los Angeles, 1986.

15 Paul de Man, *The Resistance to Theory*, Manchester University Press, Manchester, 1986.

16 Bill Griffiths, 'Cycle 1' in *Future Exiles: 3 London Poets: Allen Fisher, Bill Griffiths, and Brian Catling*, Paladin, London, 1992, p. 212.

17 Eric Mottram, *Elegies*, Galloping Dog Press, Newcastle, 1981, pp. 91–2.

18 cris cheek, *A Present*, Bluff Books, London, 1980; Mud, Spanner/Open Field no. 3, London, no page numbers.

Robert Hampson

5

Producing the unknown:
language and ideology
in contemporary poetry

I
The new and the unexpected

Neither 'the new' nor 'the unexpected' can be used to provide legitimation for innovatory poetic practice. Pound's injunction 'Make It New' has to confront the fact that 'the new' is also used to sell the latest car or weapons system.[1] How does one distinguish between what Jameson calls 'the disalienating excitement of the new' and the 'dynamic of permanent change' which is the ' "permanent revolution" of capitalist production' and the engine of alienation?[2] Other problems are raised by 'the unexpected'. In the first place, while one of the pleasures of reading poetry might come from encountering a succession of small surprises, disruptions of expectation, if the text is completely 'unexpected', the reader has no means of access into it. A second series of problems arises around this figure 'the reader': not only are the reader's expectations specific to a particular time, place and culture, they also depend upon the extent and the kind of training of the individual reader. An exchange between Rosmarie Waldrop and Bruce Andrews during the Friday night series at The Wolfson Centre for National Affairs in New York (November/December

1988) drew attention to the danger of fetishising the idea of 'countering readers' expectations'.[3] A purely formalist model of disrupting readers' expectations assumes an homogenised readership, which is at odds with the conditions of poetry publishing and poetry reading. As Waldrop observed, the reader of Susan Howe (or, indeed, of Waldrop herself) brings quite different expectations to poetry to the reader of (say) Adrienne Rich. To put it in other terms, the reader of *fragmente* or *Talus* has quite different literary expectations from the person who reads poems in the TLS or the *London Review of Books*.[4] There is, then, the paradox – which Andrews asserts – that, if this tradition of the new is defined in terms of 'countering formal expectations', it produces poetry which, in practice, is sought out by readers who expect 'challenging' texts, whereas those readers who would really be challenged by these texts are unlikely to engage with them.[5] The interest, value and legitimation of this poetry, then, have to be found elsewhere.

II
Allen Fisher and the representation of the real

In *Language, Thought and Reality*, Benjamin Whorf argued that 'the forms and categories by which the personality not only communicates, but also analyzes nature, notices or neglects types of relationship and phenomena, channels his reasoning, and builds the house of his consciousness' are 'culturally ordained' through language.[6] David Miller's essay 'Notes on poetics' took this as its starting point in order to argue for a poetry of moment-by-moment composition, involving 'the significant disruption' of the conventional meaning-code in a way which is 'not merely nonsensical' but produces 'a transformation of the cultural basis of the representation of the real'.[7] Allen Fisher's poetry was (and continues to be) an exemplary instance of such an attempted transformation. In 'A few notes for clarification: On Allen Fisher's *Place. Book One*', Miller emphasised Fisher's poetic concern with 'identifying, laying bare, certain problems in the *structure* of a culture'.[8] As Miller remarked, this explained Fisher's interest in

(and use of) writers like Alfred Watkins who 'broke down paradigms', and it is accompanied by an engagement with 'the uses of
disorder', manifested in attempts to open out the structure of the
poem. Fisher himself described the thematic concerns of Place as
'place of living, locality, house borough city country planet. place
of being, body, breath, brain. place of receipt and dispatch'.[9] This
in turn can be contextualised by reference to a passage from one
of the two works which influenced the start of the 'place' project,
Raoul Vaneigem's The Revolution of Everyday Life:

> The man of survival is man ground up by the machinery of hier-
> archical power, caught in a mass of interferences, a tangle of
> opposive techniques whose rationalisation only awaits the patient
> programming of programmed minds.
>   The man of survival is also . . . the man of total refusal. Not a
> single instant goes by without each of us living contradictorily, and
> on every level of reality, the conflict between oppression and
> freedom.[10]

Fisher's geographical/geophysical, historical/political, epi-
demological/biological exploration of South London in Place can
be read as a survival programme: through its accumulation of
information, knowledges, it works towards both a critique and an
escape from a culture marked by unhealth – by alienation and
oppression, by ecological catastrophe, by the violence of its
power relations, and by the violence engendered by the
'emotional plague' of sexual repression:

> STAB! STAB!
> the blood comes through teeth tasting of metal
>   poisoning our giblets
> swelling our nerves into holocaust
> the holocaust that will follow
>   the one we have ignited
> that will throw our thinking into the vault
>   the despair   we have tempered
>   with our own acids
>
>   below me from here
>   dogs circling the verge
>   slowly we blind them in tetrachloride lead

if we spoke
   we would tell them what is unproven doesn't exist
what their bodies know we will help them forget
   even their paths follow the roads we have torn
haemorrhaging their senses into factual non-sense
                  that some call intelligence[11]

It is, as Clive Bush has argued, a poetry informed by a sense of the moment as a complex of occasions, as the meeting-place or crossroads of a multiplicity of codes and forces:

we are part of an interaction
ununified
electromagnetic & gravitational

fields contradict
birds sensitive
to axis not polarity
fish
thru sea water see
through a moving conductor
flowing
past the lines of force
thru the magnetics
setting up perpendicular current
a direction
of flow and field
contradicting reason[12]

The fluidity of the syntax enacts the 'ununified' interaction it describes, while the interrogation of the perceptual by the conceptual both exemplifies Fisher's use of scientific knowledges in his transformation of the cultural bases of representation and gestures towards the 'unknown' (or one kind of 'unknown') by invoking non-human modes of perception. It is an attempt, as Fisher said in an interview, to express 'interrelationships beyond direct perceptual experience'; it is, as he puts it in *Place*, 'a matter of making/ and breaking/ the connections'.[13] Accordingly, he turns to scientific discourses for their mapping of phenomena beyond direct perception, and he juxtaposes or intercuts different discourses, different systems of knowledge, in order to challenge, subvert, break open their paradigms. At the same time, moving from discourse to discourse produces the shifting contexts that enable his own texts to acquire meaning.

   Place was conceived of as a ten-year writing project in five books: 'Book III is a partly distorted mirror of Book I, and Book II again acts as a mirror to the other two, and Book IV again is a mirror, so that Book V is a composite mirror if you like.'[14] Books I and III were seen as 'thematic' with Books II and IV as 'excursionary reflection' upon them, and the books were seen as locations, as components of a structure, not as the basis for a linear, chronological project. The sets that constitute each book were shuffled, re-shuffled, cut into each other to lay bare the constant re-presentation and re-vision of the work, the work as praxis not object, the notion of 'open-field composition' (deriving from Olson) combining with the desire to de-mystify the process of composition. It repeated the stance of an earlier collaborative project, *Re'un'anz*:

> – living in a wood of informations
> – the receiver makes the message.[15]

Two of Fisher's other projects during the ten-year period of composition (1971–81) also reflect on *Place*. The first, *Listen* (completed in 1973), made use of a methodology gathered from the work of John Ashbery:

> The process was to underline words in an already printed pile of articles, collecting them together in the order in which they appeared and making sentences out of them as I proceeded so that the sense of each became my imposition rather than the system's and that collectively the sentences made their syntaxis.[16]

Here Fisher was exploring and working with the mind's ability to 'make sense' out of materials presented to it, creating frames of reference to connect unrelated items. The second project, *Convergences, In place, of the Play*, was seen as an extension of Jackson Mac Low's work with systems and strict procedures: Fisher took 'vertical columns of phrases and sentences' and made 'a new syntactic arrangement horizontally', reading across as many as 'ten columns of different informations' while also allowing for reading separately down them.[17] These explorations of language and consciousness lead towards Fisher's later works such as *Imbrications* or *Brixton Fractals*:

> This gravitational song meted against displacement
> The slow movement of holding you
> *By the lake, deep amid fir and silver poplar*
> Dream sleep's energetic function
> During meditation each finger rayed in cactus spikes
> Blake crossed out sweet desire, wrote iron wire
> It was the discovery of human electromagnetism
> *made a sign, opened curtains, revealed the garden*[18]

The processing of perceptions, the constant shifting of images, voices, contexts, work to de-familiarise the dominant reality principle in order to operate a critique of it.

III
Charles Madge, David Miller
and discontinuous coherence

The neglected work of Charles Madge provided Miller with an earlier instance of 'the significant disruption' of the conventional meaning-code.[19] A poem like Madge's 'Countries of the Dead II' (written in 1936) 'punctures' the line and progressively breaks up and re-forms syntax:

> There is a passage   from the vault
> into an adjacent   invisible bedroom of
>   those were flies   crawl boring or
> spaces filled with bodies, universal catacombs.[20]

As the poem proceeds, through what looks like a process of associations or perhaps a process of deletions (as in Fisher's *Thomas Net's Tree-Birst* or Tom Phillips's *A Humument*), the 'passage' from the vault becomes a text, part of 'a labyrinth of prose'; the 'bedroom' acquires 'a bride'; the 'flies' are joined by 'bookworms' and 'centipedes'.[21] For Miller, Madge's major work was 'Bourgeois News', a 'subtle, complex and powerful montage' of what seem to be sentences taken from business reports and newspapers, with Madge cutting between sentences and within the sentence in a way that anticipates the cut-ups of Burroughs and Brion Gysin, the disparate pieces of information converging and diverging 'to perform a critique, sociological-cum-political', of the society of which the material is a reflection. In opposition to the 'collective spell' of 'a brutally divided and alienated society', whose reality is maintained partly through 'cultural and ideological "delusions" ', Madge's work, Miller argued, works at a double disclosure: 'it seeks to uncover and to demystify the myths of capitalist society; and to also disclose a fundamental richness and beauty in both the life we do live and, importantly, the life we could live but may be prevented from living'. And it does this while creating 'a new whole, discontinuous and yet coherent'.

Miller's own poetry in this period deployed both montage and the punctured line in pursuit of precisely this 'new whole, discontinuous and yet coherent'. A poem detailing his work experiences, in the sequence *Appearance & Event*, ends with a montage, in which discursive language is disrupted by a series of sharp cuts, the lines and half-lines canted against each other:

> Rich people are abounding in resources, productions, etc.;
> they are fertile & well-filled;
> they are precious, costly; high-flavoured & fat.
> They will not come out & play.
>
> When you get bitten in the neck it leaves a small wound
> instantly recognizable. It's o.k. They're beautiful, you're
> beautiful.[22]

The first three lines interrogate the word 'rich' through a series of definitions and synonyms, which ironically elides 'precious' into 'costly' before producing the shock of the cannibalistic 'high-flavoured & fat' – an echo of the class-war graffito 'Eat the rich'. The final three lines juxtapose successively and disconcertingly the discourse-types of children at play, vampirism and sixties hip-talk, in which the easy acceptance of the sixties is subverted by the reverberations produced by associating the power and privilege of the rich with vampirism.

The sequence of ten short poems that make up *Primavera* represented more radical experiments with significant disruption.[23] The sequence begins

> that I loved them, & that meant
> loving them forever a small window
> that for me it would be an *eternal*
> memory
> lost a darkness utterly black
> travel no visible record

The emotional statement (involving love, loss and memory) coheres across the disruption ('a small window'), riveted by syntactic parallelism (the repeated 'that' introducing parallel noun-clauses and a divergent relative clause), by the interplay of pronouns ('them', 'them', 'me'), and by the interaction of 'loved'/ 'loving' and 'forever'/ 'eternal' (a play of similarity and difference along a past/future axis), while the 'window', which at first reads like a notation of perception, is set against and cancelled by the 'darkness', and then re-appears in the sequence as a motif that is revalued in subsequent poems.

In his review of the volume, Gil Ott drew particular attention to the third poem of what he saw as a 'sequential collage':

> white chalk on a blackboard
> blue chalk on a blackboard
> green chalk on a blackboard
> yellow chalk on a blackboard
> white blue green yellow
> chalk on the pavement[24]

What is remarkable about the poem is its mode of operation, its simplicity of means and sense of self-containment: the minimal variation of the first four lines; the quiet interplay between the adjective/noun phrase that starts each line and the compound noun that ends it (an interplay comparable to the revivifying of dead metaphor); the apparent recapitulation initiated in the fifth line, and the transformation in the sixth line of that recapitulation into a new item, syntactically parallel but semantically divergent. This patterning can be read in two ways, depending on whether the signifier or the signified is foregrounded. On the one hand, it can be seen as drawing attention to the materiality of language, and the pattern of repetitions and substitutions can be read as an exploration of signification, of the production of meaning. Alternately, it can be read (as Gil Ott does), as working to suggest the mysterious this-ness of things through its 'objective opacity'. Where the epigraph to *Appearance & Event* drew attention to that sequence's 'sceptical study of the nature of reality and the false nature of re-creation', *Primavera* seems closer to the project outlined in *South London Mix* 'to reassert the value . . . of ordinary things'.[25] In a letter which Gil Ott cites in his review, Miller explains: 'Description is . . . a setting-forth of something in its presencing . . . responding to & bringing forth (something of) the plenitude of being inherent in things'.[26] Or, as Richard Palmer put it, 'things step forth in their being through the saying of language'.[27] The poems in *Primavera* enact a dialectic between love and loss, alienated distance and the setting forth of presence. In the final poem in the sequence, alienation gradually dissolves in a tracking from distanced notation, through self-conscious aesthetic appropriation, to an epiphanic moment:

> a wood a forest my own youth
> city material images of high contrast
> footsteps through a doorway to follow the differences
> in how we walked
> between some fragments O light of spring

The poem progresses steadily from notation to vision, but the 'meaning' remains 'open', suspended by the uncertain connection between its words.

In contrast to Whorf's idea of language as a culturally ordained system of forms and categories, Miller has moved here to a Heideggerian view of language as 'the house of Being'. Nevertheless, there are continuities. As Miller observed in his essay 'The theme of language in relation to Heidegger's philosophy', the human existent (*Dasein*), in Heidegger's early philosophy, can relate to the world of meanings in one of two fundamental ways: 'he can take up those meanings in such a way as to make them his own; or he can have the meaning-relations of his existence dictated to him'.[28] In the latter case, 'the everyday, inauthentic mode of existence', as in Whorf's theory, 'one is *spoken by* the culture, by the anonymous public voice'. In the former case, however, Heidegger seems to allow for a speaking that is not culturally ordained, even though, in this authentic, resolute mode, 'each individual speaks out of a community of speech, and from a tradition of speech'. In Heidegger's early philosophy, words are used by *Dasein* to bring something to light, but, in his later philosophy, Miller observes, language is not an object or an instrument – it is 'the house of Being', that which brings beings into the light of unhiddenness. Subsequently, through the eighties, Miller worked on an aesthetic of the epiphany drawing on the work of Gadamer, Ricoeur and Levinas.[29] His study of Hudson, *W. H. Hudson and the Elusive Paradise*, offered a reading of Hudson's fictional and non-fictional works through 'affirmative' and 'negative' epiphanies: the first 'affirms the earthly by intuiting the divine through or within it'; the second 'negates the earthly by opening up a yawning, dizzying chasm . . . an abyss of affliction, evil, or oblivion'.[30] In both cases the epiphany is produced by 'attentiveness to the visible world'.[31] Miller's own attentiveness to the visible pushes this aesthetic in the direction of another kind of 'unknown'. His introduction to the *Boyd & Evans* Flowers East catalogue similarly attends to the 'epiphanic moment of experience', the 'apprehension of some invisible or suprasensible dimension, through attention to the particulars of the visible world'.[32] An important part of this aesthetic is the idea of a 'coherence' that cannot be explained through 'an act of rational comprehension' (*Boyd & Evans*, p.6). His essays on the more abstract work of Jennifer Durrant take this aesthetic further.[33] He explores Durrant's use of disparate elements to avoid 'closure' (i.e. recuperation into 'a rationally comprehensible relational system') while achieving coherence; he outlines a conception of the symbolic, which involves the disclosure of 'some aspect or dimension of being which cannot be expressed adequately in any other way', while resisting totalisation; and he argues for the hermeneutic inexhaustibility of the art work. This idea that 'disclosure of meaning inheres in the concrete details and their organization, in such a manner that we can always encounter the work anew' clearly has its roots in Miller's earlier work on Heidegger.[34] Miller wrote of the inexhaustible plenitude of being in late Heidegger:

> Anything that has being, is always capable of being seen, experienced, encountered in such a way that it is seen or experienced anew: what we thought to be merely familiar becomes revealed as unfamiliar; it is revealed in a different light – as something 'more' or 'other' than what we had formerly known.[35]

The work of art keeps back part of its meaning: it is always more than the reader/viewer can at any time grasp. At the same time, as a disclosure of 'what is', it is also a disruption of habitualised seeing and thinking. This, then, is a conception of art 'where we are concerned with what we don't already know, and with what is never really "known" in the sense of a reduction to the level of mere factual data'. And this conception of art lies behind Miller's more recent poetry – in Unity, Orientation and Losing to Compassion – with their careful negotiation between attention to the visible and apprehensions of the spiritual through a montage of precisely rendered fragments.[36]

IV
Ken Edwards, Adrian Clarke: location and resistance

Veronica Forrest-Thomson, in Poetic Artifice, argued that poetry 'must assimilate the already-known and subject it to a re-working which suspends and questions its categories, provides alternative orderings' (p. 53).[37] In opposition to various critical strategies of 'naturalisation' (i.e. attempts to 'reduce the strangeness of poetic language and poetic organisation by making it intelligible' (p. xi), she emphasised poetic artifice as the means by which poetry can 'challenge our ordinary linguistic orderings of the world, make us question the way in which we make sense of things, and induce us to consider its alternative linguistic orders as a new way of viewing the world' (p. xi). The most fully-documented programme of challenging 'our ordinary linguistic orderings of the world' is that of 'language-centered poetry'.[38] Coming, in part, out of the non-referential work of Clark Coolidge and Robert Grenier, this poetry marked (as George Hartley has argued) a shift of attention from the referential to the syntactical, from the metaphoric to the metonymic, from a poetry of the signified to a poetry of the signifier.[39] By foregrounding the materiality of the signifier and, in particular, by its use of 'the multivalent referential vectors that any word has', 'language-centred poetry' draws attention to the role of syntactic frames in the creation of meaning and hence engages with ideology.[40]

Ken Edwards and Adrian Clarke have, in different ways, been associated with 'language-centred poetry'. Edwards, as an editor, introduced work by 'language poets' to English readers, although his own work has its roots in an older Anglo-American modernist tradition.[41] In *The New British Poetry*, he describes poets of his generation 'discovering the work of Prynne, Mottram, Raworth, Harwood, Cobbing or Roy Fisher' and then 'proceeding backwards through these to Pound, Williams, Olson, Ashbery or O'Hara'.[42] Clarke, whose work is much closer to 'language-centred poetry', aligns himself with 'an alternative modernism', which is not so much an alternative tradition but rather 'a radical challenge to any attempt to ground a tradition': it is exemplified by work by 'Schwitters, Khlebnikov, Kharms, Zukofsky, Heissenbuttel, Sanguineti, Balestrini, Pleynet, Coolidge, Albiach, Raworth and Andrews'.[43] Both poets, however, can be related to different aspects of Allen Fisher's work: Edwards takes over the idea of a locatory action as the basis for cultural criticism and an opening of the language; Clarke's work has affinities with Fisher's polyphonic texts and poetry of resistance.

Edwards' poetry in the late seventies and eighties proceeds from a version of the modernist 'mythic logic method' in *Lorca* and *Tilth*, through a flirtation with non-referentiality in *Tilth Dub* and a foregrounding of self-conscious production in *A4 Portrait*, to a reinstating of the first person in the discursive style of *Intensive Care*, *A4 Landscape* and *Lyrical Ballets*.[44] In *Lorca*, Edwards used the figure of the Spanish poet as a way of exploring (and expressing the opposition between) creativity, fulfillment, freedom, on the one hand, and sexually and politically repressive forces on the other. The basis of the poem was a locatory action: the triangulation 'London, Southern Spain, New York', three areas of personal importance to Edwards, that are integrated and interrelated through the figure of Lorca. The triangulation is underpinned by Lorca's visit to New York in 1929, by Lorca's death at the hands of the Fascists in 1936, and by Franco's long-drawn-out death at the time of the poem's composition, but the poem is not so much an account of the historical Lorca as 'a photomontage/ of the known and the possible'. Lorca's life is imaginatively transformed ('Lorca sinks into mythic existence') to articulate anxieties about contemporary forces of reaction. Thus, at the sight of 'Guernica' in the Museum of Modern Art

> a thought stumbles into words
> & with it the gun & with it
> danger
>
>> the poet assassinated
>> the siren in the dream
>> the endlessness of this road

The poem then responds to the apprehension of entrapment within historical processes with a kind of desperate, fantastic humour and a slide into the language of commercial promotion:

> History, & after that
> more history
> at an incredibly low subscribers price
> no commitment to buy
> wars & revolutions
> cancel your subscription at any time

The third section of the poem then cuts from London in 1976 to Spain in 1930, and subsequently back to Tariq and the entry of the Moors into Spain, but it is constantly returned to modern times by reminders of the concentration camps and the complicity ('non-intervention') of 'the democratic powers' in the rise of Franco. In Section 4, the figure of Lorca, recreated as a Spanish immigrant in the United States, is used in another fantasy attempt to escape the 'nightmare of history'. From behind this mask, Edwards produces a semi-hallucinatory impression of New York, drawing on Lorca's *Poeta en Nueva York* and the Whitman/Ginsberg long line:

> New York, writes Lorca, you have my undivided attention
> instantly feels his rhythm coming back to well
> & well all is well or if all is not well beneath the savage moon
> then at least the possibilities are open right there on the flesh
>   of the sidewalk
> but even as he writes there is too much heat & it is not all
>   in the air but some of it burrowed under skin
> just deep enough to feel as lethargic persistence
> so that the garages the disused buildings have shadows painted
>   with black shoe polish

Again, however, the attempted escape into fantasy is blocked, and the final section of the poem comes back to the question 'who assassinates the poet?', to which the historical Lorca supplies the answer.

In *Tilth*, Edwards used 'Kubla Khan' as the main structural device: the three sections ('Citizen K', 'Ancestral Voices', 'Singing of Mount Abora') correspond to the divisions of Coleridge's poem. In 'Citizen K', Kubla Khan's 'twice five miles of fertile ground' are reduced to the 'acreage of delight' of Lower Green Farm and introduce the central trope of gardens and gardening; 'Ancestral Voices' involves a not completely successful attempt to use, as counterpoint, the treated voices of South London social work cases; 'Singing of Mount Abora' plays decay and ruin against a meditation on light and growth:

> towards the light, six seedlings
> in the space between the panes
> south facing, forth push
> green shapely bursting heads
> clear as if etched on pearl, interweave
> 'like a nest of startled snakes'
> above & to the right
> of where he sleeps & dreams & severally is

Through a locatory action in terms of home, work and the

'muscle & meat of "everyday life" ', Edwards negotiates the binary opposites of city and country, culture and nature, growth and decay in search of the utopia:

> where the work streams out
> untrammelled lets loose
> all one may delight in

Tilth combined passages of description and notation with found material, cut-up and Poundian collage:

> just on the vestibule of consciousness
> where the sleepy images maintain
> walls & towers
> when conscious control had been suspended
>
> slowly the bubble lifted
>
> there were machines of various sorts

In this instance, fragments from Coleridge's letters and from 'Kubla Khan' are interwoven with John Livingstone Lowe's commentary to enact 'the point at which waking slips over the verge into sleep' before opening on a Wellsian dream (or nightmare).[45] In *Drumming & poems*, notation and narrative are combined with experiments with chance procedures, phrasal permutations and a two-line stanza, new in Edwards's work, which is played against enjambement and sudden changes of direction to produce a more disrupted, unsettled poetic surface:

> Geraniums
>
> seen through lattice
> of heavy iron. Butter melts into
>
> riot as rain
> & soil
>
> ('Geraniums, South London', p. 16)

The fifteen poems in the volume are each associated with a piece of music, but the nature of the connection between the poem and the music constantly changes. Sometimes he seems to seek a poetic equivalent of the musical procedures; sometimes he seems to aim at reproducing the mood of the music; at other times, the connection seems some private association not available to the reader. The two most powerful poems are two public poems, 'Southall', which is constructed from eye-witness accounts of the April 1979 demonstration against the National Front meeting in Southall and the accompanying police activities during which Blair Peach was killed by a member of the Special Patrol Group, and the title poem 'Drumming', which intercuts (again, presumably, by chance procedures) the death of Blair Peach, the British Nationality Bill, the virginity tests on Asian women at Heathrow and Isaac Gordon's account of his experiences as an immigrant in England. In these poems, Edwards uses the violent juxtapositions produced by cut-up to express the violence English society directs against black and immigrant communities:

> When I came to this country
> to take up the metal
>
> I feed in the metal
> straight into the knife
>
> When I came to this country
> straight into the knife

('Drumming (Slow Return)', p. 41)

The accident in which George Isaacs lost his fingers (as a result of unsafe machinery) becomes an emblem for the experiences of black citizens in England, as Edwards's interweaving of that incident with other material discloses a continuum of racist violence from attacks in the street through to the institutionalised racism of the state.

Adrian Clarke's work offers a much more dislocated linguistic surface. His first publication, *Ghost Measures*, consisted of four sections of sixteen poems each: each poem had sixteen lines, each line had four words.[46] Clarke took these voluntary limitations (which correspond to the I *Ching*), and within them produced an intense and powerful poetry that cuts between discourses and, like the poetry of Waldrop and Raworth, changes direction by turning on a word:

and outside nothing is
only error circumlocution semantic
thickness leaves soak in
the rain distracted Nature
countersigns the weather's work
shredding her manuscript and
rising from her desk   (p. 72)

After hesitations over the grammatical status of 'outside' and the
precise meaning of 'is', these lines arrive at a vision of 'outside' as a
dense and uncertain linguistic universe ('error circumlocution
semantic/ thickness') only to flip over to another image of 'outside' as 'the/ whole world of things': the leaves soak both in
'semantic/ thickness' and in 'the rain'. This exterior, however, is
almost immediately metaphorically transformed into an interior,
the bureaucratic office, while Dickens' Circumlocution Office
seems to hover as a ghostly presence over both the world of
words and the world of things.

   In 'Listening to the differences', Clarke talked about appro-
priating Lyotard's idea of 'the phrase' as a linguistic strategy to cut
across categories and evade closure: 'With phrases we are set
adrift from narrative and logic to struggle with what they present
without hope of return to safe ground'.[47] Lyotard argues 'that the
linking of one phrase onto another is problematic and that this
problem is the problem of politics'.[48] In opposition to the state,
which 'knows no reality other than the established one' and
'holds the monopoly on procedures for the establishment of
reality' (The Differend, p. 4), Lyotard asserts the need 'to find new
rules for forming and linking phrases' (p. 13), and uses Gertrude
Stein as an example. In her work, the phrase is 'an event'. Lyotard
remarks: 'To save the phrase: extract it from the discourses in
which it is subjugated and restrained by rules for linking ...
seduced by their end' (p. 68). Clarke's poetry of the phrase resists
such seduction. This resistance is most obvious when, as in some
of Edwards' work, it seems to offer a deconstruction of the symbolic order of the mass media:

forecast cloudy with rain
max temp 10 to
12C traffic congested
in the outer suburbs
Friendly Persuasion a crackle
of static Sir Geoffrey
believes progress can be
made busy with clerical
work clue 9 across
change my one solution
charred corpse legitimate target
either inapt before THE
QUEEN AT 60 moon
rises 4 snarled in
clematis persisting light aspires
to flesh and blood   (p. 20)

The language of the newscast is disrupted by cutting, while the
compression of the short lines encourages the floating phrases to
form new links: thus the 'static' that produces the 'crackle' of
radio interference momentarily creates a 'static Sir Geoffrey' who,
ironically, believes 'progress can be/ made'. In the same way, the
numbers seem to connect (as signs from the same sign system),
break (because they are taken from different genres of discourse),
and then reconnect again on a meta-level (because of their aesthetic use in the poem). The allusion to crossword puzzles, with
its reminder of the register of crossword questions, prompts the
reader to decode the next two lines, and 'charred corpse
legitimate target' cracks to disclose a memorial of the 1986 US
bombing of Tripoli. Clarke's poetry is conceived as a poetry of
resistance to what Lyotard calls the 'hegemony of the economic
genre'. Where freedom and resistance are thematised in Edwards'
work, in Clarke's work they are implicated in the poetic artifice as
part of the language use. The first poem in the sequence begins:

after so many deaths
to walk the ice
between withered chrysalids and
the breath of stars

o my only light
for ice read virgin
well why not read
tabula rasa do I
need to tell you
connect to the descriptive
system and we're off
BRACKET conjoined OBLIQUE disjunct   (p. 5)

What looks like a lyric poem in the descriptive mode quickly
undoes itself by drawing attention to the signifier, the reading
process and its own textuality. At the same time, these are poems
which are aware of the ways in which resistance can be
recuperated to the economic genre:

each individual consciousness raised
a single iota is
up for grabs Marie
Bashkirtseff feminist classic think
we don't own you   (p. 34)

Hartley argues that Althusser's conception of ideology as 'representation' of the imaginary relationship of individuals to their real
conditions of existence 'points to literary practice as a mode of
intervention in ideological struggle'.[49] This might also suggest
what is at stake in this contestation of language, syntax and representation and provide legitimation for certain kinds of innovatory
poetic practice.

Notes

I am grateful to my colleagues Andrew Gibson, Alison Light, Adam Roberts
and Katie Wales and to the students of the Royal Holloway and Bedford
New College 'Contemporaneities' seminar for comments on an earlier
version of this essay.

1 Ezra Pound, *Make It New*, Faber and Faber, London, 1934.

2 Frederic Jameson, 'Foreword' to Jean-François Lyotard, *The Postmodern Condition: A Report on Knowledge*, Manchester University Press, Manchester, 1984.

3 Charles Bernstein (ed.), *The Politics of Poetic Form*, Roof Books, New York,
1990, pp. 69–70.

4 *fragmente*, ed. Andrew Lawson and Anthony Mellors, 8 Hertford Street, Oxford; *Talus*, ed. Marzia Balzani, Hanne Bramness, Stephen Want, Shamoon Zamir, Department of English, University of York.

5 In his essay 'Julia Kristeva, Susan Howe and avant garde poetics', in Antony Easthope and John O. Thompson (eds.), *Contemporary Poetry Meets Modern Theory*, Harvester Wheatsheaf, Hemel Hempstead, 1991, Peter Middleton engages with a related issue: Kristeva, in *La Revolution du langage poétique* (Seuil, Paris, 1974), argued that 'some literature can weave together the relations of the unconscious, the subject and society, in a manner which both destroys and reconstructs', but she 'never resolves the issue of whether she is arguing that such texts did have a revolutionary impact, or that they have a continuing potential' (pp. 82–3)

6 'We cut nature up, organize it into concepts, and ascribe significances as we do, largely because we are parties to an agreement to organize it in this way – an agreement that holds throughout our speech community and is codified in the patterns of our language', Benjamin Lee Whorf, *Language, Thought and Reality*, ed. J.B. Carroll, Chapman & Hall, London., 1956, pp. 213f.

7 David Miller, 'Notes on Poetics', *Alembic*, 6, Summer 1977, pp. 42–4; reprinted *Paper Air*, 2.2, 1979, pp. 53–5.

8 David Miller, 'A few notes for clarification: On Allen Fisher's *Place*. Book One', *Poetry Information*, 16, Winter 1976–77, pp. 23–6.

9 Allen Fisher, *Prosyncel*, Strange Faeces Press, Penfield, New York, 1975, p. 9.

10 Raoul Vaneigem, *The Revolution of Everyday Life*: trans. John Fullerton and Paul Sieveking, Practical Paradise Publications, 1972, p. 2. The other book which 'played a large part towards the thinking behind the work' was Charles Olson's *A Special View of History*, 'Intuitions and interactions', *Prosyncel*, p. 9.

11 Allen Fisher, *Place I–XXXVII*, Aloes Books, London, 1974, I and VI.

12 *Place*, XXXV; see Clive Bush, ' "Moving the boundaries of settlement": the acts of continuing in Allen Fisher's Poetry', *Talus*, 5/6, Spring 1991, pp. 22–61.

13 *Prosyncel*, p. 25; *Place*, IX.

14 'An interview with Allen Fisher', *Alembic*, 4, Winter 1975/76, pp. 49–57.

15 *Prosyncel*, p. 7.

16 *Prosyncel*, p. 37.

17 *Prosyncel*, p. 37; *Convergences, In place, of the Play*, Spanner, London, 1976.

18 Allen Fisher, *Imbrications*, Lobby Press, Cambridge, 1981; Allen Fisher, *Brixton Fractals*, Aloes Books, London, 1985. The quotation is from the opening lines of 'Around the World', *Brixton Fractals*, p. 13.

19 David Miller, 'Disclosures: Notes on the poetry of Charles Madge', *Great Works*, 7, May 1979, pp. 54–63.

20 Charles Madge, *The Disappearing Castle*, Faber & Faber, London, 1937.

21 Allen Fisher, *Thomas Net's Tree-Birst*, Edible Magazine Poisonous Edition, London, 1970, an 'auto-destructive' version of Wordsworth's *The Prelude*, Book First; Tom Phillips, *A Humument*, Thames and Hudson, London, 1980, a 'treated' version of W. H. Mallock's *A Human Document*.

22 David Miller, *Appearance & Event*, Hawk Press, Paraparaumu, New Zealand, 1977.

23 David Miller, *Primavera*, Burning Deck Press, Rhode Island, (no pagination), 1979; reprinted in *The New British Poetry*, Paladin, London, 1988, pp. 312–14.

24 Gill Ott, 'Springtime Held', *Tamarisk*, 1980.

25 David Miller, *South London Mix*, Gabberbocchus, London, 1975, 1. 20.

26 David Miller to Gill Ott, 28 March 1980.

27 Richard Palmer, 'The postmodernity of Heidegger', *Boundary 2*, IV, 2, Winter 1976, p. 423.

28 David Miller, 'The theme of language in relation to Heidegger's philosophy', *Paper Air*, 3:1, 1982, pp. 91–100; p. 93.

29 See, particularly, Hans-Georg Gadamer, *Philosophical Hermeneutics*, trans. D. E. Linge, University of California Press, Berkeley and Los Angeles, 1977; Paul Ricouer, *The Symbolism of Evil*, trans., E. Buchanan, Beacon Press, Boston, 1969.

30 David Miller, *W. H. Hudson and the Elusive Paradise*, London, Macmillan, 1990, p. 15.

31 *W. H. Hudson*, p. 16.

32 David Miller, foreword to *Boyd & Evans*, Flowers East, London, 1991, pp. 4–5.

33 David Miller, *Imagination and Unity, & The Poetics of Painting: Two Essays on the Art of Jennifer Durrant Stride*, Exeter, 1989.

34 'Jennifer Durrant and the poetics of painting', (no pagination).

35 'The theme of language in relation to Heidegger's philosophy', p. 98.

36 Unity, Singing Horse Press, Blue Bell, Pennsylvania, 1981; *Orientation*, Bran's Head Books, Frome, 1982; *Losing to Compassion*, Origin Press, Kyoto, 1985. Miller's work is most readily accessible in *Pictures of Mercy: Selected Poems*, Stride, Exeter, 1991.

37 Veronica Forrest-Thomson, *Poetic Artifice*, Manchester University Press, Manchester, 1978, p. 53.

38 The term was first used in Steve McCaffery's 1976 essay 'The death of the subject', *Open Letter*, 3.7, Summer 1977 (revised and reprinted as 'Diminished Reference and the model reader' in *North of Intention: Critical Writings 1973–1986*, Roof Books, New York, 1986) to mark a distinction from referent-centred writing. For a sample of the language-centred work associated with the magazine L=A=N=G=U=A=G=E, see Bruce Andrews and Charles Bernstein (eds.), *The L=A=N=G=U=A=G=E Book*, Southern Illinois University Press, Carbondale, Ill., 1984.

39 See George Hartley, *Textual Politics and the Language Poets*, Indiana University Press, Bloomington and Indianapolis, 1989.

40 Charles Bernstein, 'Semblance', *The L=A=N=G=U=A=G=E Book*, p. 115.

41 Work by Alan Davies appeared in *Alembic*, 4, Winter 1975/6; work by James Sherry appeared in *Alembic* 5, Autumn 1976, and 6, Summer 1977; work by Lyn Hejinian and Rae Armantrout appeared in *Alembic*, 8, Spring 1979;

subsequently, 'language-centred' writing was a significant strand in *Reality Studios*. *Reality Studios*, 2.4, April/May/June 1980, under the sub-title 'death of the referent?: some trends in contemporary american poetry', constituted a colloquium on 'language-centred' writing, complete with extensive bibliography.

42 Gillian Allnutt, Fred D'Aguiar, Ken Edwards, Eric Mottram (eds.), *The New British Poetry*, Paladin, London, 1988, p. 267.

43 Adrian Clarke, 'Listening to the differences', originally delivered at the Sub Voicive One Day Colloquium 'No One Listens to Poetry?', 20 July 1991, printed as *RWC Extra*, 2, November 1991, no pagination.

44 *Lorca: An Elegiac Fragment*, Alembic Editions, Orpington, 1978, (no pagination) *Tilth*, Galloping Dog Press, Newcastle Upon Tyne, 1980; *Tilth Dub*, Reality Studios, London, 1980; *Drumming & poems* Galloping Dog Press, Newcastle upon Tyne, 1982; *A4 Portrait*, Spectacular Diseases, Peterborough, 1984; *Intensive Care*, Pig Press, Durham, 1986; *A4 Landscape*, Reality Studios, London, 1988; *Lyrical Ballets*, Torque Press, Southampton, 1990.

45 John Livingston Lowes, *The Road to Xanadu* (1927), Picador, London, 1978, p. 326.

46 *Im'mediate Measures (ghost measures 2+3)* Alighieri & Co, London, 1986; *Ghost Measures*, Actual Size Press, London, 1987; *Spectral Investments*, Writers Forum, London, 1991.

47 Adrian Clarke, 'Listening to the differences'.

48 Jean-François Lyotard, *The Differend: Phrases in Dispute*, trans. G. Van Den Abbeele, Manchester University Press, Manchester 1988, p. xiii.

49 Hartley, p. 27; Louis Althusser, *Lenin and Philosophy*, trans. B. Brewster, New Left Books, London, 1971, p. 162.

Helen Kidd

6

The paper city: women, writing, and experience

maybe just me, and a thin wind wrinkling
winterdusk comes up unsticking
leaves, could be outside the dressing room;
then this crowdsudden,
                    "What a mob! What a jostle!
Someone should do something here."
                              Ease up.
just set the river there on the left under
hills in the West fumbling the sky over
a damp moulder of ground where marsh spooks stand.
though in an offhand corner something unpeels,
flaps on its billboard hinge against
the smudges of late. could be a wing
                         cannot   see
it stumbles and creaks, could be an empty hand's
frantic salute, or maybe a creature, its last limb
that lolls and twitches out of the eater's mouth, or
does it idly heft its cantle over this cranny
where Bosch-painted mushroom bums are sprouting
pink innocence, nuzzle the peached cheek of black?

fire-crackers, trumpets out there,
                         but over the river
the ghosts still look like winning. and I?

am coming unstuck again. the small flaps its half-
seagull, and slowly, but slowly, as snail-nails
emptying teaspoons of glass, tunnels off
                              out of the frame.[1]

I

When I wrote this poem in 1985 I was just beginning to investigate
the politics of the writing subject. I began writing seriously in
1980, and initially I was interested in finding appropriate linguistic
energy to communicate the textures and topographies of the
states of mind which lie on the perimeter of consciousness. But
the question persisted. How to write a political poem? I was an
active peace campaigner at the time, and I wanted to find a
suitable form in which to express the nature of nuclear destruction, and the effects of living on the brink with them. These
considerations contributed to my growing commitment to
feminism, as only feminism seemed to offer a critique which is
wide and radical enough to analyse the situation, not only of
women, but of the marginalisation and oppression of other
silenced peoples and issues. Its possibilities for further development and also for survival strategies seemed the most promising.

   In tackling such issues, if I were to use the subject position 'I'
confidently and authoritatively, my words would always begin to
sound hollow to me. The implications of fixed authority and all its
attendant rhetoric carried by the assertive 'I', leave me feeling that
such an attitude begs the presence of an abyss, a gaping absence
underlying the brittle and temporary subject. It has always felt like
an empty vessel. The notion of a single identity with which to face
the world, of the self as a constant, and likewise the notion of a
single poetic voice, have left me feeling profoundly uncom-
fortable.

   By 1985 my studies had introduced me to feminist thinking
on subject identity. What I had been attempting, including
exploring the great shifter 'I', suddenly didn't seem so far out on a
limb. Furthermore, to move about the page space in an eccentric
way, to play with the rules of syntax and punctuation began to

make theoretical sense. Sadly, I had read an amount of work by women which had left a great many questions unresolved. Anthologies were curiosities, valuable in their presence, but patchy in their choice. In many the poetry had been sacrificed to statement and polemic, while other writers tended to concentrate on the idea of women as writers at the expense of feminism.[2] However, discovering Barthes, Hélène Cixous, Kristeva, Mary Ellman and others, I began to feel my experiments were justified.

I came to understand my need to move about the page and use space as a creative component within the making of a poem. It releases the poem from the tyranny of stanzaic form into a more multi-dimensional approach. Words or phrases are enabled to move about one another as a mobile might move in the air, or, in a more sculptural way, they can appear in blocks as Gertrude Stein used them. Similarly, punctuation can impose a strait-jacket on meaning, whereas removing it can allow a lexical item to spill over into an entirely different or ambiguous usage, thus deepening the poem's field of association. For example 'over' in line nine of 'The Paper City' can be read to refer back into its own line as meaning 'all over the sky' or it can connect with line ten as 'over a damp moulder of ground'. By placing it at the end of the line it effects a double movement, backwards, as I have said, and also forward, operating as an open link with the following line. I am particularly fond of what I call 'hook words', that is to say connectives and prepositions onto which the next line can be hung. By placing and using them like this some of the bones of the poem show through as well, which pleases me, as I enjoy allusions within the poem to its own making process.

I can only understand truth as an ongoing and relational phenomenon, and poetry I enjoy as a means of questioning this. I prefer to eschew any suggestion of absolute truth or revelation. I am more interested in the question of how to be fully human, and that means being flexible, and whatever else may be beyond life is merely there to assist that. If the poet sets him- or herself up as an utterer of universal truths this inevitably closes off creative possibilities for the poem and for the reader. We are all capable of making, rather than simply consuming, and poetry is one, and only one, manifestation of this, and one in which the reader is an equal, not an inferior who has come to drink at the fount of wisdom. It is the poet's responsibility to open the poem, including the play of its making, towards the reader as co-creator.

Now I recognise that these ideas need not be termed specifically feminist, but they are derived from the socialist–feminist critique of patriarchy with all its hierarchical implications. It is certainly true that men also use this technique of revealing the bones of the poem, or of opening the poem towards the reader[3]. The use of ambiguities, playing with language and giving oneself licence to explore those half-articulated states of subject identity where the subject is either dissolving or re-forming in a continuous state of flux, is an important recognition of the way in which, at present, female subject identity is formulated. Therefore it is important to examine the varieties and possibilities offered when subject identity ceases to be seen as a single, phallic, separate, defensive, and therefore brittle but essential quality, but something which is constantly relational, interactive, context-based, moving between self and other.

To elaborate this point more fully, in 'The Paper City' the creation of identity is pictured as a precarious business which is prone to dissolution both by the predations of more aggressive subjects, and also through more organic means. This dissolution is not, however, entirely without its rewards. There is an erotic gain made through returning to a condition where the unconscious allows taboos to be lifted and repressions to be removed, as for example in 'over this cranny/where Bosch-painted mushroom bums are sprouting/pink innocence, nuzzle the peached cheek of black'. I wanted this part of the poem to return, as it were, to the pre-Oedipal innocence of the sensory and sensual awareness of infants. Nancy Chodorow explains this state and how it is never fully repressed in female individuation. Thus, although it is common to both male and female, and can be demonstrated in the writings of both, women writers enjoy easier access to it:

> Women's mothering . . . produces asymmetries in the relational experiences of girls and boys as they grow up, which account for crucial differences in feminine and masculine personality, and the relational capacities and modes which these entail. Women and men grow up with personalities affected by divergent boundary experiences and differently constructed and experienced inner object-worlds, and are pre-occupied with different relational issues. Feminine personality comes to be based less on repression of inner objects, and fixed and firm splits in the ego, and more on retention and continuity of external relationships. From the retention of pre-Oedipal attachments to their mother, growing girls come to define and experience themselves as continuous with others; their experience of self contains more flexible permeable ego boundaries. Boys come to define themselves as more separate and distinct, with a greater sense of rigid ego boundaries and differentiation. The basic female sense of self is connected to the world, the basic masculine sense of self is separate.[4]

I recognised those states of dyadic unity where mother and child interact almost as one entity before having the psychoanalaytic terminology to explain them, and I can clearly recall them from my children's early years. Furthermore, at these times memories of my own pre-Oedipal phase were awakened.

Whether we dress it in the rhetoric of high moral or spiritual truth and seriousness or not, it seems to me that much of the poetic impulse is based on exploring the materials to hand, in this case langauge.[5] Thus even to make sublime poetic nonsense like Edward Lear, Phyllis April King and Ivor Cutler,[6] is to exercise a subversion which alters the reader's view of the possibilities of language which celebrates the flux, or pulsations of feeling, described by Kristeva as being part of a pre-Oedipal babblement.[8] Once the child in us has been liberated then pleasure cannot be far away. In fact I will go further and use the word *delight*, which somewhat approaches Roland Barthes's and Cixous's untranslatable 'jouissance'.[9]

The further we move from delight, then the further we move into humourless reductivity and intolerance. We move into the realm, rhetorically speaking, of absolutes rather than the relative, and from the possible to the imperative.

II

In a long poem called 'Las Madres de la Plaza de Mayo', I explored the significance of the lost children of Argentina and other South American countries, coming to the conclusion that once the child in us is lost or destroyed or denied then we ourselves are profoundly lost.

. . . .
Listen, man, who passes by so busily;
until they have returned, our children,
your children, the land will stay hollow.
What use are gardens without play?
What use is a ball without hands to catch it?
Until they return your world will stay broken,
your pages lie empty. Shades of the vanished
will ache on the thresholds, frost over your windows.

Ely, Carmen, Cozne, Lina, Nelida
calling for Los Niños.
Our songs write themselves on the Plaza.
'Appariçion con Vida!' Let them appear alive.
Appariçion con Vida.
Appariçion con Vida![10]

The poem differs in approach to 'The Paper City' because of the nature of the subject-matter, which is a question of human rights. Although it was written six months earlier, it is more easily accessible. In the poem I use the technique which I call 'fold-in', which I prefer to the more violent associations of 'cut-ups'.[11] The stanzas are a collaboration between myself and the poems of the mothers themselves. I found a book of poems by the mothers of the Plaza de Mayo and then came across an article describing how American dollars are still supporting the military regimes in South America. I used material from both of these, re-wording some of the poems slightly, in the interests of poetic economy. I included the dramatic monologues spoken by torturers, police chiefs and morgue attendants, but also a direct quote from Ronald Reagan. The poem becomes therefore a development of a collective voice, or plea. It is not so much a collage as a chorus, and a simple contrast between grief and inhumanity, impersonal power and dispossession.

What I enjoy about fold-ins is the crossing of boundaries between self and others, just as in 'The Paper City' the boundary is crossed between painting and words, as it is, on one level, a painting without a picture. In other poems I have used space in a more sculptural way, or I use interactions with music. In 'The Bower Meadow' I explore the idea of women talking together as being like a dance. It is based on observations of how women interact together and how, in conversation, threads are dropped, picked up again, sentences unfinished and then re-formulated later on. There is room and space for interruptions, and a great deal of playfulness. Women as mothers are used to interruptions and are also exposed to children's word play, and they do not necessarily assume that they will be heard out from the beginning to the end of a discussion, but if it is important they will be able to pick up the thread of an idea later. They do not expect to occupy a public platform as an automatic birthright, but are more often expected to make supportive noises rather than authoritative pronouncements.[12]

The consequence is a particularly creative use of dialogue, of give and take, which some men find hard to handle. It is one of the qualities celebrated by the Irish poet, Eavan Boland, who specialises in capturing the nuances and qualities of what she calls 'the woman in the ordinary'[13]. She explores those reclaimed and creatively used moments which women find for themselves, feeding babies at dawn, between flights of stairs at dusk, quilting, or all the other varieties of making that accompany domestic moments, normally unsung, and so often belittled. Her meticulous and evocative observations are a celebration, and also a valuable recognition of the slighted aspects of women's lives. At the extreme end of the scale, this disregard has resulted in the disempowerment, and in many countries, severe oppression of mothers and children. The more women's lives and ways of being are written and celebrated the less they will be relegated to the place of silent and silenced otherness.

'The Bower Meadow', as a title, was taken from a sketch by Burne-Jones for the painting of the same name. The sketch shows two women, who are in the background of the finished painting. They are dancing together and, as well as the movement of their dresses, he also pays attention to the positions of their feet. They both look light and nimble, but also very well earthed so that they will not fall.

As a dance might so the speaking or
as circling to and fro maybe me and you
a movement on about around that this
and several curlicues along a drift

the maps or traces throughing air
toe light foot fall heel quiets it
is womantalk the choreographies along
its outer-edged and sea-surled crest where
we friends and laughter
lip and wonder on the language reef.
as a dance might so the speaking or
as circling to and fro you and maybe me
       a movement
    an about around
      heel light foot fall toe light taps it
is womantalk and wanderthrough
          laughter and friends
     the choreographies

The cross-over between self and other and the cross-over between the other arts, painting, sculpture, dance, music and so on, is an important parallel, in that both involve dialogue, interaction and a dissolution of rigid compartmentalisation. Rigid categories may be useful as analytical tools, but in practice collaborations and interactions create and inform texture, depth and complexity in any artistic event. These events do not exist in isolation but continue to feed one another, and can be seen to do so, even if we examine writing in the narrow confines of canonical definitions. It can also be seen in action during the early Modern period, when performance arts such as ballet and concerts allied with poetry and art, as in for example, Walton's

Facade. The sixties was another period during which media and art forms interacted.[15] Poetry reappeared as a performance art, particularly with the Liverpool Poets, and rock musicians considered their lyrics to be as important as their music, particularly the Beatles, Joni Mitchell and Bob Dylan. Artists such as Warhol were exploring cinema and comics at the same time, for new source material and techniques.

Whereas 'The Bower Meadow' mimics the movement of conversation and dance, 'Pansexuality' returns to the fold-in technique, with the emphasis on a chorus of women's voices. It includes more textual play, what I would call textual erotics, than was possible in the more declarative 'Las Madres'. By the very nature of its subject-matter 'Pansexuality' poses a redefinition of sexuality, not only in the arrangement of the voices, but also in the movement and textures of langauge, making them as erotic and open as possible. It is a celebration of non-prescriptive eroticism in which biologism, heterosexism and end-directed sexuality are marginalised. For this reason Lorca is included on the side of the angels, and D. H. Lawrence, Freud and Lacan are included only as voices from the margin, their comments being placed in brackets. They become, in contrast to the celebrants, examples of reductivity and the aridity of scientific, or quasi-scientific, authoritative assumptions.

. . . .
Then we, the women, recite our litany,
the feminary of the vulvas; compare them
to apricots, pomegranates, roses, pinks,
peonies or marguerites. A web in the light,
the pubic fleece, the mons pubis. The labia
majora like two shellfish halves; the labia
minora, their hidden face, purple of Sidon,
tropic coral: the clitoris, the prow of a ship,
its stem the comb of a shellfish, it is mercury,
it is quicksilver, impatient for pleasure;
we have called it a cherrystone, a bud,
a young shoot, a shelled sesame, an almond,
a sprig of myrtle, a dart, the barrel of a lock.

(. . . the fantasy of being a man, in spite
of everything, often persists as a formative
factor over long periods. This 'masculinity
complex' in women can also result in a manifest
homosexual choice of object.)

or we might lie along the very cool
and damp of grass at midnight dark;
the earth folds into you, salts body
creases. Or on the heat of sand,
its grain and dry salt on your breasts
on mine are travelling in silver on
your belly over and my tongue explores
your feet, hips, hollow of your back
(When a man seeks a woman in love, or
in positive desire, he seeks a union,
he seeks a consummation of himself
with that which is not himself,
light with dark, dark with light.)

Let them have their oneness, with its dominations,
its solipsisms like the sun. Let them have
their strange divisions by couples in which
the other is the image of the one, but an
image only. We simply say we will not
garner or store the symbols that we used
to need to show that we were strong. We will
not compare the vulva to the sun moon stars,
we do not say the vulvas are black suns
                    in the shining night.[16]

In order for the medium to become its own message the poem
allows the textual/textural erotics of language as a surface, or
linguistic skin, to take over from the flat, Latinate and controlling
language of the so-called experts. The introduction of an I, an
erected subject, in the swimming section, 'Then I/spurtle through
the smoothy skin . . .', is included as an element, but an element
only, in the process of sensual and sexual interaction.

Unlike Freud and Lacan I do not see the phallus as the
necessary principle controlling writing and individuation,
sexuality and the social order. Admittedly Lacan does separate the

phallus from its physiological counterpart, the penis, and points out that it is indeed symbolic. This is supposed to reassure us that it is assumed by authorities such as Lacan that we women still relate psychologically to a particular system which defines us as lacking. As Elizabeth Grosz points out, this is indeed a problem and, although Lacan's distinctions are useful, in that they underline the linguistic and symbolic (rather than the biological), indicating the possibility of change, nevertheless:

> In spite of Lacan's claims, the phallus is not a neutral term functioning equally for both sexes, positioning them both within the symbolic order. As the word suggests it is a term privileging masculinity, or rather the penis. The valorization of the penis and the relegation of the female sexual organs to the castrated category are effects of a socio-political system that enables the phallus to function as the 'signifier or signifiers', giving the child access to sexual identity and speaking position within culture. Its position as a threshold signifier is symptomatic of the assumed patriarchal context in Freud's and Lacan's work ... he is ... responsible for positing a metonymic relation between an organ and a signifier ... although Lacan's account is directed to the phallus as a signifier not the penis as an organ, it is committed to an a priori privilege of the masculine that is difficult if not impossible, to dislodge.[17]

I do not wish to deny the existence of the phallic aspect of individuation, for clearly it still exists and still influences us, and it is both a psychological response to biological function, and at the same time a symbol of an ordering principle of Western capitalist patriarchy. What I want to do is invest significance in other ordering elements, and simply acknowledge it as only one element among many. Once the notion of play is introduced, and of sexuality as interplay between self and other which colours every aspect of life, then the urgency of end-directed sex, with all its implications of closure and death, can be avoided. We can return to the vitality of child-like (not childish) perceptions of the world. We can return to a non-penetrative text which engages with, and becomes another aspect of, the fluidity and pulsational process of flux.[18] For women the skin is an important erotic element. Enjoyment is not centred on one site alone. It is ex-centric. As

Cixous says in the early part of the poem 'our depth is density of body/of touch, "all over" ...'. Once the entire surface is celebrated it is also sensitised, and that surface, be it the poem's, or an individual's skin, becomes an interface which might interact with other surfaces, sand, bark, water, air, and so on. To be sensorily awake is to be alive, and there is therefore no need to quest for meaning, for control, or for the ultimate sexual conquest/object. That is a form of consumerism inculcated by a particular brand of patriarchy called capitalism. I see pansexuality as a continuous process which can overcome such an emotional boom and slump pattern in sexual interaction. There is no reason why men should have to continue focusing on one aspect only of their sexuality, that of penetration and orgasm. What reinforces such attitudes is the re-enactment of old and unsatisfactory notions of how to relate through the 'us and them' rhetoric which science and much of psychoanalysis still produces. In a later section of the poem the scientific community, 'we', the experts, set themselves up against their objects of study, women, who are described as having 'peculiarities', a value-laden term, suggesting that this group only assumes itself to be normative.

> (... for both sexes only one genital, namely the male one, comes into account. What is present therefore is not a primacy of the genitals but a primacy of the phallus ... Unfortunately we can describe this state of things only as it affects the male child; the corresponding processes in the little girl are not known to us.)[19]

Freud's writings imply that 'Woman' has meaning only in relation to the reproductive process, and that human beings are not so much interactive and social, as reproductive, whether or not reproduction is any longer an urgent necessity. What is not productive in female physiology, that is to say the clitoris, is labelled 'virile' and 'peculiar', regardless of the fact that it is unique sexually in that it exists only to give pleasure. (Elsewhere he explains it away as part of an infantile stage of sexuality, which he dismisses as inferior.) I chose the following passage for the poem to marginalise, '(a further complication ... the clitoris, its virile character, continues to operate in later female sexual life. We do not, of course, know the biological basis of these peculiarities in women . . .)'.[20]

Here again the scientist is baffled by the presence of difference, and at a loss to explain it. It is not clear whether the clitoris is called virile because it contains erectile tissue (so do many other parts of the body), or because of its pleasure-giving properties. Given the capacity for and variety of pleasure that women may experience without reproductive sex leads me to the conclusion that men might appear to have been suffering from a form of clitoris envy.

III

It must surely be possible for men to engage with the continuum of self and other, and some male writers' work would strongly suggest this.[21] It is surely entirely possible for both sexes to enjoy the sensory, the erotic, the play of surfaces, skin, taste, touch, smell, sight and sound, the kind of responsiveness which 'Pansexuality' celebrates.[22] Thus we need to re-define power to encompass those qualities hitherto marginalised and marked as being 'feminine'. One way is to unpick the rhetoric of power, including the scientific texts which reinforce social assumptions.

Writing 'Pansexuality' felt dangerous. It felt like a transgressive activity, and although I was already engaged in reading feminist theories with other women, I had very little contact with other women writers with whom I could discuss the techniques I was using. I was used to working in a workshop situation and found the practical advice of other poets extremely useful. However, my experiments with fold-in and questions about feminism and writing had usually drawn a blank. The poem was originally published in an A4 leaflet called *Tyromachia*, dreamed up by Bill Herbert and Keith Jebb[23] as a playful echo of the (in)famous magazine *Blast*.[24] I collaborated on this leaflet and also co-edited, with them, *New Poetry from Oxford*. They were working with language and form in a challenging way. Nevertheless I felt uneasy about only having the approval and encouragement of fellow male poets.[25] Male writers may still situate themselves in a poetic terrain which has been pioneered and mapped in Britain, on the

Continent and in America. Modernism and post-modernism have been generally defined as inhabited by male writers from Eliot and Joyce onwards, regardless of Gertrude Stein, Mina Loy and many others.

Women writers confront many problems, and the most urgent of these is how to write without writing ourselves back into the corners patriarchy has created for us. Thus a form of self-censorship operates for many writers. Sexuality is a difficult subject to deal with for women, and I still feel there are things which I cannot write, not because they are unsuitable poetic material, but because I am a woman. Lifting the constraints on language is very much part of my concern and therefore such silence is annoying. But this is exactly why 'Pansexuality' felt transgressive for me.

IV

The difficulty I have in transforming personal experience into poetry partly stems from my attitude to writing. I cannot see my life as subordinate to my craft. Only once have I managed to write a successful 'confessional' poem, and that was long after the event. It deals with a stillbirth, and I very deliberately used the event to parallel the sense of dispossession which I felt generally and with regard to language.[26] I had not yet come to criticise Lacan's view that the phallic is the important factor in the symbolic order, particularly in language. Neither had I negotiated a way out of the Kristevan siting of women on the side of the unconscious, the silenced and the repressed.[27] All I felt was a profound sense of alienation from the world of letters, from the symbolic order, and, largely because my questioning had led me to this point, I felt like the absence Freud depicts women as being. I used the stillbirth poem both as an elegy for my lost daughter, and as an expression of this uncertain and painful alienation. The last line of the poem knits the two together, 'Silence grates on a broken edge'.

Whilst writing the poem I felt guilty of using a situation and manipulating it. And yet now I feel strongly that all writing is a remaking, a distortion, an appropriation, a bricolage. Nevertheless, I felt then that in making this poem I had somehow prioritised writing at the expense of life. Many male writers that I have talked to don't seem to suffer from this problem, perhaps because defining and separating off identity is part of their experience of individuation. They are also encouraged to situate themselves authoritatively in the identity of 'poet'. I feel partly envious of such uncomplicated subject positions, and yet I know that if I were to make writing my *raison d'être* I would be devaluing the rest of my life, and also compartmentalising my writing, placing it in a hermetically-sealed category which would deprive it of those fluid boundaries and edges which language explores. The following poem is a critique of the 'poetry [or writing] is my life' attitude, a criticism of the construction of the fiction of the great male writing 'I', which transforms and absorbs everything into its own subjectivity.

'Will Our Hero be Dashed to Pieces on the Jagged Rocks Below?'

Whatever he wrote he wore,
poems like all sorts of socks . . .
silk hand-made paper birds –
nest paper Japanese hand-made paper
satellite map weather map fishing
fly Guatemalan worry doll fly
firecracker pastel . . .

It was the perpetual loon of thought
on the lake. A state of happy repose
of the boulevardier on holiday, exhausted
by his nocturnal activities. And now
he spoke in mellow leather brogues
with all the style and elegance
of a Duncan's walnut whip.

He looked up towards his gonads
in the last uncreated light,
heard the chorus of this curious tale
                                begin:

'Hidden deep within the Hertfordshire countryside
in the village of Ayot St. Lawrence,

stands the home of George Bernard Shaw.
Four rooms downstairs are unchanged
since his death. His hats hang in the hall.
His pens, dictionaries and typewriter
are on his desk; his personal
treasures are on view, and at the bottom
of the garden . . .' is the bottom
of the garden and the revolving summer.[28]

I am not suggesting that all male poets necessarily adopt this elitist
position, but it is a very real danger for any writer to build the
fiction of a single I-dentity, and Shaw, who features in this poem
seems to me to epitomise it. Wendy Mulford speaks of the writer
and identity thus:

> . . . 'Poet', 'Poem', and 'Poetic Tradition'. I think these concepts
> need to be seriously challenged and defetishized. They are not
> rooted in the objective relations of our society and they encourage
> and prop up the idea of this art as a magical art, which must be
> performed by elite beings-apart. The prevalence of these notions in
> poetry, and the failure to challenge them, is a very real indication of
> the problem facing high art in a capitalist society – how its practice
> is tied to and legitimated by society precisely because in its hier-
> archical and elite nature it reinforces the ideological hierarchy of
> aspiration and remains the property of the few. I'd suggest that
> men can use these concepts in support of their particular artistic
> practice (even when in other ways the implications of what they do
> point in another direction) because they can still more easily be
> spokesmen of their own culture, culture which because of gender
> is never ours in the same way, even though because of class it is not
> theirs either, and they/you too are working to deconstruct it.[29]

Meeting Wendy Mulford and Denise Riley I felt that at last I had
found other women who were exploring, stretching and questioning language. Yet these were also women who were not
prepared to lose sight of the politics of gender and sexuality in the
interests of pursuing the politics of the text. It felt like coming
home and finding a community at the same time.

One of the features that interests me about Wendy
Mulford's writing is that, like me, she is interested in using landscape images, and also images of the sea. I call the latter

'metaphors of mutability' and they serve several purposes. Firstly, they are suggestive of the fluid boundary of the self/other axis. Then they are also evocative of the oceans of untapped consciousness within us. They are also resonant of the tides and movements of language which underlie every utterance, and in this way they can serve as a writerly image in which the poem can talk metaphorically about its own making. Finally they possess a primal and pre-Oedipal pull, re-evoking the fluidity of being and sensations before individuation takes place.

In her *East Anglia Sequence*, Wendy Mulford uses the sea and its erosion of the land as a suitable image for the negotiations which surround subject identity. This occupies a liminal and shifting site which has to be continuously redefined. It is never fixed and is constantly remaking itself and its relationship to the world outside.

'The Coriolis Effect'

> Temporarily composed
> The church of St. Nicholas
> top left, tacked to
> a wide band of steel blue
> a narrow band of gold strips
> of dun bluff dunes
> plough pitted tractors cows
> deepn hedge curling the lower slopes
> at my back the east wind blows
> from off the land, from off the sister sea

In the waters near Britain the effect of wind is generally more important, producing a wind-driven current which, piling water up against the coastline, or against the continental shelf, causes the rise in level. However the direction of the current is not directly down-wind, thus a surge which formed on the West Coast of Scotland will have progressed to Wick in four hours, four hours later to the Tyne, six hours later to Lowestoft, arriving at the Thames estuary after another three hours and thence to the coasts of Holland and Germany.

> One seagull
> holding its place in the air-currents
> I on the stubble-hill breast

>fronting the glittering points of the sea
>to compose a view
>hold the church steady
>while the sea withdraws
>its commercial lure
>the heathland hugs
>its barrowed secrets
>sacred places flattened
>beneath bracken beds
>underworld stumble[31]

The focus is on a liminal landscape, the salt-marsh land where the writing subject is located, and simultaneously defined as a fiction necessary to the composition. But there is also an insistence on ebb and flow, on the shifts between stanzaic and prosaic sections. Although the prose sections read as found information on tidal behaviour, nevertheless they possess a musicality and poetic quality of repetition, parallelism which echoes the subject, the sea, and they have the unshaped expansive movement of prose which evokes the sea.

The second stanza connects the image of 'one seagull/ holding its place in the air-currents' with 'I on the stubble-hill breast'. The lack of punctuation allows for a play of alternative readings and the implication is that to be sited on land is no less fluid than the 'sister sea', merely different. Indeed the passages about the sea also imply that the sea also has some recognisable patterns of behaviour, which could be described as its harder 'glittering points', so there is a play here between fixing the unfixable, and unfixing the seemingly fixed. The poem discusses the process of composition, whilst revealing it as temporary, a suggestion made concrete by the topographical location, the salt-marsh and its erosion by the sea. If we read the 'I' of the second stanza in connection with line five as 'I am fronting the sea in order to compose a view', the honest subject position is revealed *vis-à-vis* the formulation of an image, but line five can also be read as a directive to the reader as to the means of creating a photographic composition incorporating an artefact, also only temporarily in view, and hence less fixed than we might imagine.

Both the 'I' and the church are like the seagull, temporarily frozen in positions by the poem and are subject to linguistic and meteorological change. This is first suggested in the initial stanza, which reveals the church as 'temporarily composed', reinforced by the words 'tacked to'. The writing subject is also associated with the 'sister sea', that is to say it is related to another fluid and altering medium, a process rather than a fixable entity. But we could also read the land as being kin to the sea, as it is described as having visual qualities akin to the sea, and is also undergoing processes of change.

Later in the sequence, in 'Pareto Optimality' intermixed snippets of found material are emphasised by an introductory line in German, and visual and tactile concretisations in two stanzas contrast strongly with the stark impersonal official register of a government report. The contrast continues in 'Danger Level', where the concrete images are concentrated in the final section and deal with the story of Gabriel Piggot's mother:

> Gabriel Piggot's mother gathered up her family to St. Nicholas' porch
> & would not budge until the landlord was compelled to take action
> to rehouse her & in the assumption of her action challenged
> robbery by wind and wave and expropriation as in the grievances listed
> loss of
> eels fish samphire grazing wildfowling flags furzes
> whins from heath and marshland. Equals
> loss of movement, shelter food.[32]

The woman is nameless herself, an inhabitant of this liminal terrain, a precarious position under threat of inundation by the sea, but also from the impersonal and officious attitude of authority, in the form of the landlord. Thus her subject position and her livelihood are doubly assaulted. She makes a defiant gesture against these two opponents by her physical statement, her choice of drowning rather than dispossession. Hereby she constitutes herself as an agent of her fate, not a victim. This is therefore an appeal to common humanity against the implacable and yet not hostile force of the sea. Her strategy of defining herself as human, and hence vulnerable subject, and her refusal to be displaced either by the elements or by faceless authority, can be compared to the writing subject. It is characterized by unsuspected shifts, in position and point of view, and it is an inhabitant of a liminal but extremely rich and detailed territory. It is necessary as an element in the process of creating the poem, and will not be located either entirely in the sea of language possibilities and horizons, nor in the abstractions of form and order, but negotiates between the two.

Denise Riley in the following untitled poem, emphasises the dialectic of order and possibility, self and other, and she uses the image of a train to reinforce the idea of movement between two states. The lack of a title indicates her resistance to the neatness and closure of labelling, and the use of couplets emphasises the notion of two sites between which process emerges as a third possibility, breaking down the simplistic economy of paired opposites. The poem also depicts writing as a crucial component in this process, which is beyond definition, continuous, growing out of dialectic, and the lack of capitalisation stresses the importance of this continuum:

> such faces bones honeycombed sockets
> of strained eyes outlined in warm
>
> light aching wrapped in impermeable
> coating of pleasure going off wild
>
> on the light-headed train   'will write
> and write what there is beyond anything'
>
> it is the 'spirit' burns in and
> through 'sex' which we know about
>
> saying It's true, I won't place or
> describe it   It   is   and refuses the law[33]

The fictions, the traps in which we are caught, the ways we might write ourselves out of them, write what we want, not what we are supposed to, this is the paper city I explore. Others also inhabit these streets, explore these avenues, ask similar questions. As Denise Riley puts it in 'A note on sex and the "reclaiming of language" ',

> The work is
> e.g. to write 'she' and for that to be a statement
> of fact only and not a strong image
> of everything which is not-you, which sees you[34]

Also, for me, the work is extending that respect for otherness, that
non-object-based view of the world, that avoidance of appro-
priating or colonising that which I love, that which I relate to, that
which I write about, whether it be Aboriginal Land Rights, or
Balinese gamelan, more state funding for Aids research and
treatment, varieties of rain in the Outer Hebrides, well-laid
hedges or Gay Rights. I am on a roller-coaster and every impression is fleeting, vivid, crucial and barely understood. All I can do is
reach for the blur with words, from this blur that is I, wherever
that may be and for the moment that it is. What I must also do is
tell you to believe in it only for a nanosecond, and then to realise
that it will change. That means using language as a changeable
fluid system, a series of floating signifiers. I want to end with a
poem by Geraldine Monk, in which the subject is a roller-coaster
hurtling through a plethora of impressions. There is also the
implication that language can foster a cuckoo-in-the nest situation, where the subject can sit heavily in its midst, inhabit it as a
secure retreat. 'Where's the cuckoo' the poem asks, the drunken
word-intoxicated subject asks, preferring the kaleidoscope to the
fixity of image and voice, and indeed the cuckoo has flown.

> 'Spring Bank'

> (I
> my(self)-per-por-trait-(or)
> roller coaster seaside
>   besides
> my undercurrent
> remains sub-
> and slightly bilious)

> the Alfa Romeo swoops downhill moor on hamlets
> inhail of stereo blastsmooth and
> swerves thick smoke/ash flying (from cradle to rocka rocka bye bye/
>   white   ashen fall

and accents dry   calcification)
for ale and whiskey

hung over
through noon to Kildale
watching climbers
a voice drifts with volcano fall-out and
moon blue mix with fluoresce of Rape and rock moss
in shadow and sunsting/whilst
high on Roxby the fox ghost silhouetting
four remarkable bottles of guinness –
                    Aeolian sounds of execution
tight warren of tunnels and doors
designed for lost souls in states of embarrassing
                                    emergencies

(The Fox is heavy)

Night and tiny finger on butterfly brooch mother
o' pearl wings and nails press then flutter
'Wher's the cuckoo'
(a short measure this)
'Where's the cuckoo'

a drunk sings high from Loftus to full and cloud split moon[35]

Notes

1 Helen Kidd, 'The Paper City', New Poetry from Oxford, 5, 1986, p. 4.

2 Carol Rumens' anthology, Making for the Open: The Chatto Book of Post-Feminist Poetry, 1964–1984, Chatto, London, 1985, contains many excellent poems, and yet the editorial comment consciously eschews feminism in a very blinkered and unrealistic way. On the other hand One Foot on the Mountain: An Anthology of British Feminist Poetry, 1969–1979, ed. Lilian Mohin, Only Women Press, London, 1980, has a sadly uneven collection of poems.

3 For two excellent examples see the poetry of W. S. Graham and Frank O'Hara. In particular, W. S. Graham, Collected Poems 1942–1977, Faber, London, 1977, and Frank O'Hara, The Collected Poems of Frank O'Hara, ed. Donald Allen, Alfred A. Knopf, New York, 1971.

4 Nancy Chodorow, The Reproduction of Mothering: Psycho-Analysis and the Sociology of Gender, Berkeley and Los Angeles, 1978, p. 169.

5 For example, Tom Raworth's wry juxtapositions of language snippets expose discrepancies and possibilities in minute microscopic close-ups of language. The humour of these observations is essentially a generous gesture which invites the reader to consider and enjoy the activity. See, for

example, his *Lazy Left Hand, Notes from 1970–1975*, Actual Size, London, 1986.

6 For Phyllis April King and Ivor Cutler's poetry the following records are recommended: *Dandruff*, Virgin, V2021, 1974; *Velvet Donkey*, Virgin, V2037, 1975; *Jammy Smears*, Virgin, 1976.

7 e.e.cummings, 'in Just', *Complete Poems 1913–1962*, New York, 1968.

8 Debbie Cameron in *Feminism and Linguistic Theory*, London, 1985, pp. 125–6, summarises Julia Kristeva's description of the pre-Oedipal phase thus:

> Kristeva discusses the pre-Oedipal Imaginary stage before language acquisition, in an interesting way. She suggests that before the symbolic order there is a semiotic order linked to oral and anal drives which flow across the child. The 'pulsions' of these drives are gathered in a choral (which means approximately, a recepticle). Later, when the child takes up a position in the symbolic order as a result of the castration complex, the contents of the chora will be repressed, but its influence will nevertheless be discernible in linguistic discourse through rhythm, intonation, gaps, meaninglessness and general textual disruption. Indeed some discourses, like art, poetry and madness, draw on the semiotic rather than the symbolic aspects of language.

9 For a useful comment on '*jouissance*' see the introduction to *New French Feminisms*, eds. Elaine Marks and Isabelle de Courtivron, Brighton, 1981, p. 36, n. 8:

> The verb jouir ('to enjoy, to experience sexual pleasure') and the substantive la jouissance ('sexual pleasure, bliss, rapture') occur frequently in the texts of the new French Feminisms. We have constantly used the English words 'sexual pleasure' in our translations. This pleasure, when attributed to a woman, is considered to be of a different order from the pleasure that is represented within the male libidinal economy often described in terms of the capitalist gain and profit motive. Women's jouissance carries with it the notion of fluidity, diffusion, duration. It is a kind of potlatch in the world of orgasms, a giving, expending, dispensing of pleasure without concern about ends or closure. One can easily see how the same imagery could be used to describe women's writing.

This is, in its turn, a development of Roland Barthes's idea of *jouissance*, which occurs in the 'writerly' text, where order is disrupted, 'the garment gapes', and disrupts the reader's expectations, bringing 'to a crisis the relation with language'. (Roland Barthes, *The Pleasure of the Text*, 1975).

10 Helen Kidd, 'Las Madres de la Plaza de Mayo', unpublished, 1985.

11 The cut-up technique was first coined and used by William Burroughs, and has been since used by writers such as Robert Sheppard, Allen Fisher and Kathy Acker and has been used as a form of social and language critique. Acker saturates the reader with violent collages of twentieth-century urban decadence, or male violence, with no contrast and with a uniformity of tone which emphasises its banality. I find her approach both bleak and voyeuristic. See Robert Sheppard, *The Frightened Summer*, Pig Press, 1981, and *Returns*, Textures, 1985; Allen Fisher, *Brixton Fractals*, Aloes Books, London, 1985 and *Buzzards and Bees*, Micro Brigade, London, 1987; Kathy Acker, *Empire of the Senseless*, Paladin, London, 1988.

12 See Dale Spender, *Man Made Language*, London, 1980.

13 For Eavan Boland's poetry see The Journey, Carcanet, Manchester, 1989, and Outside History, Carcanet, Manchester, 1990.

14 Helen Kidd, 'The Bower Meadow', Password Scop, Summer 1986.

15 Walton collaborated with Edith Sitwell, who spoke her poetry to his musical score.

16 Helen Kidd, 'Pansexuality', Writing Women, V, 3, 1988. The co-celebrants are Lorca, Hélène Cixous, Luce Irigaray and Monique Wittig. Those whom I call 'the chaperones' are Jacques Lacan, Sigmund Freud and D. H. Lawrence.

17 Elizabeth Grosz, Jacques Lacan: A Feminist Introduction, London and New York, 1990, p. 123.

18 See note 8. The foremother to this technique is, of course, Virginia Woolf.

19 'Pansexuality', Freud, see note 16.

20 Ibid.

21 See note 3. See also Basil Bunting's Briggflatts, Fulcrum, London, 1966.

22 However, as it is, in effect, an extension of that state of being which Chodorow describes, then it does tend to be harder for many men to move beyond the self-sealing notion of identity. Until this sense of separation is removed, sexuality for men, and in particular heterosexual men, will continue to be compartmentalised, end-directed and on and off like an electric light, rather than a continuum which vitalises everything. This situation is reinforced by touch taboos in the West, and by the system which rewards individuation of the separated self. To be interactive is not a condition bringing the rewards of money and power.

23 Bill Herbert writes in lalans Scots and in English, see Sharawaggi, W. N. Herbert and Robert Crawford, Polygon, Edinburgh, 1990. Keith Jebb writes in Shropshire dialect and English; his book A. E Housman is forthcoming.

24 Blast, ed. Wyndham Lewis, 1914, 1915.

25 Like Emily Dickinson I prefer to situate myself amongst writing women. I tend to think back through my literary mothers, Eilean Dubh, Mary Shelley, the Brontës, Virginia Woolf, Edith Sitwell, Gertrude Stein, Mina Loy, H. D., Marge Piercy, Adrienne Rich, and across cultures to other women, Sunita Namjoshi, Ntozake Shange, Rabia, Joy Harjo and Huang O.

26 Helen Kidd, 'For the Stillborn', unpublished, 1985.

27 Julia Kristeva, Revolution in Poetic Language, trans. M. Walker, New York, 1984.

28 'Will Our Hero be Dashed to Pieces on the Jagged Rocks Below?' This is an extract from the poem, which is unpublished, written in 1986.

29 Wendy Mulford, 'Notes on writing. A Marxist/Feminist viewpoint', On Gender and Writing, ed. Micheline Wandor, Pandora, London, 1983, p. 35.

30 Another poet who employs such images is Eric Mottram. See Elegies, Galloping Dog Press, Newcastle, 1981.

31 Wendy Mulford, The East Anglia Sequence; this extract from Reality Studios, 18, 1986.

32 Ibid.

33 Denise Riley, 'such face bones . . .', *Dry Air*, Virago, London, 1985, p. 19.

34 Ibid., p. 7.

35 Geraldine Monk, 'Spring Bank', *Tiger Lilies*, Rivelin, London and Bradford, 1980, and *The New British Poetry*, eds. Alnutt, D'Aguiar, Edwards and Mottram, Paladin, London, 1988, pp. 317–18.

Case studies

David Miller

7

Heart of saying:
the poetry of Gael Turnbull

I

In spite of the publication of a virtual Collected Poems from a
well-known publisher in 1983,[1] and the respect of many of his
peers, Gael Turnbull remains a neglected poet, whose work has
been little discussed.[2] Although he has published books and
chapbooks since 1954,[3] and two significant and fairly comprehensive volumes were made available in 1968 and 1970 respectively,[4] he has been noticeably absent from critical accounts of
British poetry in the post-second-world-war years.[5]

The reasons are, I would say, various. There is a quietness to
his work, a lack of the dramatic, 'showy' or spectacular that would
catch the attention of those who are not attuned to less obvious,
but one might argue, truer poetic qualities. The man himself has
never been in the least self-advertising; and while as he has not
followed any of the more acceptable paths laid down by influential British mainstream critics, he has, presumably, been too individual and non-doctrinaire to suit the liking of some of the more
rigid and dogmatic proponents of 'advanced' or 'innovative' writing. I should add, to be fair, that Turnbull's oeuvre is somewhat
uneven, and his more 'conventional' poems are not, I think, as
successful or as interesting as his work with exploratory forms.[6]

However, there remains a body of distinguished and exciting work, which deserves much greater attention than it has hitherto received.

II

Because Gael Turnbull remains a semi-visible (which is also to say, semi-invisible) figure, it would not be amiss to set down a few biographical facts. Turnbull was born in Edinburgh in 1928, and educated at Cambridge University and the University of Pennsylvania.[7] He spent periods in Canada, England, and the USA during the years 1940–64, settling in England in 1964, where he remained until his retirement from the medical profession and a move to Scotland in 1989. These facts are significant, because Turnbull's residence in Canada and the USA made him aware of developments in poetry in those countries. In 1953, the Canadian poet Raymond Souster put him in touch with Cid Corman, one of the prime movers in what came to be known as 'the new American poetry', and through Corman and his excellent and influential magazine *Origin*, he came to know the work of Robert Creeley, Charles Olson, Robert Duncan, and others. When he returned to England in 1955, he served as a link between American and British poetry, making work available through his Migrant Books (later Migrant Press), as well as through his circulation of books from such US presses as Divers, Origin and Jargon. He published a selected poems by Robert Creeley, *The Whip*, in 1957, and had plans (never realised) for bringing out Olson's 'O'Ryan' sequence (later published by White Rabbit). While he was still in England, he received a visit from Louis Zukofsky, one of the most important of twentieth-century American poets, but at that time still little-known. During this period, he also established contact with various British poets, including Roy Fisher, Charles Tomlinson, and the veteran modernist Basil Bunting. Turnbull went back to the States in 1958, and began publishing the magazine *Migrant* in 1959. With Michael Shayer in Worcester as a contributing editor, *Migrant* lasted until its eighth issue, in 1960. That same year, Turnbull resumed publishing chapbooks (under the name of Migrant Press), and during the next six years such poets as Edward Dorn (writing on Olson's 'Maximus' poems), Roy Fisher, Matthew Mead, Ian Hamilton Finlay, Anselm Hollo, Edwin Morgan, and Turnbull himself appeared under the Migrant imprint.[8]

Turnbull published a good deal in these years. He was a contributor to both Origin and Black Mountain Review, amongst other journals, and he also brought out a number of chapbooks, including one from Corman's Origin Press in Ashland, Mass. (*Bjarni Spike-Helgi's son and other poems*, 1956). The Cape Goliard/ Grossman collections, *A Trampoline* (1968) and *Scantlings* (1970) were his major collections until *A Gathering of Poems* in 1983, but mention should also be made of three individual publications: *Twenty Words, Twenty Days: A Sketchbook and a Morula* (Migrant Press, Birmingham, 1966), *Residues: Down the Sluice of Time* (Grosseteste, Pensnett, Staffs., 1976), and *Residues: Thronging the Heart* (Aggie Weston's, Belper, Derbyshire, 1976); these three long poems are, I would maintain, Turnbull's most important works. He has continued to publish chapbooks, but no large collection has appeared since *A Gathering of Poems*.

III

In the Preface to the 'New Canadian Poetry' issue of *Artisan*, Turnbull wrote:

> Poetry can't afford place names. British? American? These appellations don't mean too much. Except as an individual, working at his craft, may happen to reflect the circumstances of speech in which he is involved. Only in this sense may one speak of a 'national' idiom in writing.
>
> To look for such an idiom in 'tradition' is to miss the point. The cry 'Make It New' doesn't mean abandoning what we have. It means finding what we have, what is now; and not what was.[9]

There is a common prejudice to the effect that modernism and postmodernism are somehow foreign to British writing. To confirm a dominant American (or European) influence on radical poetry in the UK may in some respects set up a false emphasis, obscuring what is genuinely individual (and British, whether one defines this in the limited sense Turnbull gives to 'a "national" idiom' or in a stronger sense depending upon a particular set of characteristics) in the work done by modernists like David Jones and Basil Bunting and postmodernists like Tom Raworth and Thomas A. Clark.[10]

It would be true to say that, amongst his peers and his elders, it is certain American poets whose preoccupations link up most strongly with Turnbull's. We can see this by simply quoting two remarks of Louis Zukofsky's. In his seminal essay 'A statement for poetry', written in 1950, Zukofsky declared that the poet's 'ear is sincere, if his words convey his awareness of the range of differences and subtleties of duration. He does not measure with handbook, and is not a pendulum.'[11] He asks: '... what specifically is good poetry?' and answers: 'It is precise information on existence out of which it grows, and information of its own existence, that is, the movement (and tone) of words. Rhythm, pulse, keeping time with existence, is the distinction of its technique.'[12]

However, in contradistinction to a range of poets who privileged such notions as impulse, process, and spontaneity[13] – Allen Ginsberg, Charles Olson, Jack Spicer, and Robert Duncan are notable examples, in their different ways – Zukofsky's work is informed by a dialectical or dialogic movement between impulse and plan, or between heuristic process and projection of structural determinants.[14] In this regard, Turnbull is nearer, in his most important poems, to Zukofsky than he is to most other American poets in the sixties and seventies.

In their own quite different ways, Basil Bunting and Roy Fisher can be seen as sustaining similar concerns.[15] I emphasise Bunting and Fisher amongst British poets, because Migrant Press published or acted as distributor for their work,[16] and Turnbull has also written essays on them; also because Bunting was, with David Jones, pre-eminent amongst Turnbull's elders in British poetry, as Fisher was amongst his contemporaries. Bunting addressed himself to a poetry rooted both in direct experience, and in complex patterns of sound, image and meaning distinct from the more conventional orderings found in 'closed' verse.[17] Turnbull's admiration for Bunting is evident throughout his essay *An Arlespenny. Some notes on the poetry of Basil Bunting . . .* (1965).[18] He writes, for example:

> For myself I re-read Bunting's poems for many pleasures, but chiefly these: The conviction of direct knowledge of physical experience; and, an unfailing devotion to the poem as a construction of words to be both said and heard, and not merely read with the eye. . . . But it is by the voice that I am held. Not sound in any way cultivated for itself, as separate; but spoken and heard with the full sense that it is only by articulate speech that we can know anything, and that no word exists until it is spoken and heard.[19]

More to the point, at least in terms of my argument in this essay, is Bunting's concern with a 'structure of meanings . . . [which] are organised according to a musical architecture – that of sonata form',[20] and at another level, the schematic or diagrammatic structure which Bunting claimed was the basis of the complex exploratory patterns of *Briggflats*.[21]

Turnbull's rambling text about Fisher, 'Resonances & speculations, upon reading Roy Fisher's *City*',[22] centres upon Fisher's (and Turnbull's) sense of landscape as *human* landscape;[23] upon the fact that Fisher 'is concerned to perceive and to declare his perception';[24] and that, in common with many of their American peers, they had found that:

> in writing, it is not a matter of a certain material which is *there*, as a fixed thing, upon which the writing feeds and works. The act of writing also serves to nourish the material. When we speak of something, we affect it. It isn't quite the same. As we cannot altogether 'will' what we would say. The very language we use is not 'mine' but is only 'ours'; and what we would say, of any material, is shaped by those others both past and present; as it is also shaped by the meanings which are in the material itself, meanings which perhaps we discover rather than create.[24]

Much of Fisher's best work arguably results from the combination of 'perceptual attentions'[25] with a methodology dictating particular sets of formal/structural determinants, and the use of various 'defamiliarising' techniques. If one quotes Fisher's own comment on 'The Ship's Orchestra': '. . . along with a lot of things I do, it was rigorously composed in an additive form. That is, each section was written in an attempt to refer only to what I had already written in that work, and without any drive forward at all',[26] it's entirely possible to see why Robert Sheppard should have asked Fisher, in *Turning the Prism: An Interview with Roy Fisher*, whether 'Twenty Words, Twenty Days' had had any influence on the form of 'The Ship's Orchestra' and 'The Cut Pages'.[27] Fisher replied: 'Not a direct influence, but [it was] one of those things where there is common ground . . .'.[28]

IV

Roy Fisher reviewed 'Twenty Words, Twenty Days' in *tlaloc*,[29] after Turnbull's poem-sequence had appeared as a pamphlet from Migrant Press. The review is worth quoting at some length. Fisher writes that:

> It is a reflective poem which progresses by means of a game, a set of comparatively abstract propositions of no particular significance in themselves, which both stimulate and limit what goes on.
>
> The game was a simple one, of the order of *bouts-rimés* or charades. It consisted, apparently, of picking a word at random from a dictionary each day for twenty days, and working associations from it. The interesting thing is that, apart from one or two instances where the 'given' word happens to be intransigently arch or bland so that the game plays the player, the exercise is not a mechanical work-out leading to a set of studied variations; it is made to produce a very personal poem, having a rhythm, continuity and consistency of its own and carrying the twenty words and days along with it. The game was in fact a stalking-horse; the poet's way of getting himself to recognize what was on his mind.
>
> Something more follows from this. It would have been very easy, I think, for Turnbull to have removed from the poem most of the evidence of how he came to write it; to have vamped up a title or a topic out of what turned up (Kennedy's assassination for one thing, as it happened) and to have passed it off as something less arbitrary than it is. But attention is directed to these matters: . . . the twenty words are left, capitalized and screwed into their particular

sections, and are obviously meant to be obtrusive, almost like the ideograms in the *Cantos*.[30]

Fisher concludes the review: 'You get the impression of a man accused and challenged by this selection of words as if by dreams, and with no way of answering except by the inconsequential-looking truth. In this, he picks up a type of preoccupation found in many of his shorter poems, and gets a good deal further with it.'[31]

'Twenty Words, Twenty Days' has, as I have already stated, a particular importance in Turnbull's *oeuvre*, together with 'Residues: Thronging the Heart' and 'Residues: Down the Sluice of Time'. Without wanting to denigrate the shorter poems – and indeed, I think that such poems as 'An Irish Monk on Lindisfarne About 650 AD', 'Black Spruce, Northern Ontario', 'Homage to Jean Follain', 'A Hill', 'Thoughts on the One Hundred and Eighty-Third Birthday of J. M. W. Turner', and 'George Fox, From His Journals', are remarkable and finely achieved pieces of writing – the three long poems are arguably his best, and are certainly his most developed and sustained attempts at a poetry that proceeds from both plan and impulse, as well as continuity and dis-continuity, and a sense of tradition and a sense of moment-by-moment 'flow'.[32]

'Twenty Words, Twenty Days', in the way that it works from random selections from the dictionary embedded as isolated words in the movement of a language seeking to disclose the 'heart', i.e. the emotional strands of personal being which come together as if to form the 'core' of one's existence, and from an almost diaristic regard for what occurs in the writer's life (including memories and reflections), throws both the details of language and the details of living into relief. In other words, language and experience are foregrounded in their intersecting, their interplay; so that they are clearly *not* treated as if identical, or as if either might be simply 'transparent'. Turnbull keeps his attention on both the particulars of language and the particulars of 'lived' modalities of being. (And as he states in 'A Hill': 'The joy is in the attention.')[33] The connections are sometimes oblique, odd,

in relation to the process of inserting a chance-derived word/
concept into the occurrences of a particular day (which, as I have
said, include what might be termed 'subjective' or perhaps more
correctly 'interior' occurrences), but the semantic contiguities of
these passages set up a field or matrix of energies, tensions,
suggestive of Olsonian 'composition by field'.[34] It is often extraordinary with what grace Turnbull effects a paradoxical marriage
of continuous and discontinuous impulses:

awakening this morning, as the alarm rang, a guilt –

unexpectedly remembering a girl I met once years ago,
while on holiday, out walking in the Appalachians –

how I came upon her on the trail, high on the ridge,
having seen no one for two days: she in shorts, with
rucksack, plodding the same direction but more slowly,
a student from some university and taking . . . what
was it? . . . geology? –
        and she wanted to talk, so it
seemed, a bit lonely too I suppose, a gawky kid and more
than slightly eccentric to be way off there by herself –

and I turned, turned from her because my mind said that
she was ugly, not attractive, a physical aversion, a
disdain, not the woman I imagined for myself at such time
and such place –
        and I walked on ahead as quickly as I
could, as if in flight, as if actually pursued –
             as I flee
the vague guilt, the regret that follows me closely even
to this moment –
        that I should have feared such an
ordinary smile, of someone out there on that mountain,
trudging the same route, sweating the same pack, seeing
the same endless trees –
        assuaging the same oppressions
heavy on me –
        yes, surely the same, surely, however
different –
      or at variance –
         and yes, PRECONCERTED –

the whole thing 'fixed', 'rigged', a 'set up' –

       granted

the facts of my birth, natural disposition, upbringing,

and so forth –

     no escape; and all now escaped, gone –

before I knew fully, without possibility of appeal –

as I do appeal, nonetheless, not knowing to whom –

              as

gesture –

   and indictment –[35]

I want to note here the largely conversational 'tone', the non-rhetorical and anti-decorative, spare and economical (although not highly compressed) language, and the quietly stated, or understated, impress of emotion. These qualities should not make one miss, however, the sometimes abrupt and fragmented concatenation of phrases (more evident, admittedly, in other sections than here), nor the charged quality of the 'turn' in the movement of the poem, at 'PRECONCERTED', which word Turnbull lets himself be led by in a heuristic process, so that the diaristic recording of a memory and its attendant emotions is allowed to crystallise into a broader, deeper sense of things.

'Twenty Words, Twenty Days' is, apart from its visual/rhythmic shifts like those of 'verse' lineation,[36] a close kin of that 'poetry in prose' which is so notable in contemporary writing, whether standing alone or in conjunction with lineated poetry; I am thinking, for example, of much of David Jones's work, of John Ashbery's 'Three Poems' and 'The Ice Storm', of Roy Fisher's 'City', 'The Ship's Orchestra' and 'The Cut Pages', and of Robert Lax's 'The Circus of the Sun' and '21 Pages'.

V

'Residues: Down the Sluice of Time' and 'Residues: Thronging the Heart',[37] are so closely related that they can be considered together. (In fact, 'Residues: Thronging the Heart' reads very much as if a continuation of the other, longer poem.[38])

To use Kenneth Cox's term, these poems may seem 'bipolar' in their structuring process, except that the 'terms' are involved in something more like a dialogue (as Cox admits). To put this another way: Turnbull's concern with observation or 'reporting' on the one hand and personal feeling or reflection on the other, is paralleled by a 'binary' concern with continuity and discontinuity, in the actual writing, but these concerns are treated as intersecting, rather than forming an absolute opposition. This fundamentally dialogic approach is extended to the more thematic strands of the poem: time as moment-by-moment experience on the one hand, and time as tradition (the bearing of the past upon the present), time as transmission or endurance (or conversely, loss); or again, the 'hard', 'dark' aspects of existence, such as suffering, disease and death, and the epiphanic, joyful, or humanly engaging aspects.[39] Through sudden shifts, juxtapositions, interruptions, Turnbull assumes the complex task of illuminating the 'lived' modalities of existence, especially the 'heart' and its relationship to 'saying': 'not there, not there – voice of/ the heart – what's dear and near, gone/ out – returning – turning in the/ heart – and on the air'.[40] In much of what he writes in these poems, I am reminded of what Turnbull said of Basil Bunting: 'The central "concern" of Bunting in his poems is the slightness of the individual under the span of Time, and before Death; and the courage, absurdity, pathos, and sheer variety of means by which men face their destiny. One such "means" is the making of poems.'[41] The unflinching attention to grim details of human existence may also, at times, bring the great American poet Charles Reznikoff to mind:

> no use to deny
>   last quarrel with his wife, in a fury
>   struck her, knocked her down the stairs,
>   saw she was dead, took gun from wall, went
>   upstairs, smashed in the children's skulls
>   before they woke and then the dog, went
>   down, took paraffin, set fire to the
>   cottage, back upstairs, lay down on his
>   bed, muzzle to mouth, blew out his brains –[42]

Elsewhere, we are drawn into an epiphanic moment, a revelation
of luminosity and splendour within experience, leading back to
'the heart'. 'Residues: Down the Sluice of Time' ends:

> and at midnight, cold and old, in
> the absolute of their vastness, far,
> the stars are strewn in the dark:
> a precipitate of shimmers, mica seeds,
> of milky crystals, hoarfrost grains,
> a dust of spicules, flaring glints,
> a spume of shivered silver, diamantine
> flecks, an archipelago of quivered light

> from an edge of iron
> against a grindstone, thrust –
> for a moment held
> against the wheel of time

> snow flakes on the wind –
> and her finger tips graze chill
> beneath my shirt – along the ridge
> and furrows of my ribs –
> questing for home, for warmth
> in the heart's fold –
> till skin and sinew quake
> and pulse rewake [43]

VI

In 'Residues: Thronging the Heart', Turnbull writes:

> and the auld worthies of the Kirk
> in the Catechism, their first question:
> the chief end?
> and their answer:
> to glorify

> to sublime, to heat
> to transformation

> by dint
> of each particular[45]

This 'transformation// by dint/ of each particular' is, I believe, at
the heart of Gael Turnbull's poetics. It will be fitting to close this

examination of his work by referring to one of Turnbull's rare public statements on his poetic beliefs. He begins *some resonances and speculations* with a natural event,[45] a thunderstorm, and speaks of the lightning's

> inscription/ across the blackboard of the night/ making utterance of its urgency/ declaring a transit of energy/ along a line and through time/ a graphic act, an elocution/ demanding attention, alerting splendour.[46]

He goes on to refer to human articulation in its power to 'force through incoherence/ to alert even one ear against/ all the deaf-mutes of the humdrum'.[47] However,

> it takes effort even to listen/ even to yourself, an intention/ that consumes, that uses energy/ must be directed as a blow-torch/ to burn off the rust, to smelt inertia/ or as fire in a kiln/ fed by the up-draught of the heart/ to anneal the ceramic of the will/ into an instant of conception.[48]

For Turnbull, poetry is a transformation of the humdrum, the inertia, of the everyday into a disclosure, a release, a transmission of splendour not unlike the lightning's splendour. 'Twenty Words, Twenty Days' stands, in particular, as testimony of what may be revealed by attention to the details of day-to-day personal existence. Towards the end of *some resonances and speculations*, he writes: 'inscribing lines, smearing paint/ muttering words, repeating rhythms/ neither for something or for nothing/ but because we must also transmit/ whatever radiance is trapped within us'.[49]

Notes

1 Gael Turnbull, *A Gathering of Poems: 1950–1980*, Anvil Press Poetry, London, 1983.

2 The main critical discussion of his work to date is Kenneth Cox's review-essay, 'Gael Turnbull's poetry', *Scripsi*, Melbourne, II, 4, June 1984.

3 His first collection was *Trio*, with Eli Mandel and Phyllis Webb, Contact Press, Toronto, 1954.

4 *A Trampoline: Poems 1952–1964*, Cape Goliard, London and Grossman, NY, 1968; *Scantlings: Poems 1964–1969*, Cape Goliard and Grossman, 1970.

5 To take just two examples of books in which one might have expected to
   find some discussion of Turnbull, I would mention the lack of any account
   of his work in M. L. Rosenthal's *The New Poets: American and British Poetry Since
   World War II*, Oxford University Press, New York, 1967, and A. Kingsley
   Weatherhead's *The British Dissonance: Essays on Ten Contemporary Poets*, University
   of Missouri Press, Columbia, Missouri, 1983. (Turnbull is mentioned, but
   only in passing, in the latter book.)

6 The best of Turnbull's work is written in a form of 'free verse' which
   explores the area between impulse and plan, as I will explain later. But I
   would add that in general the term 'exploratory' may be used for any work
   that seeks to explore, discover, and deal with what is unfamiliar, rather than
   compose in ready-made forms with a view to inventive and decorative
   stylisations of language.

7 My information for this section comes from two articles by Turnbull,
   'Charlotte Chapel, the Pittsburgh Draft Board and *Some Americans*: a personal
   memoir', *PN Review*, Manchester, 28, 1982, and 'Migrant – a personal
   account', *Credences*, Buffalo, NY, I, 2/3, Fall/Winter 1981–82, as well as private
   correspondence with the poet.

8 Michael Shayer and Roy Fisher were involved with running Migrant Press
   from 1963–66 and 1964–66 respectively.

9 *Artisan*, Liverpool, 6, Autumn 1954, p. 1.

10 I am using the term 'postmodernism' to imply, not anti-modernism, but a
    writing that in some sense goes beyond modernism, or explores alternative
    possibilities than those identified with so-called 'dominant' modes of
    modernism.
       I should also gloss the term 'radical', which I am using in the sense of a
    departure from the more dominant or established aesthetic norms.

11 *Kulchur*, New York, III, 10, Summer 1963, p. 52. Compare Turnbull's poem 'If
    He Sings It': 'Not the degradations/ of a metronome// or the mere con-
    trivings/ of better mousetraps// but an architecture of/ pauses// and evi-
    dence/ like a footprint.' (*A Gathering of Poems: 1950–1980*, p. 19.)

12 'A statement for poetry', *Kulchur*, p. 50.

13 See Duncan's comment:

    . . . with the *Pisan Cantos* of Ezra Pound and *Paterson* of William Carlos Williams, with
    the *Symphony in Three Movements* of Stravinsky, I began to be aware of the possibility
    that the locus of form might be in the immediate minim of the work, and that one
    might concentrate upon the sound and meaning present where one was and derive
    melody and story from impulse not from plan.

    (*Towards an Open Universe*, Aquila Publishing, Portree, Isle of Skye, 1982, n.p.)

14 Michael Heller provides a good account of Zukofsky's principles and
    practice in his book *Conviction's Net of Branches: Essays on the Objectivist Poets and
    Poetry*, Southern Illinois University Press, Carbondale, 1985. For the notion
    of structure in artistic work, see Anthony Braxton's apposite remarks in
    Graham Lock, *Forces in Motion: Anthony Braxton and the Meta-Reality of Creative
    Music*, Quartet Books, London, 1988, especially where Braxton speaks of 'a

structural situation or a language situation that has particular variables which will allow certain things to happen . . .' (p. 232).

15 Needless to say, there are considerable differences between all these poets, but I'm only concerned here with those things they have in common.

16 Migrant Press distributed Bunting's long poem *The Spoils* (published by The Morden Tower Book Room, Newcastle upon Tyne, in 1965), and published Fisher's *City* in 1961 (supplement, 1963).

17 Robert Duncan's justly celebrated essay, 'Ideas of the meaning of form', published in *Kulchur*, New York, 4, 1961, gives a good idea of the dissatisfaction with 'closed verse', beyond the question of the mere employment of traditional verse forms. Duncan points out that the whole process of poetic discovery, and the poet's concern with the unfamiliar, is occluded through emphasis upon rational control, manipulation of literary 'devices', etc.

18 Privately published. No place of publication given.

19 *An Arlespenny*, (no place of publication given), p. 4.

20 Anthony Suter, 'Musical structures in the poetry of Basil Bunting', *Agenda*, London, XVI, 1, Spring, p. 47.

21 'Once I had got the thing clear in my head as a diagram, I simply set to work and wrote it', Bunting told Peter Quartermain and Warren Tallman, in 'Basil Bunting talks about *Briggflatts*', *Agenda*, London, XVI, 1, Spring 1978, p. 17. I should, however, note that the diagrammatic structure is not at all self-evident, whereas Turnbull's structural determinants, in a work like 'Twenty Words, Twenty Days', are fairly obvious to an attentive reader. Finally, I should also note that 'Briggflatts' postdates 'Twenty Words, Twenty Days', and cannot be thought of as a precedent for Turnbull's work in this area.

22 'Resonances & speculations, upon reading Roy Fisher's City', *Kulchur*, New York, II, 7, Autumn 1962. It is sufficiently rambling to include an account of a visit to Basil Bunting, which has no overt reference to the subject of the essay.

23 For Turnbull, it is *only* the 'humanized' landscape that is meaningful.

24 Turnbull, 'Resonances', p. 27.

25 The phrase is Jed Rasula's; see Rasula and Mike Erwin, 'An interview with Roy Fisher', in Roy Fisher, *Nineteen Poems and an Interview*, Grosseteste, Pensnett, Staffs., 1975, p. 13.

26 *Ibid.*, p. 14.

27 Toad's Damp Press, London, 1986, p. 19.

28 *Ibid.*, p. 19. See also Fisher's comment on p. 18: 'Gael and I: very different people, but I suspect we influence each other in funny ways as the years go by.' Fisher's *Poems: 1955–1980* (OUP, 1980) bears the dedication: 'For Gael Turnbull'.

29 *Tlaloc*, Leeds, 13, 1966.

30 *Ibid.*, n.p.

31 *Ibid.*, n.p.

32 Kenneth Cox, in his insightful essay on Turnbull, identifies the fact that 'Each [poem] is generated from two opposing sources which alternate and interact without conflicting', and comments: 'Technically these poems are among the most original written in English during the past two decades.' ('Gael Turnbull's poetry', *Scripsi*, II, 4, June 1984, p. 97.)

33 *A Gathering of Poems: 1950–1980*, p. 52.

34 Olson, in his famous 'Projective verse' essay, insists upon an interplay and a propulsion of energies and perceptions. The essay is conveniently available in *The Poetics of the New American Poetry*, ed. Donald M. Allen and Warren Tallman, Grove Press, New York, 1973.

35 *A Gathering of Poems: 1950–1980*, pp. 78–9.

36 For example, at the phrase 'as gesture', near the end of the poem I have quoted.

37 As stated, these poems both appeared as booklets in 1976.

38 For a complementary view of 'Residues: Down the Sluice of Time', see John Freeman's review, 'RESIDUES by Gael Turnbull', *Poetry Information*, London, 16, Winter 1976–77.

39 In the most general terms, an epiphany is a moment of experience in which the world is seen *sub specie aeternitatis*.

40 'Residues: Down the Sluice of Time' (*A Gathering of Poems: 1950–1980*, p. 139).

41 *An Arlespenny*, p. 2.

42 'Residues: Down the Sluice of Time', (*A Gathering of Poems: 1950–1980*, p. 133).

43 Ibid., pp. 145–6.

44 Ibid., p. 149.

45 The title-page reads in full:

some resonances and speculations// on and/ for An Artists' Eye// and Doazy Bor/ and various ears// on/ Sunday the 21st/ of October 1979// in the Corn Exchange// at Saffron Walden/ in Essex.

The booklet itself is undated and no place of publication is given. I should note that Turnbull presumably didn't value the piece sufficiently *as poetry* to include it in *A Gathering of Poems*.

46 *Some resonances and speculations . . .*, p. 1.

47 Ibid., p. 3.

48 Ibid, p. 3.

49 Ibid., p. 8.

Since this essay was written, a major collection of Gael Turnbull's poetry has been published: *While Breath Persists*, Porcupine's Quill Press, Erin, Ontario, 1992.

Peter Barry

8

Allen Fisher
and 'content-specific' poetry

One of the symptoms of the loss of nerve and ambition which has characterised British poetry in the past thirty years is the neglect of the long poem as a vehicle for a range of concerns beyond the merely personal and anecdotal. As Donald Davie has argued, a poet of lasting significance must have 'a politics and a philosophy of history', and to abandon these entirely is to 'opt out of twentieth century endeavour in poetry', to 'cop out more or less shamefully'. But, he adds, 'that cop-out is not carried like a brand of Cain by subsequent generations of British poets'.[1] In other words, the fact that recent British poetry has been so much taken up with coastal sailing need not deter others from attempting an ocean voyage. And beyond the lists of the major presses we will find many poets who have not been content to confine themselves to our 'insular obsession' with domestic anecdote and ingenious imagery. One such poet is Allen Fisher, whose major work, *Place*, is similar in scale, and to some extent in method, to poems like Ezra Pound's *Cantos*, William Carlos Williams's *Paterson*, Charles Olson's *Maximus*, and Louis Zukofsky's *A*.

   Place and its related materials appeared in a wide range of formats and publications between the mid-1970s and the mid-1980s. Sections 1 to 37 of the poem were published as a single volume in 1976 by Truck Press (St Paul, Minnesota) under the title

Place I–XXXVII, and an extract from that volume will be discussed here.[2] The part chosen is the fourth of the thirty-seven sections in the Truck Press book, which takes up nine of the one hundred pages in the volume; four of these nine pages are reproduced in full in the appendix to this chapter, as these are the ones discussed in greatest detail. The pages used are the first two of Part IV (lines 1–35 in my re-numbering) and the sixth and seventh (lines 36–73). The remaining five pages are commented upon more briefly wherever an appreciation of the poet's line of thought seems to require some reference to them. What is attempted here is the detailed contextual analysis of a very small part of a very large work; in relation to the size of the whole it is equivalent to a commentary on just one of Pound's cantos. As in the *Cantos*, too, many different kinds of material are used in *Place*, so that the section examined is in no sense typical of the subject-matter of the whole. On the other hand, again like the *Cantos*, the method remains fairly consistent throughout, with open-field collages of quoted material and commentary being interwoven, and a range of thematic concerns and recurrent images quickly establishing themselves. In that limited sense the section discussed here can be taken as representative.

1
What is meant by 'content-specific'?

The critic L. S. Dembo, in an illuminating remark about the *Cantos*, says that they are 'not only a pastiche of Pound's reading: they are virtually a mirror of Pound in the act of reading' (*Concepts of Reality in Modern American Poetry*, p. 170).[3] This is equally true of many major modernist poems – *The Waste Land*, David Jones's *Anathemata*, *Paterson* – the focus is, in varying degrees, the author in the act of reading, so that readers need to reactivate that body of reading in order to enter the poem. It is important to realise, though, that doing this isn't just a preliminary to the reading of the poem: a reciprocal process takes place in which we read the sources in the light of the poem and the poem in the light of the sources, and this is the characteristically modernist reading experience. So the text is (to subvert a Barthesian term) readerly in two senses: firstly, it is *about* reading, as a way of engaging with and making sense of the world, and secondly, it demands the reader's sustained participatory engagement with its materials, as well as with 'the words on the page'. The kind of reading required is thus an active (often retro-active) process like study, but since there is little likelihood that the documentary sources of modernist works could be traced independently by each individual reader, it often requires the help of mediating figures (as, for instance, *Ulysses* needed Stuart Gilbert and his successors, and the *Cantos* needed Hugh Kenner).[4]

As *Paterson* is centred upon the town of Paterson, New Jersey, and *Maximus* on Gloucester, Massachusetts, so *Place* takes as its focus South London, where Fisher was living at the time of composition. The abiding concern is what Eric Mottram calls a 'locationary action', the subject's attempts to 'place' himself, within a specific locale, within his culture, and within the historical and political juncture we inhabit with him. The poem draws throughout on a number of historical sources, such as Walter Besant's popular work *South London*, published posthumously in 1912. This book was a portion of his *Survey of London*, which, as the title indicates, was intended as a modern version of the London *Survey* of the sixteenth-century antiquary John Stow. Besant's main interest was in fleshing out the bare bones of archaeological and documentary evidence, in the manner of the great Victorian dinosaur reconstructions from fossil remains. But the question Fisher poses in Part IV of *Place* (the focus of the present chapter) goes beyond mere antiquarian contemplation of the past and asks what can be learned of and from it for present use in these rows of streets 'strung out in rhythm with the railway'?

The overt subject-matter of Part IV concerns the many tributary rivers of the Thames which were covered over and lost to view in the course of London's development in the nineteenth century. Fisher's written source is Nicholas Barton's *The Lost Rivers of London* (Leicester University Press, 1962), a meticulous work which documents the fate of these tributaries, for the most part now buried forever beneath London's streets. Fisher walks the course of each of the lost rivers, and this section of Place records his thinking and reading about the significance of these buried rivers, rather as Richard Long's photographs record his reflective 'land art'. As Fisher has said in interview, he used these rivers as, among other things, a metaphor for thought.

In his use of the London rivers as a way of thinking about ways of thinking Fisher shows the 'Martian' poets how metaphor might actually be *used*, with heuristic intent, as a way of exploring our construction of reality, rather than just as a brightly-coloured, high-tech form of entertainment which merely ruffles the surface of a world which is accepted and unquestioned. Using his modernist working methods of collage, juxtaposition, and 'open-field' techniques he subjects this highly specific content to the greatest possible pressure, so that the fullest range of implication and resonance can emerge. He is no mere imitator of his modernist predecessors, and one of his main innovations is this detailed use of scientific and historical data, as exemplified by the 'lost rivers' material discussed here.

It might be useful to have a name for poetry of this kind, poetry which explores highly specific materials and data with heuristic intent and as implicit metaphor. A useful analogy is with the kind of art known as 'site-specific' work, typified by the large-scale public sculptures and installations of David Mach. His installation 'Here to Stay' of 1990 used over 100 tons of magazines and newspapers to construct twelve giant columns around the cast-iron supports of the Tramway exhibition centre in Glasgow. 'Site-specific' work like this is built into and integrated with its display space: it therefore challenges the most basic assumptions about art objects (for instance, that they should be permanent, portable, and saleable) and demands new kinds of interaction between art-work and audience (for instance, it deconstructs the basis of conventional aesthetic judgements and values). Likewise, poetry such as Fisher's is fully integrated with the scientific, his-torical, and social data which is built into it, thereby challenging preconceptions about what constitutes the poetic, and demand-ing the kind of 'study reading' mentioned above. We might there-fore call such work 'content-specific' poetry.

2
Using the 'Lost Rivers'

As would be expected, Fisher makes particular use in Part IV of Barton's chapter 'The lost rivers of the South' which begins with a comment on Besant's theory that in pre-Roman times 'the Thames in the London area spread out into a vast shallow lagoon, covering almost the whole alluvial plain' (Barton, p. 40). In fact, says Barton, 'the level of the Thames today is some fifteen feet higher . . . than in Roman times, since Roman huts have been found at Tilbury thirteen feet below the present high water mark'; the Thames may not have been tidal as far up as London, since there was 'a yew forest at the period on the marshes below Dagenham', and nor is there evidence of 'the construction of embankments at this period' (pp. 40–1).

This is the information compressed by Fisher in lines 1–7 (see Appendix. From here on line numbers of cited passages will be given in brackets). Besant's 'old lagoon' theory was an attractive hypothesis which accounted for a good deal of otherwise puzzling data, enabling him, too, to offer an etymology for the name 'London' itself as being derived from *Llyn*, a lake, and *Dynas*, a dwelling. But the discoveries at Tilbury are conclusive proof that the synthesis was premature and must be abandoned. The 'old lagoon' then becomes emblematic in the poem of the urge to escape the pressures of complex and multifarious data by rushing to conclusions. It is thus a counterweight to an image used elsewhere in *Place*, that of the 'oak in miniature', whereby the bonsai, the miniature tree in its glass container, symbolised the need to crystallise the sprawling mass of disparate data which enquiry always throws out into a neat concept or guiding thesis, no matter how provisional this might be. However, with the warning of the 'old lagoon' in mind, all the conclusions reached or posited in section IV are provisional and tentative: Remarks such as 'I couldn't get to the matter of this' (45) and 'I was uncertain of the trouble here' (70) are typical of its meditative tone; the 'measure' throughout the section, as throughout much of the whole work, is that of the mind thinking; it faithfully reproduces the characteristic hesitations, doublings, and parentheses of all original thought, what Coleridge memorably called 'the *drama* of reason' (letter to Poole, January 28, 1810). Thus, as the speaker looks across the river at night to the Tilbury container-ship berths ('the fairy lights east of Dagenham') he thinks of the Roman huts and the yew forest which once occupied the ground, and of the implications of these simple facts:

> the embankments do not mark a new river
> they hold the old
> as it rises   (5–7)

There is, then, continuity *and* change, and hence no completeness of either, and if the situation is as complex as this in the case of the mainstream, then it will be even more so in the case of the tributaries.

In the pages which follow Fisher continues to draw on Barton's chapter five, focusing in turn on several of the 'lost rivers'. Lines 7–35 concern the Falcon Brook, which flows from Battersea to Balham, while the three pages not reproduced here deal with the Effra, which runs from Norwood to Lambeth, and the Earl's Sluice, which runs from Bermondsey to Camberwell.

3
The double-headed Falcon (lines 7–35)

The Falcon Brook, Barton tells us, is:

> quite a large stream rising by two heads in Balham and Tooting, which united near Clapham Common and ran north-north-west to Clapham Junction Station, where it turned west. A small creek still shows where it joins the Thames at Battersea. The original name was 'Hidaburna'   (p. 41).

Fisher makes complex use of this information: he first posits a simple following of this river, from the sources in Balham and Tooting to the outlet into the Thames. But then he reminds himself that neither of these three stages (source, course, and outlet) is in fact clear-cut:

> the source in the springs
> is not the actual source
> but the first visible source (15–17)

This is a point which will bear meditation, and Fisher makes an immediate application of it: similarly, he says, the thinking of Ezra Pound (which has different origins from the 'mainstream' and a special influence – note the aptness of the metaphor – on the poet's own praxis) cannot be said to originate with Pound's speaking or writing of it, for 'this originality has come because of previous accumulation' (20). What is being meditated on here is the Poundian notion of the 'paideuma', which 'originated' with Frobenius (though the word 'originated' itself is one which this section of *Place* systematically deconstructs). Pound calls the paideuma the 'tangle or complex of the inrooted ideas of any period' and adds 'I will use paideuma for the grisly roots of ideas that are in action'. In Fisher's line of thought, Pound's ideas, though out of the 'mainstream', do not fall from the blue, but are linked with *some* paideuma, even though it be one which, like the Falcon Brook, has long been forced underground and has been largely forgotten. And since the Falcon Brook begins, not in Balham and Tooting, but in complex geological processes, it becomes difficult, too, to use that word without an awareness of how problematical the notion of a beginning is.

The situation is jut as complicated at the other end of the process where the stream flows into the Thames from the 'small creek' at Battersea: the Falcon Brook cannot be said to 'end' here, since it flows on, mingled with the larger stream:

> the tail into the Thames
> is not the final result
> but the last visible result   (21–23)

This taking up of the particular by the general is the poet's ideal for his own work, for he writes in the preface to *Place* (quoting the 1960s radical theorist Raoul Vaneigem) that 'in Vaneigem's words/ I await the day when this book will lose and find itself/ in a general movement of ideas'. Of course, it follows from the logic of this reasoning that it is impossible, too, to say that the Falcon

Brook ends where the Thames ends, for both flow on 'towards an ocean or cloud' (27), becoming lost in a general movement. There is a rationale here for the gathering of encyclopaedic amounts of information, but the mind may prove unable to cope with dizzying proliferations of data, and therefore make little headway in disentangling 'the roots of ideas in action'. And the more the mind contemplates the course of the Falcon Brook – following it 'backwards' through whatever geological processes produced its course, and 'forwards' through cycles of evaporation, cloud-formation, and rain-fall – the more likely it is that these vertiginous accumulations of information will become useless. Thus, the Falcon Brook is another warning to the poet: a synthesis may turn out to be false (like that of the shallow lagoon) or it may 'over-tame' its materials (like the oak in miniature). But the intellectual risk of reacting to this fact by constantly deferring conclusions and accumulating more and more data is that one may in the end fall victim to the double-headed Falcon, which sours all intellectual endeavour by holding out the impossible goal of achieving a final synthesis based upon comprehensive data.

4
The Effra and the Earl's Sluice

The course of the next river is followed with these complexities in mind ('when I took the Effra/ I bore this with me'). As Barton tells us: 'the Effra passes under South Lambeth Road at Cox's Bridge, before falling into the Thames just upstream of Vauxhall Bridge . . . . In 1880, the raised banks for spectators around the Oval cricket ground were completed by using earth excavated during the enclosing of the adjacent Effra' (pp. 42–3). The information about the Effra's fate near the Oval is used by Fisher, including Barton's comment about its name: Besant had speculated that it came from the Celtic *yfrid*, meaning a torrent, while Ruskin thought it a shortened form of *Effrena*, signifying the 'unbridled' river. The fate of this river, bricked over and turned into a sewer, its swift current 'carrying the waste of a dozen villages', reintroduces ideas from Part II of *Place* about connections between the patterns of occurrence of certain illnesses and the clotting of water sources. It also enables Fisher to return to the Poundian 'interweave' of lines 7–35, for in the Effra, 'the course becomes sewer/ where our roots suck for vertu'. The Poundian notions of the 'vertu' and the 'forma' designate both the moment when 'ideas, as it were, tremble on the edge of expression', when an idea in the 'paideuma' is on the point of entering into action. Thus, the question which the Effra poses for Fisher is that if the sources (the *Zeitgeist*, though Pound warns us not to equate this with the paideuma) which are the base material of ideas (and hence, in turn, the ultimate producers of action) are themselves polluted, then where are we to look for the beginnings of a dynamic of change? And if the causeways, the rivers, and the roads of past London are all now buried, lost, or destoyed, then how is the 'used diary' of the past to be read, and how can we be sure that the information now lost was not in some way essential to our future well-being?

These are the questions Fisher has in mind as he traces the next of his rivers:

> by the time I came to the Earl's Sluice
>   it was   the shedding I had in mind
>   what we give to the stream of things
> what we take from it

There is a pun here on the word 'shedding', which can mean either a sloughing-off and leaving behind, or a strengthening and shoring up, since 'shedding' is the term for the timbers or other materials which are used to strengthen a river embankment. Barton describes the Earl's Sluice as 'running along the southern border of Walworth Common (now Albany Road)' and mentions the fact that 'the stream received a tributary from Peckham Rye which was known locally as the Peck, and whose bed is still visible in Peckham Park. The main part of the stream was enclosed as the Earl Main Sewer in 1820–3, but the section nearest the Old Kent Road remained open until 1831' (p. 44). But though buried and turned into a sewer, the stream yet remains above ground, not

physically, but as an idea, or, at least, as the interface between
ideas, for its line marks a multiplicity of boundaries: 'the Earl's
Sluice divides Bermondsey and Rotherhithe from Camberwell
and Deptford . . . it used to be the boundary between Surrey and
Kent, and still divides the boroughs, the parliamentary con-
stituencies, and even the Police Divisions' (Barton, p. 63, incorporated by Fisher into his fifth page).

Here, then, is another sense in which a stream escapes
simple definition: it may be more accurate to consider it (and, by
implication, any 'line' of thought) not as a particular directional
movement, but as

> a meeting line of different sheds
> a source of ideas
> distribution of ideas
> to and fro the general flow

So it is not just physically that a river becomes lost 'in the general
movement', the river-as-idea is similarly beyond ultimate
definition, and itself becomes a means of distributing and
circulating ideas. Though buried its influence is continually felt.

5
The Neckinger (lines 37–56)

Fisher's sixth page, on the Neckinger, compresses Barton's information into its first eight lines. Barton (p. 45) tells us that the
Neckinger was:

> the name of the stream which ran down from Bermondsey Abbey
> to the Thames . . . it was also presumably this stream of which
> traces were found 'a little while ago near the Elephant and Castle'.
> No doubt it was in part artificial . . . The same may be said of the
> connecting watercourse between the Neckinger and the Earl's
> Sluice

The remainder of the page is a meditative interweave which
ponders the processes for which these buried rivers act as the
correlative:

> I couldn't get to the matter of this
> if our streams are becoming artificial
>   our old sources will dry
> and the trees we have planted to sup them
>   will wither with them
> nervously striking out for more nourishment
>   to find a poison flow
> that they are no longer strong enough to filter   (45–52)

Thus, the sources of energy once available to us are now buried and stagnant, so that when our roots 'suck for vertu' they ingest only the outpourings of 'drains clotted with the phlegm of programming' (as it is expressed earlier in the poem). So instead of the tributaries remaining efficacious, when they join the larger flow there is simply a process of homogenisation, so that 'the many channels become alike/ and indistinguishable/ and our course is one of habit/ disregarding any process we may need'.

6
The Ditch at Nine Elms

These prescient images of detritus and congestion are powerfully reinforced on the next page, which concerns the Ditch at Nine Elms. Fisher draws here on Barton's chapter seven, 'Dubious lost rivers', which contains an account of the Ditch:

> It divided the parishes of Lambeth and Battersea, and may have been, in part at least, artificial, like Parr's Ditch. On the maps of Speed and Veitch, however, it appears to form a communication with the Falcon Brook. This may be the remnant of a backwater which once made Battersea into an island . . . A tidal loop such as this, open to the Thames at both ends, would certainly be very susceptible to flooding and rapid water movements. (pp. 58–9)

A 'river' of this kind, which has the river as its 'source' *and* empties into it, is the perfect image of intellectual congestion, for it contributes nothing to the mainstream but what it has taken from it, and is merely an ironic parody of that 'distribution of ideas/ to and fro the general flow' which should constitute the intellectual 'eco-system'. Far from being a source of innovation, such a tributary is greatly at risk of flooding by the discarded debris of the mainstream, which it will, yet again, recycle:

> the remnant backwater filled with
> the dead fish it spawned
> . . .
> the Thames it fed flooded it
>   and the more it flooded the more it cycled   (63–4, 68–9)

At this point Fisher skilfully brings in Pound again, warning himself against setting up an intellectual system which is a closed tidal loop of this kind:

> I read Pound who calls me to read Dante
> who gives me better sight to read Duncan
> who suggests I read Pound   (71–73)

This reminder that any intellectual economy needs openings ('towards an ocean or cloud' (27)) is a timely one, and the last six lines of the following page describe another stream which is partly artificial. This is the so-called Canute's Trench, dug by King Canute to get his ships past the enemy-held London Bridge without having to go under it. As Barton relates (pp. 79–80) Maitland, in 1739, claimed to have traced out the course of this trench across South London. The route looks long and intricate, and seems at first to have involved a super-human amount of excavation, but in fact it makes cunning use of natural watercourses:

> His route went up the Earl's Sluice, across the Old Kent Road south-east of the Lock Hospital, then via the Lock Stream to Newington Butts, passing south of the Elephant and Castle and continuing its course by the Black Prince in Lambeth Road it runs west-and-by-south, through the Spring Garden at Vauxhall into the Effra.

Thus, an artificial river makes use of natural ones, not taking the easy way out, but seeking the only way through ('not because easier/ but to make possible', as Fisher says on the same page). The poet accepts that our sources must, in part, be manufactured by our own ingenuities; we are not restricted to what is 'given', by 'nature' or by the past.

7
The significance of the rivers

Hence, the last page of Part IV introduces new dimensions into
the explorations of the rivers:

> and then our journey became less instinctual
> more rational
> that is logical

It is not a question, then, of choosing *between* the Roman grid-iron
of streets on the north side of the river, which imposes its
synthetic, imperialist form on the landscape, and the streets of
Southwark on the other side, which follow the land-contours
(one of the basic distinctions used elsewhere in *Place*); rather, we
choose *from* them, making a judicious blend of the two. The blend
Fisher discusses on this page is from Barton's chapter nine, and it
concerns the case of a railway line which is laid along the bed of a
former canal, another example of one line of energy being super-
imposed upon another (like the road which was laid along the
track of the tidal causeway in Part II). As Barton tells us, 'the
[railway] line from Croydon to Rotherhithe is built in the bed of
the old Croydon Canal, and the lock-keeper's cottage can still be
seen from the train at Brockley' (p. 79). That there is an ingenuity
here akin to Canute's is evident – the new course makes use of
the old in a way that is 'less instinctual/ more rational', and a
similar conjunction of road and railway is the subject of Fisher's
next lines, on the river Wandle. Barton describes an early scheme
to use Wandsworth (on the Wandle) as a port to be connected to
the South Coast by an iron railway from Portsmouth:

> The value [of Wandsworth] as a harbour is shown by the route of
> the iron railway, authorized by Act of Parliament in 1801, which
> was to run from Wandsworth, as a port, to Portsmouth. In fact, it
> never got any further south than Merstham, near Redhill, and this
> lay almost entirely in the Wandle valley. The rails were so made that
> anyone could, for a small fee, use them for his own carts. (p. 82)

In the *Dunciad* Pope describes the Wandle as 'the blue transparent
Vandalis', the phrase used by Barton as the ironic caption to his

first illustration (which shows the now polluted river near Earlsfield in Wandsworth), and by Fisher in his final remark on the Wandle. The last detail on Fisher's page, concerning the Effra, gives another example of a 'less instinctual' use of one of these rivers, this time as an ornamental motif in a garden. Barton writes 'Fifty years later [1780] the Effra, "a pleasant stream, overhung by laburnums, hawthorns, and chestnut trees" [quoting Besant], was used to make an ornamental water in the garden of one of Adam's houses, "Belair", in Gallery Road, Dulwich: this is the only part of the Effra still visible today' (p. 96).

Thus, Fisher's section IV on the 'lost rivers' of South London ends on a surprisingly positive note: though these watercourses have nearly all been interfered with in some way, this has not meant in every case that former carriers of 'vertu' have now become mere shifters of effluent. Though there is this danger of their becoming merely the indices of a stagnant intellectual economy, their 'less instinctual' uses can be a safeguard against this. The human ingenuity which allows boats to pass London Bridge without going underneath it is emblematic of the fact that *Place* is not in any sense the expression of a sentimental wish to escape a polluted present-day culture by reverting to a more 'natural' past. On the contrary, it is guardedly optimistic about the possibility of salvaging a future by an eclectic blend of the recoverable past and the decipherable present. If we can break our habits of thought, Fisher seems to say, we can perhaps hope to do more than just survive. If we don't, the evidence increasingly shows, we can hardly hope to do even that.

This discussion of a section of *Place* has the double purpose of both drawing attention to a significant modernist work and sugesting the general nature of a category into which it might fit – the 'content-specific' poem. It might be helpful, therefore, to end with a brief summary of some of the characteristics of this category. Firstly, poems of this kind make direct use of hard data (scientific, technological, sociological, and so on), often incorporating some of it into the poetic text in more-or-less 'raw' or near-verbatim form. Secondly, it therefore challenges, or deconstructs, prior notions of what constitutes poetic material, since this data is not just 'background' to which we might be referred in a footnote, but makes up a substantial part of the poetic text. Hence, the notion of authorship itself is made problematic by these procedures. It follows, thirdly, that the kind of reading required becomes a study process in which the sources and the poetic text are, so to speak, read into and through each other, roughly as the above reading of section IV of Place demonstrates. This has, fourthly, a number of consequences, one of which is to put considerable difficulties in the way of the casual reader, and it is not suggested here that these difficulties are easily solved. Inevitably, though, any solution will have to involve a change in the 'tradition of critical silence', discussed in footnote three. An ideal solution, fifthly, would recognise that content-specific poetry is often constructed on collage principles, and that a suitable publication format might be some form of parallel printed text, of the sort experimented with in post-structuralist publications. As this implies, finally, this kind of work questions conventional ideas of the nature of the speaking subject in poetry. There isn't the reassuring, containing, ironic, wry, reflective voice of the humanistic individual, which is pervasive in most poetry (not excepting, of course, poetry which uses the device of the non-authorial 'persona'). Rather, the pages often have a dialogic structure featuring several voices, including those of the 'source authors', and they lack a privileged and authoritative overview, being instead 'open-field' structures in the classic modernist way. In a phrase, content-specific poetry often takes poetry readers into cultural space they have not previously entered.

Notes

1 Donald Davie, Under Briggflatts: A History of Poetry in Great Britain, 1960–1988, Carcanet, Manchester, p. 256.

2 The complicated publishing history of the Place project is, in outline, as follows, these items being listed not in chronological order of publication but in the order of the five main books:

Place Book One, Aloes Books, London, 1974, republished by Truck Books (St Paul, Minnesota), 1976
Unpolished Mirrors (Place Book Two), Reality Studios, London, 1985
Stane (Place Book Three), Aloes Books, London, 1977

Becoming (*Place Books Four and Five*), Aloes Books, London, 1978

Much of this material also appeared in various small-press journals, and there were several items related to the *Place* project published in the late 1970s and early 1980s.

For briefer samples of Allen Fisher's work see *Angels of Fire: An Anthology of Radical Poetry in the '80s*, ed. Sylvia Paskin, *et al.*, Chatto, London, 1986, and *The New British Poetry*, ed. Gillian Allnutt *et al.*, Paladin, London, 1988. The latter contains an extract from *Unpolished Mirrors* (Book Two of *Place*). See also *Future Exiles: 3 London Poets: Allen Fisher, Bill Griffiths, and Brian Catling*, Paladin, London, 1992.

3 L. S, Dembo, *Concepts of Reality in Modern American Poetry*, University of California Press, Berkeley, 1966.

4 The poets discussed in this book can be said to represent a distinct tradition of poetry, with its own characteristic cultural practices. One of these is what D. J. Ellis (in the present book) calls the 'convention of critical silence'. This involved a general reluctance to annotate or explicate poems closely, a feeling that they should speak for themselves, and an inhibition about assuming the role of critic or explicator, on the implicit grounds that to do so would be to claim a spurious authority which would infringe egalitarian principles. Hence, small-press booklets were usually devoid of information about the author, or any kind of commentary, annotation, or analysis, in spite of the considerable difficulty of much of the poetry published in this way. This resulted in a 'theory gap' (Robert Hampson's term), a general dearth of material explaining what poets were doing and providing a critical terminology in which it could be discussed. Hence the non-appearance of the 'Stuart Gilbert' figures. What I am describing here is the general situation during a particular period, the 1970s. There were, of course, exceptions – Eric Mottram, for instance, wrote influential essays on several important figures. But most of the writing about this poetry tended to be celebratory rather than analytical, on the one hand, or else would simply list and record what had been published. However, the convention of critical silence seemed to lose its force as the 1980s progressed, partly because of the example of avant-garde American poets whose work was accompanied by polemical and explicatory essay writing which assured them serious attention, linked them with prestigious movements in criticism, and made current a critical terminology which could make sense of what they were trying to do.

Appendix
Pages from Section IV of *Place*
(Page breaks in the original are indicated by an asterisk)

What is lost

the Thames fifteen feet higher
                              not below the old lagoon
under the fairy lights   east of Dagenham   the yew trees

the embankments do not mark a new river   5
      they hold the old
          as it rises

 *

if I take a river to its source

  and in the case of the Falcon Brook
  this is 2 springs   10

& follow its course
  from head to tail
  to the Thames

I may arrive from at least three projections

       the source in the springs   15
       is not the actual source
       but the first visible source
       so that if Pound said it
       it is original
this originality has come because of previous accumulation   20

the tail into the Thames
  is not the final result
  but the last visible result

  before we consider the Brook Hidaburna
  as the source   or A source   25

and the Thames as the course
  towards an ocean or cloud
  so that if Pound said it
  it is part of what has been said
leading us on to what will be said   30

it is also that the course of the Falcon
       is all that need concern us
       as its source or the source
          it will create
       is already part of it   35

 *

after the Sluice walked upstream
  along a connecting stream to Neckinger

(the course between Bermondsey Abbey and Thames)
parts of the flow are artificial
   to make matters worse   40
   Kent says the streams near the Elephant temple
   to be the Tygris
and this too partly artificial

took the bus south   45
I couldn't get to the matter of this
if our streams are becoming artificial
   our old sources will dry
and the trees we have planted to sup them
   will wither with them
nervously striking out for more nourishment   50
   to find a poison flow
that they are no longer strong enough to filter

so that the many channels become alike
   and indistinguishable
and our course is one of habit   55
   disregarding any process we may need

*

I retraced my steps
   took the Ditch at Nine Elms
which forms a communion with the Falcon Brook
   making an island of Battersea   60
   inside a tidal loop

this too in part artificial
   the remnant backwater filled with
   the dead fish it spawned

   too far from its source   65
because of false changes
   its communications breaking
the Thames it fed flooded it
   and the more it flooded the more it cycled

I was uncertain of the trouble here   70

I read Pound who calls me to read Dante
who gives me better sight to read Duncan
who suggests I read Pound

Robert Sheppard

9

Lee Harwood and the poetics of the open work

1
The catalytic text

For Lee Harwood and many other writers of the new British poetry of the 1960s, modernism was not the alien and spent force Movement writers had taken it to be a decade earlier.[1] They realised that what Jerome Rothenberg has called 'a tradition (or poetry) of changes' involved not only a set of poetic techniques, wider and more experimental than the limited possibilities of Movement verse, but an acknowledgement of a highly complex and experimental attitude to life antithetical to the empiricism and social decorum of the Movement (Rotherberg, p. 28). Commitment to it involved a necessary openness to that multifacetedness of experience written of by Charles Olson: 'Any of us, at any instant, are juxtaposed to any experience, even an overwhelmingly single one, on several more planes than the arbitrary and discursive which we inherit can declare' (Olson, *Human universe*, p. 164). While the self becomes an experiential collage, writing becomes a kinetic process, not only in the sense described in Olson's 'Projective verse' essay, but also as the process of the constant coming into being of meaning itself, against the commonsense notion of a linguistic struggle for the expression of independent 'thoughts'.[2] As Derrida points out, 'It is because writing is inaugural . . . that it is dangerous and anguishing. It does not know where it is going, no knowledge can keep it from the essential precipitation toward the meaning that it constitutes and that is, primarily, its future. (Derrida, p. 11). Whether this late modernism can be called postmodernism or not, it is clear that Lyotard's definition of postmodern epistemology, in *The Postmodern Condition*, as the play of undecidables presents a useful homology for the work of much of the new British poetry, which is also 'producing not the known, but the unknown' (Lyotard, p. 60). Its rules are not normative and fixed. In Lyotard's characterisation of the writer's work, 'rules and categories are what the work of art itself is looking for . . . Hence the fact that work and text have the characters of an event' (Lyotard, p. 81). Both events, of writing and reading, will involve *indeterminacy* and *discontinuity*.

Umberto Eco in his 1959 essay 'The poetics of the open work' also cautiously draws parallels between scientific worldviews and the procedures of the most vital post-war art, and sees these two terms – each derives from a major strand of physics – as relevant. Indeterminacy is regarded in both science and phenomenology 'as a valid stepping-stone in the cognitive process'; discontinuity is understood 'not as an element of disorientation, but as an essential stage in all scientific verification procedures and also as the verifiable pattern of events in the subatomic world' (Eco. p. 58). Artworks which bear analogous orientations Eco calls 'open works'; it is important to stress that their procedures do not necessarily reflect the terrifying cultural and existential disintegration which is often read into early modernist works, as in the fragmentation and juxtaposition of Eliot's *The Waste Land*, but can be more positively regarded as the 'possibility of thought and action made available to the individual who is open to the continuous renewal of his life patterns and cognitive processes' (Eco, pp. 60–1).

Such a description fits the work of Lee Harwood. An early affinity to Dada and Surrealism – and his dedication as the translator of Tristan Tzara's work throughout the 1960s – meant that

from the beginning he was committed to discontinuous structures presenting multiple points of view. In 'As your eyes are blue'
(1965), a homoerotic concern with the presence and impending
absence of the lover is balanced against collaged perceptions,
memories and dream:

> you know even in the stillness of my kiss
> that doors are opening in another apartment
> on the other side of town   a shepherd grazing
> his sheep through a village we know
> high in the mountains the ski slopes thick with summer flowers
> and the water-meadows below with narcissi
> the back of your hand and –
>
> (Harwood, 1988, pp. 15–16)

Subsequent texts of the 1960s were self-conscious
narratives, parodic fragments that often presented the absurdities
of heroic quest with a particular concentration upon colonial life
or some extremity of mock-heroic behaviour which is submitted
to a textual dispersal. One such piece, 'The Argentine', ends:

> The journey had to be made and the horsemen were right
> But the weight of possessions held on to
> if not for love of them, then for some sense of duty
> and fear

> These accounts of past and future journeys
> became boring . . . and any violence that might have been
> has now grown limp like the vase of dead flowers
> that the efficient house-keeper will surely clear away   (p. 56)[3]

The level tone throughout the discontinuities and
indeterminacies of the story (such as accounts of *future* adven-
tures) emphasises the stasis of this world, as does the rather
aristocratic domesticity of its final metaphor. The influence of the
New York school, particularly of John Ashbery here (but elsewhere of Frank O'Hara), had served Harwood well. Its adap-
tation of surrealism for narrative ends Harwood had made
his own to such an extent that when he went to live temporarily in
New York the work he wrote there won the Poet's Foundation
Award for 1967. But he was soon to abandon this discursive

mode. F. T. Prince's gentle criticism of the poems of The White
Room – that Harwood was 'pattering on' – convinced him that this
mode was becoming pure production (Harwood, 'A conversation', p. 13).[4]

In Harwood's work there is often a tension between such
fictive elegance and a more 'straight-talking' discourse; Harwood
calls this his 'puritan-cavalier routine' (Harwood, 'A conversation', p. 13). This was not merely an understandable escape from
influence, for it had a supplementary political and moral
dimension. By 1974, writing in terms which reflected his recent
reading of Ezra Pound, he noted, 'A country rises and falls – and
the indicator is always its use of language, maybe even the cause.
How "straight-talking" its leaders, educators, press, population
are' (Harwood, 'Bob Cobbing', p. 7). And how 'straight-talking'
the poets, those unacknowledged legislators, are too, he seems to
imply. Turning from the New York artificers to the Black Mountain poets, such as Charles Olson and Robert Creeley, he discovered 'that it is possible to write directly, in a personal way, but
. . . it must be straight, and it must be set in contexts' (Harwood, 'A
conversation', p. 14). This may seem an odd, unusually literal,
reading of The Maximus Poems, but Harwood's emphasis upon
'context' ensured that a clearer, sparser diction was not an aban-
donment of modernist complexity. Freed from fictive elabo-
ration, 'facts' and information could become part of the poetic
text and context.

Harwood takes delight in work which demands a certain
fusion of interpretation and participation, something his fictional
mode occasionally precluded. The word 'maybe' which he read
in a descriptive passage in the original version of Roy Fisher's City
meant that the reader 'had to decide whether to put in a road or
not, and that is an exciting experience' (Harwood, 'A conversation', p. 12). Even with such minimal indeterminacy, 'the poem
becomes a catalyst' (p. 12). This metaphor of the catalytic text was
repeated often by Harwood between 1970 and 1973 and is central
to his notion of the open work during the writing of 'The Long
Black Veil', the text I will examine in the second part of this essay.

'Ideally,' Harwood commented in 1972, 'I want the poem to

be like a beautiful object, a box that's all slotted together; then I leave it on the table and leave the room, and you come in and pass it on' (Harwood, 'Extracts', p. 8). A poem is thus not primarily self-expressive. It is objective, and only completed by the reader, though here Harwood does not have in mind the ideal reader of recent reader-response theorists, one 'constituted' or 'implied' by the text, but the multitude of readers who actually do engage with the poem-catalyst; it causes various changes within different readers without itself altering its objective form. Nevertheless the subject's responses must fuse horizons with the poem as the reader 'reacts to the play of stimuli' to which 'the individual addressee is bound to supply his own existential credentials' (Eco, p. 49). Eco's definition of the open work as a 'construction kit' loosely matches Harwood's own catalyst model. In the late 1960s, particularly in *The Sinking Colony*, Harwood's use of indeterminate forms and discontinuous textual lacunae and fragmentation similarly had as its aim, 'getting the audience involved in the poem' (Harwood, 'Extracts', p. 9). One such poem, 'Linen', ends:

> touching you   like the
> and soft as
> like the scent of flowers and
> like an approaching festival
> whose promise is failed through carelessness   (CFR, p. 113)

Harwood glosses his own text by pointing out that 'each of us has got a different concept of what touching is like, right? And so I should respect your view . . . So we've got to leave this room for people, and here it's very consciously leaving half-lines and areas of doubt' for the reader's intervention (Harwood, 'Extracts', p. 9). But the text is not a blank page for the reader to inscribe his or her self; the lacunae are underwritten, as it were, by Harwood's own Ashberyesque concluding similes, which provide a necessary context for the passage. Eco calls such texts 'works in movement': 'the *possibilities* which the work's openness makes available always work within a given *field of relations*. As in the Einsteinian universe the *work in movement* is the possibility of numerous different personal interventions, but it is not an amorphous invitation to indiscriminate participation' (Eco, p. 63).

The problem with suspended textual lacunae is that the reader may well simply read the utterance as incomplete and not attempt the participation desired by Harwood. There are less successful texts of Harwood's where the informational load is so low there seems little point in a reader combining its elements. If this operation occasionally fails to offer examples of creative response, it does, however, offer a metaphor for the operations of a work in movement, such as the larger scale processes of 'The Long Black Veil'.

2
'The Long Black Veil': the comprehension of process

In his 1975 volume *HMS Little Fox*, Lee Harwood described the long work 'The Long Black Veil', with which the volume begins, as 'the end-product, the "flower" of my work to date' (Harwood, *HMS Little Fox*, dust jacket). Written between 1970–72, it was Harwood's longest and most ambitious poem at that point in his career: a single work in poetry and prose, a collaged notebook in twelve parts. Strands of earlier work are collected in this paradoxical text which appears at once both openly notational and obsessively concerned with a semi-clandestine love affair (the poem's title alludes to a country and western song about adultery). The schema of the poem is such that it represents, chronologically speaking, a montage: 'one actuality in time set (beside) another, causing waves to go between the two' (quoted in Mottram, p. 33). Film had always provided Harwood with important structural homologies, but his description here echoes Eisenstein's theory of montage which regards the combination of discrete shots not as a simple sequence, but as the creation of a new conceptual unit. A literary parallel is Pound's dynamic practice of imagist-vorticist theory in the *Cantos*, in which diverse discourses are juxtaposed. The resulting discontinuity is productive of a broadening of conceptual and imaginative horizons. 'The Long Black Veil' provides such discontinuity and indeterminacy in a movement not simply limited to the two 'times' of the text, but one of constant de-centreing.

One epigraph of the poem is from Pound's 'Canto 77':

> 'things have ends (or scopes) and beginnings.   To
> know what precedes   and what follows
>   will assist yr/ comprehension of process'

(CFR, p. 129)

Process is indeed the concept that turns collage to montage, imagism to vorticism. It allows temporality to expand beyond the single instant and – in a sense that is relevant to this poem – it allows sexual contact to develop into relationship. The 'Preface' to 'The Long Black Veil' poses several questions about this last aspect:

> a year passed
> I think of you
> it's early on a sunny morning in June
> and think of your thinking of me
> possible

> How do we live with this?
> yet live with this

> What have we left
> from all this?

(CFR, p. 130)

Memory and anguished yearning remain constant although Harwood uses the Borgesian image of a pile of coins, each repre-senting a memory of the previous memory to show the distortions and simplifications of its processes. He repeatedly makes a distinction between vital insistence and dead repetition:

> two years repeated   'Oh Jung'
> the cycle not repeated
> only the insistence

(CFR, p. 130)

'Oh Jung' is itself an insistence, echoing paradigmatically both a previous quotation and a future reference:

> 'Concepts promise protection
> from experience.

The spirit does
not dwell in concepts.   Oh Jung.'
(Joanne *Kyger* – DESECHEO NOTEBOOK)
(CFR, p. 130)

There can be no sheltering from the insistences of experience in conceptualisations, in the repetitiveness of intellectual systems. The 'Preface' ends: 'But what of the essence of this? "Oh Jung's" insistences. The Sufi story of the famous River that tried to cross the desert, but only crossed the sands as water "in the arms of the wind", nameless but' (CFR, p. 131). The parable demonstrates that existential movement or process will always involve metamorphosis, a point endorsed by Jung.

Book One is haunted by the distance between word and thing, unhappy nominalism a reflection of the narrator's erotic isolation; his 'how I ache now' is mysteriously parallel to the 'endless skies/ that ache too much' (CFR, p. 132). The text is hesitant, constantly revising itself: 'It's light/ I mean your body'. The body is the only constant but absent referent in this general failure of reference: 'the words?   how can they . . .' (CFR, p. 132). The book ends

dawn – light – body – words – skies – ache – distance – valley –
sun – silos – farms – ridge – creek – each other – birds – wind
The Flight – BA 591   (CFR, p. 133)

These nouns, isolated from preceding lines, are both inadequate summary and alienated, essential detail. What survives the 'distance' implied by the flight number is an enigmatic and poignant impression of the single noun phrase of the list, 'each other', caught like a cinematic sequence, frozen in its frame; process arrested as language ceases to be of use:

you stop and half turn
to tell me . . .
that doesn't matter
but your look
and this picture I have
and at this distance

(CFR, p. 132)

Book Two contains this important prose reflection upon the capabilities of the mind: 'I will call anything that goes on in my head "a dream", whether it be thoughts or imaginings, day-dreams or sleep dreams. They all give pictures of "the possible", and that is exactly their value' (p. 135). This attitude could be either egocentric or utopian, and Book Two favours the former: 'I hold you to me in a small room – the night air so heavy. Inside "the dream" . . .' (p. 134). Nevertheless the 'dream' recurs again in various locations, another paradigmatic insistence, to offset the apparent tranquillity and singleness of love-making. At the end of Book Two, one version of the 'dream' is a nostalgic and self-conscious harking back to the fictions of The White Room, which hints, in a sudden change of focus, that movement and location never cease:

> the two warships ploughed out to sea
> waves flowed between them. . . .
> Not the first   but one of many
> such expeditions
>
> (CFR, p. 135)[5]

Book Three suggests that such fictions can be unnecessary evasions of the ordinary life that is celebrated in the prose journal passages that are placed throughout the work:

> There's no steamer bringing you to me
> up-river at the hill-station
> No long white dress on the verandah
>
> It is . . .
> I hold you.   isn't this enough?
>
> (CFR, p. 137)

The colonial fiction reasserts itself to decentre the poem's obsessive moments of physical intimacy, though the landscapes of the travel notes are occasionally swallowed by a polymorphous pathetic fallacy, becoming 'only a description of my love for you' (p. 137). No sooner are fictions dismissed than the reader is drawn again into their beguiling exotica:

At the hill-station   all the bearers fled

the delighted naturalist was left unconcerned
carefully placing his specimens in the black metal box

(CFR, p. 138)

The naturalist is as absorbed as the narrator by his obsessions, both to the point of ignoring the wider contexts that surround their activities. Literal notations of continual travel in North America and Canada fill Books Four and Five as well, juxtaposing notations of love-making with travel jottings, as though travel were an attempt to escape the 'dream' that still continually disrupts it. Book Four ends: 'felt so good this morning – as though I woke up beside you' (CFR, p. 139).

Although montage and the ideogrammic methods are ways of dealing processually with both original and secondary material, the concept of *collage* emphasises citation and quotation, the principal components of Book Six. As the French group Mu argue of this technique: 'each cited element breaks the continuity of the linearity of the discourse and leads necessarily to a double reading: that of the fragment perceived in relation to its text of origin; that of the same fragment as incorporated into a new whole, a different totality' (quoted in Ulmer, p. 146). Yet such a totality is always shifting under the imbalance of its elements. It is in Book Six – mid-point through the text –that 'the questions of complexity' are dealt with most fully. Harwood quotes Forster's obituary for Gide which praises Gide for transmitting 'life's complexity, and the delight, the difficulty, the duty of registering that complexity and of conveying it' (CFR, p. 142). This is almost an internal epigraph for the second half of 'The long black veil'. It is by making a collage using Jung's essay 'Marriage as a psychological relationship' that Harwood fully develops a theory for a constantly de-centreing process in his work and for a model of late twentieth-century human consciousness, a structural homology for the 'comprehension of process' demanded by Pound:

The distinctions

"Oh Jung" (1875–1961) on "Marriage . . ." (1925)

The container *and* the contained
not *or*

one within the other
a continual shifting   and that both ways
– more a flow – from the simplicity to the complexity,
"unconscious" to conscious,
                              and then back again?
and the move always with difficulty, and pain   a pleasure
                                                    (CFR, p. 142)

In Jung's theory of marriage the container is a complex
character, the contained simple and psychologically dependent
upon the other. There are pleasurable but also painful resolutions
of the disparities between them as the container looks in vain for
his or her level of complexity in the partner, whose simplicity is
also disrupted by the search. The contained, however, comes to
accept his or her position and ultimately finds some complexity
in his or her limited self. The container eventually becomes
acutely aware of the necessity for self-fulfilment.[6] Harwood, however, subverts the underlying submissive-dominant polarity of
Jung's theory with his emphatic '*and*' which suggests that the roles
are interchangeable, dynamic and discontinuous. The process is
both a mode of consciousness and a method of communication:

not so much a repetition
but a moving around a point, a line
– like a backbone – and that too moving
(on)

                                                    (CFR, p. 142)

There can be no single fixed view, since the point is also moving,
dynamic; the poem reflects this in that the straight talking and the
artifice, the journals and the quotations, the poetry and prose are
like complementarities in quantum theory: mutually exclusive
positions that support one another. And it is the very journey, a
narrative of fragments, that is supported, also, by the 'double
readings' of citation and reference. Taoist complementarities, yin
and yang, enter the poem ideogrammically to suggest the
wholeness of sexual union yet this does not take precedence over

an ironical quotation from Stendhal's *Le Rouge et le noir* in which Julien Sorel's love is described as 'still another mode of ambition' (CFR, p. 143).

Jung himself commented upon the relationship between twentieth-century physics and Taoist philosophy, and he also furnished the introduction to Wilhelm's translation of the I Ching, which is quoted in the collage of Book Six. (Thus Jung's thought provides both philosophical support for, and becomes a critical object of, this central book.)

> Before Completion   Wei Chi/64
> But if the little fox, after nearly completing the crossing,
> Gets his tail in the water,
> There is nothing that would further.
>
> (CFR, p. 143)

Harwood omits from this citation of the 'Judgement' the word 'success' as though to again resist finality; interestingly the accompanying 'image', which Harwood also leaves out, describes 'the condition before transition' (*The I Ching*, pp. 248–9). 'This hexagram,' the commentary to the oracle explains, brings 'The book of changes' to 'a hopeful outlook'; it exemplifies the flux in which Harwood's text restlessly moves: 'a time when the transition from disorder to order is not yet completed', when the little fox is poised between success and failure (pp. 248–9). Harwood continues with an example of such a transition, a not entirely convincing image of the lover:

> in the half light . . .
> A minotaur? a cat? tiger?   Her face
> a metamorphosis   seen   at once   many times.
> Our powers generating . . .
>
> (CFR, p. 143)

In Book Seven Egyptian mythology provides another analogy for the Taoist dualities of the masculine and feminine, and the operations of heterosexual love: 'Horus, the rising sun, enters Hathor, the sky./ Obvious enough.' (CFR, p. 147). However, the presence of a third deity, '*Anubis* – the jackal headed god, the guardian of the dead', complicates this 'obvious' identification and prepares for his re-appearance (CFR, p. 146). Harwood is careful to avoid conventional religion, the Egyptian powers representing 'No godhead, no gospel, but "a multiplicity of approaches, each in its own right, each immanent in nature"' (CFR, p. 147). Yet even this gentle pantheism in the unidentified quotation is de-centred in Book Eight where the Sufi poet, Ibn 'Arabi, provides a return to the obsession: 'God's face is the face of your lover' (CFR, p. 148). This book is entitled 'England' and the complementarity of the mythological and the 'immediate/ God's face' has itself to engage the charged landscapes of erotic exchange:

> the green sea and the hills behind the town,
> like some giant sandwich
> and our love in the filling of it
>
> (CFR, p. 148)

The simile is deliberately banal, courts sentimentality and embarrassment, reflecting both a need to de-centre Harwood's mythological and learned borrowings and his returning mistrust of his manner of expression:

> My heart weeps
> Who would ever have thought I'd write that?
>
> (CFR, p. 149)

The advocate of 'straight talking' who in Book Ten states that 'the word grows emptier the farther it moves/ from the flesh', finds himself resorting to an abstract metaphor, not sure whether this discovery is a success or a failure, and some readers may well feel the same of this deflationary passage (CFR, p. 152). But they don't have to wait long before the text transforms itself freshly, into a record of anguished hypersensitivity that contrasts with such innocence:

> As though a monster haunts us – continually aroused at
> each 'wrong' word, each 'wrong' action, and roaring out from
> its darkness to terrorize us again.
> A giant and indestructible serpent filled with anger and venom,
> nightmare.

'Each single angel is terrifying.' (*Rilke*)

(CFR, p. 149)

The angels of Rilke's *Duino Elegies*, the first of which is quoted here (and more fully in the twelfth book), are non-Christian symbols of a state of completeness that transcends the ordinary world of flux and change. They are appealed to as witnesses to the sort of mortal love Harwood celebrates in the earlier part of the book, and their terror derives from their sheer beauty, perfection and otherness. But while accepting the challenge of Rilke's late Romantic image of inhuman transcendence, it is not equivocal enough for Harwood. Book Eleven begins:

> Is this the Rilkean dream or 'home' we come to?
> At dusk the skyline obscure.
>
> Yes and no. (CFR, p. 154)

Again there is complementarity – between positive and negative, between fixity and movement, between the new and the familiar:

> Many pictures – the surface apparently the same.
> A series of events, but the marks they leave
> varying.   Things happen, have qualities.   (CFR, p. 154)

Later lines characteristically de-centre this passage:

> But the quality
>
> The dreams do happen –
> But there is no 'home' we come to
> – but on this earth, and open to its powers (CFR, p. 154)

Yet the dream here is the familiar Harwood 'dream' of potent possibility, the ghosts and the god Anubis returning to guard against the terrifying aesthetic transcendence of Rilkean completion and stasis:

> The dead watching over us, surrounding us with a tenderness
> – as though they were gravity – they hold us, their arms around
> us, however we move.
>
> And Anubis guiding the dead through their journey.
>
> (CFR, pp. 154–5).

Home is neither here nor there in a world of transformation and movement, the dream reflected, as always, in the variety of locations (and texts) that the poem negotiates.

Book Twelve, 'California journal', brings the continual shifting of place and movement to poetic fulfilment if not completion. Consummation, as in the love-making that is described, can only be transitory, particularly as the beginning of Book Nine draws back the 'long black veil' of the poem's concealment just enough to suggest the material condition of the adulterous lovers' separation:

> Today, lying on the grass in the park
> by your house
>   We were very close
> Your husband, your children, you go
> about your duties, you love
> and care for them   (CFR, p. 150)

So the 'final' lovemaking is indeed 'like the sweetening of the body before burial, before our parting' (CFR, p. 160). The conclusive and private 'lie naked upon the bed' exists in irresolution with the 'lying on the grass' of public precariousness. Yet 'the dream echoed again and again in many parts' (CFR, p. 160):

> The ritual of – repeated again – No. We make love – to each other –
> in turn. The body glowing, dizzy . . . walking through clouds. The
> faces transformed again.   (CFR, p. 161)

This metamorphic ritual is a necessary insistence, not a casual repetition. Jung's fixities are dissolved in ritual exchange, in the momentary whole of yin and yang.

3
Conclusion

The restless de-centreing of 'The long black veil' 's own contrasting discourses is part of the postmodern condition that Lyotard defines as 'an incredulity towards metanarratives' (Lyotard, p. xxiv). In the face of multiply coherent realities there can only be a poetics of indeterminacy and discontinuity and little resort to what Lyotard calls 'the narrative function', which is, in any case, 'losing its functors, its great hero, its great dangers, its great voyages, its great goal' (p. xxiv). Already in his fictions of the 1960s Harwood was charting this loss. But in 'The long black veil' he was dispersing his narrative energies into what Lyotard calls 'clouds of narrative language elements – narrative, but also denotative, prescriptive, descriptive, and so on' (p. xxiv). In this classic open work, the elements are left in a discontinuous relation so that the reader becomes an active co-producer of the text as he or she is drawn along the trails of its dispersal by the 'double reading' of the collage elements, by the multiple references of its juxtapositions and complementarities.

'The long black veil' represents a summation of Lee Harwood's aesthetic quest over the previous decade, and it also pointed towards some features of subsequent work. The restless tensions between obsession and allusiveness, narrative and lyric, information and personal statement, poetry and prose, as well as 'cavalier' fictiveness and 'puritan' straightforwardness were all to be explored in differing combinations. A poetic agenda had been set. Harwood's volume of selected poems, Crossing the Frozen River (1988), bears testimony to the centrality of 'The long black veil' as much as it demonstrates Harwood's continuing diversity of approaches.[7]

Notes

1 For a general account of Movement aesthetics and its orthodoxy see Morrison (1983); for the best critical article, see Crozier (1983).

2 See Olson, 'Projective verse', in Allen and Tallman, pp. 147–58.

3 'The Argentine' was originally published in The White Room, but the page reference here is to Harwood's Crossing the Frozen River, henceforth CFR.

4 For my own assessment of Harwood's work of the 1960s and the relation to the works of Bob Cobbing, Roy Fisher and Tom Raworth, see Sheppard (1992).

5 The phrase also seems to echo Harwood's previous description of the dual time scale of the text.

6 See Jung (1971), pp. 170–2. There is also an element of subversion in the fact that the poem's obsession is not with marriage but with adultery.

7 In one sense 'The long black veil' was a dead end; the notebook format,

with its plain style, so attractive for this long work, proved less efficacious for its successor, 'The notes of a Post Office clerk', in Harwood (1977). Whereas 'The long black veil' is reprinted in full in Harwood (1988), only a few lyric fragments of the later text are reprinted.

Bibliography

Allen, Donald and Warren Tallman (eds.), *The Poetics of the New American Poetry*, Grove Press, New York, 1973

Crozier, Andrew, 'Thrills and frills: poetry as figures of empirical lyricism', in Sinfield, A. (ed.), *Society and Literature 1945–1970*, Routledge and Kegan Paul, London 1983, pp. 129–233

Derrida, Jacques, *Writing and Difference*, Routledge and Kegan Paul, London and Henley, 1978

Eco, Umberto, 'The poetics of the open work', in *The Role of the Reader*, Hutchinson, London, 1979

Fisher, Roy, *City*, Migrant, Worcester, 1961

Harwood, Lee, *The White Room*, Fulcrum Press, London, 1968

Harwood, Lee, *The Sinking Colony*, Fulcrum Press, London, 1970

Harwood, Lee, 'Extracts from a conversation with Lee Harwood' (Victor Bockriss), *Pennsylvania Review*, 1, 1970, pp. 11–14

Harwood, Lee, 'Bob Cobbing', in Mayer, P. (ed.), *Bob Cobbing and Writers Forum*, Coelfrith, Sunderland, 1974, pp. 7–13

Harwood, Lee, *HMS Little Fox*, Oasis Books, London, 1975

Harwood, Lee, 'A Conversation' (Eric Mottram), *Poetry Information*, 14, Autumn/Winter, 1975–76

Harwood, Lee, *Boston–Brighton*, Oasis Books, London, 1977

Harwood, Lee, *Crossing the Frozen River*, Paladin, London, 1988

The I Ching, trans. R. Wilhelm, Routledge and Kegan Paul, London and Henley, 1951

Jung, Carl G., 'Marriage as a psychological relationship', in Campbell, J. (ed.), *The Portable Jung*, Viking Penguin, New York, 1971

Lyotard, Jean-François, *The Postmodern Condition: A Report on Knowledge*, Manchester University Press, Manchester, 1984

Morrison, Blake, *The Movement*, Oxford University Press, Oxford, 1980

Mottram, Eric, 'Beware of imitations: Writers Forum poets and British poetry in the '60s', *Poetry Student* 1, 1975, pp. 6–7, 32–35

Olson, Charles, *The Maximus Poems*, Jargon/Corinth Books, New York, 1960

Olson, Charles, 'Projective verse', in Allen and Tallman, pp. 147–58

Olson, Charles, 'Human universe', in Allen and Tallman, p. 164

Rothenberg, Jerome, *Pre-faces*, New Directions, New York, 1981

Sheppard, Robert, 'British poetry and its discontents', in Moore-Gilbert,

B., and Seed, J. (eds.), *Cultural Revolution?* Routledge and Kegan Paul, London, 1992

Ulmer, Gregory L., *Teletheory*, Routledge and Kegan Paul, New York and London, 1989

Index